the giant awakens

PUNJAB

INDUSTRY & GROWTH

the giant awakens
PUNJAB
INDUSTRY & GROWTH

Dr. Gurpreet Maini

India Research Press
New Delhi

India Research Press
B-4/22, Safdarjung Enclave,
New Delhi – 110 029.
Ph.: 24694610; Fax : 24618637
bahrisons@vsnl.com
contact@indiaresearchpress.com
www.indiaresearchpress.com

ISBN : 81-87943-38-6

Cataloguing in Publication Data
Dr. Gurpreet Maini © Text
The Giant Awakens: Punjab Industry & Growth
by Dr. Gurpreet Maini

Includes bibliographical references and index.
1. Punjab 2. Indian Economy 3. Industry
4. Development 5. Title 6. Author

ISBN : 81-87943-38-6

Printed in India at Focus Impressions, New Delhi – 110 003.

Contents

Abbreviations

ASR	:	Amritsar
CII	:	Confederation of Indian Industry
CRRID	:	Centre for Research in Rural and Industrial Development
CMIE	:	Centre for Monitoring Indian Economy
GNDU	:	Guru Nanak Dev University
NCAER	:	National Council for Agricultural and Economic Research
PFC	:	Punjab Financial Corporation
PSE	:	Punjab School of Economics
PHDCCI	:	Punjab, Haryana, Delhi Chamber of Commerce & Industry
PSIDC	:	Punjab State Industrial Development Corporation
ICICI	:	Industrial Credit and Investment Corporation of India

Preface

Amidst the currents of Indian history, whether they flow from the Ancient, Medieval or Modern segments, Punjab's role is pivotal. Whether as the earliest abode of the Aryans or as a sentinel for Indian frontiers, a buffer of the Colonial empire, its vivisection as a corollary to Independence, the custodian of free India's agricultural endowments or capsized by terroristic violence, it has always created major news in past and present records. Post Green Revolution, it has been clichéd with epithets like prosperous and progressive, particularly compared with the rest of India. It reflects a high per capita income, owing to its agricultural buoyancy. However, in the contemporary context, a replete assessment of progress is inclusive of economic growth, of which industrial development is a major determinant, in this respect. However, compared to states like Maharashtra and Gujarat, Punjab's statistics remain abysmally poor.

So a comparative analysis reflects, that the state's agricultural statistics soar whilst the industrial statistics are comparatively rockbottom. This phenomenon, depicts an unusual antithesis, that with all the prevalent parameters, a community marked by dynamism, enterprise, hard work and resilience, agriculture which boomed in response to the Borlaug seed and culminated in the spectacular Green Revolution, agricultural surpluses should have spurned industrial strides, as elsewhere but Punjab's achievement fell far short of expectations.

This disparate development became more pronounced, when in the recent past, the state was gripped by terrorism causing turbulence in its entire socio-political structure. This lacuna in Punjab's body politic, i.e. agriculturally pronged development was pronounced by eminent analysts as a major cause for youth falling prey to the malaise of terrorism. The causative factors for terrorism, were discussed at length in various seminars, papers and theses. However, this vital core issue of industrial lag has been only perfunctorily discussed. As a student, subsequently as a teacher, having lived in this region for a major part of my life, later as a witness to history evolve as a chapter of terrorism, I became enthusiastic about pursuing research in this specific region with a contemporary focus.

The staggering industrial growth of Punjab did necessitate an indepth study, moreover a historical inquiry, as this was the core issue for the onset of terrorism, which plagued the state for almost a decade. The prospect of culling the causes for a sluggish industrial growth from a historical perspective was challenging, fascinating yet contemporary. My endeavour was to examine the major social, political, economic and geographical strands of Punjab's history, then present them in a coherent, analytical, contextual and historical framework focusing on its industrial growth.

Punjab's historians have worked extensively in the contemporary sphere on the social, political, cultural and religious themes. However, economic history is an emergent and relevant theme, closely allied with the possible cause and effect relationship of historical events. Whenever studies have been conducted in Punjab on violence, they have paid scant attention to certain structural roots of violence stemming from the distortions in its economic structure. Various studies conducted on the subject suffer from this theoretical inadequacy; a neglect of the process of economic growth simultaneous with its social and cultural evolutionary process. Modern Punjab was the focus of my study, as this would be relevant in the present context to construe linkages with industry in the rest of the country, as well as with the historical past. The industrial lag as a problem has manifested itself in the present day and its repercussions have been contemporary.

For a systematic study and to extract the pith and marrow

of each historical event, the chapterization has been done keeping the specific historical episode at the core of the discussion and its linkages with the industrial theme. I commenced my study by a reconnoitre of Punjab's historical past, which is essential. Since many subsequent occurrences are seeded in the past, it was also imperative, to analyse the psyche, ethos and cultural moorings of the people of the area under study. History no longer unfolds in a watertight compartment, sociological and geographical factors coexist. So I have attempted a temporal study of economic events and their imprint on historical evaluation from not merely a theoretical perspective.

During the course of my research, I have charted out the major historical events which shaped the evolutionary process and thereby analysed its economic fallout. The colonial impact could not be overlooked, as it played a major role in steering the state towards agricultural prosperity by laying its foundations in an extensive canal network, not without tampering with the social fabric. Partition was cataclysmic, it left scathing scars on the psyche, the economy and the topography of the state. The task of recuperation and reconstruction was stupendous. The terrain, would scarcely have time to recoup and some political or border aggression would erupt. This seems like a pattern inherent in its historical past.

The next historical occurrence, which had repercussions in a vivisection of the state, was the Punjabi Suba movement. Therein lay the germs of subsequent communalism, all these socio-political occurrences brought forth major repercussions, so they had to be probed into. The Green Revolution was undoubtedly, like a magic wand ushering in a proverbial gilded era but it brought forth major distortions in the social and political fabric of the state, in determining its future policies. The wave of prosperity, which the Green Revolution brought created a large employable workforce, but did not create conditions and opportunities of employment. The unemployment, a glaring gap in wealth distribution, led to unequal conditions for availing of opportunities and aggravated rural poverty giving rise to individual and social anger, a resultant sense of insecurity made it easy for resulting retrogressive religious ideologies to seed and flourish, in terrorism which rocked the state. This was a major phase of history to be scanned and retrospectively analysed. For the progress of industry in the state, a study of industrial policies and acts, whether central or state were essential which was done in a separate chapter. Finally, as the winds of liberalization blew over Punjab, they were juxtaposed fortunately, with peace and tranquillity with the elected government of Beant Singh, the impact of democracy and peace on industrialization were discussed. In the conclusion, the ultimate findings of my work are synthesized and presented.

After making a sound foundational survey of the historical backdrop, it was imperative to pursue my study on historical methods by tapping the primary sources, to provide a deeper insight into the subject. I visited the Directorate of Industries, Punjab, where records and documents are maintained pertaining to this specific field, so as to provide all the vital clues to make a start. These records, reports, industrial policies were accessible and the officers were helpful with their oral versions on various queries.

The Statistical Abstracts from the Statistics Department of Punjab, State Industries Corporation, other Corporations and Boards have been useful for the collection of specific data and figures, significant for the eventual historical analyses and conclusion. The Punjab Chapter of the PHD Chamber of Commerce and Industry has prepared various papers on industry in Punjab, these were useful. In addition, to these primary sources, the field work, reports and data available at the Centre for Rural Research and Industrial Development are extensive, as well as intensive, on the subject. Though most studies on Punjab are largely obsessed with terrorism and its repercussions, I had to sift material pertaining to my topic. The Punjab State Archives, which has shifted partially from Patiala to Chandigarh, houses primary sources for reconstructing important milestones in Punjab's chequered history — the colonial period, partition, resettlement and bifurcation. I spent some time looking at the Primary Sources there, i.e. Punjab Administrative Reports, files on Commerce and Industry, various acts of the Punjab Government and monographs on industrial products.

No thesis on Punjab is complete without reference to the old copies of *The Tribune*. I scanned the copies on microfiche. The private papers of individuals—Lord Mountbatten and Jawaharlal Nehru were also scanned, so as to resurrect the early period of my study, at the Nehru Memorial Museum Library, New Delhi. On request the Shiromani Gurdwara Prabandhak Committee at Amritsar, a few records of Master Tara Singh and Sant Fateh Singh (in Punjabi) were browsed through, though, unfortunately, a lot of archival material was destroyed during Operation Blue Star. The Home Department, Political, as well as the Commerce Department files 1920-46, housed at the National Archives at Delhi gave some inkling to the British attitudes towards initial industrial development in Punjab. In order to make the study empirical and get a first hand account of the subject, some businessmen from major industrial towns of Punjab were interviewed.

In Delhi, the Federation of Indian Chamber of Commerce and Industry Reports and Confederation of Indian Industry Reports were from where I assessed the general trends of Indian industry, notifications and policies of the Government of India, which had subsequent repercussions in Punjab. The National Council of Applied Economic Research at New Delhi, has been bringing out surveys like the Techno Economic Survey on Punjab, these again have been most useful. Data were also collected from the Annual Survey of Industries issued by the Central Statistical Organization.

For the ultimate culmination of my study first as a Phd thesis and then as a book , the dramatis personae was varied. Before my thesis took a final shape, I faced innumerable obstacles, the greatest blow was the death of my guide Dr. R.C. Jauhri, who died when my thesis was in its final stages, I owe the utmost of gratitude to him for all the inspiration and guidance he provided me always. At this juncture of despair and despondency, Dr. J.S. Dhanki bailed me out. I must thank him most profusely for agreeing to supervise my remaining research work with tremendous patience and care. My colleague Dr. Sukhdev Sharma deserves special gratitude for his help at every stage during the journey of my research work. I must not overlook the valuable tips provided by Dr. G.S. Bhalla and Dr. G. K. Chadha of JNU who are connoisseurs on the subject of Punjab's Green Revolution.

Apart from the academic support, emotional buffers in every venture are essential – thanks to my husband, Jivtesh for keeping me on the track of sanity, when I was at my wit's end in the course of my research work and thanks to my children Preetesh and Tridivesh for being patient with a mother, who was perpetually buried beneath layers of books and papers. The utmost gratitude to my parents for always encouraging me to pursue academics, particularly, my father who still wants me to embellish my academic accomplishments. I hope this is a step in that direction. Behind the evolution of every font in print, there is the publisher without whom these pages could never emerge as books. I must thank Anuj Bahri for that.

Foreword

When the British ruled India they were particularly partial to the Punjab as it was the home of the martial races, the Sikhs and the Punjabi Muslims, whom they gave first preference in the recruitment for the British-Indian army. Owing to this fact, the Punjab benefited from the remissions of the pay of the soldiers, a source of income which no other province had to such an extent. These remissions were literally ploughed back into agriculture. In the fertile land of the Five Rivers investing in agriculture was a sound proposition. The Punjab was known as the granary of India and it richly deserved this designation. Under colonial rule, industry was neglected throughout India. There was little incentive to invest in it at that time. Therefore, it was not surprising that the agricultural wealth of the Punjab did not give rise to an equivalent growth of industrial investment.

When the British left India, they divided the country. This vivisection of India—as Mahatma Gandhi called it — affected the Punjab greatly. The dividing line cut across the areas inhabited by the Sikhs. Most of them left the Western part of the Punjab which became part of Pakistan and settled in the Eastern part which remained in India. Since many of them had served in the army during the war, they were well-trained and resourceful people, who could start from scratch and still work wonders. But the Sikhs also had to adjust to the new policy of recruitment for the army adopted by the government of independent India. There was no draft in India which would have automatically led to a proportional representation of all parts of the country in the army. On the other hand, employment in the army was coveted everywhere. A democratic government could not be partial in the recruitment for the army. Accordingly, the Sikhs saw the numbers of their recruits dwindle, whereas across the border in Pakistan, the Punjabi Muslims retained their privileged position in the army. The people could not be blamed for resenting this. They also felt neglected by the Government of India in many other ways. This government sponsored heavy industry in other parts of India, but did not do so in the Punjab. From the point of view of the central government, the Punjab which always headed the list of per capita income in India, did not need any special help. Poor states were far more in need of central assistance but this was no consolation for the Punjabis.

A further problem which affected the Punjab arose from the political ambitions of a certain section of Sikhs who wanted a state of their own. The resentments described above nurtured these ambitions. But the Indian Constitution permitted only the establishment of linguistic states and not of states for religious communities such as the Sikhs. When Indira Gandhi finally consented in 1966 to divide the Punjab along linguistic lines, this did not solve the problem but created further complications. The new Punjab consisted only of 60 per cent of Sikhs. Under such conditions political parties had to either follow a communal line, so as to capture most of the votes of the Sikhs or try their best to cross the communal divide in order to gain support among Sikhs as well as Punjabi Hindus. Central meddling in Punjabi politics was endemic under such conditions. Finally, the state drifted into a welter of terrorism and internecine destruction. Fortunately, the fertile land of the Punjab yielded its harvests regardless of political turmoil. But industrial investment could not progress under such conditions. Even after this turmoil had been overcome, the Punjab did not make rapid strides so as to catch up with other industrialized states of India such as Gujarat and Maharashtra. The wounds of the past had still to heal and this would take quite some time.

Gurpreet Maini has made a valiant attempt in this book to analyse the development of the Punjab bearing all these facts in mind. Her study is a good example of "political economy" in the most comprehensive sense of the term. Nowadays, economic studies often have a very narrow focus and do not take political and institutional factors into consideration. On the other hand, historical studies usually bypass the difficult field of economic analysis. In this book the fate of the Punjab has been portrayed in such a way as to cover history and economics in a most convincing manner. It is to be hoped that a study like this will contribute to the further development of the Punjab.

Heidelberg, January 2003 Dietmar Rothermund

these lines in mind. His study is a good example of political economy in the most comprehensive sense of the term. Nowadays, economic studies are often very narrow and do not take political and institutional factors into account. On the other hand, historical studies usually bypass the difficult field of economic analysis. In this book the path of the Mughal state is portrayed in such a way as to cover history and economics in a most convincing manner. It is to be hoped that a study like this will contribute to the further development of the [illegible].

Heidelberg, January 2004 Dietmar Rothermund

Introduction

Before embarking onto a study of Punjab in its contemporary economic content, a review of its historical evolution is imperative. A transparent perception would be possible only after examining the currents of history, as they flowed for this particular segment of the subcontinent and the emergent peculiarities marking its identity. The annals of Punjab's history present interesting phenomena. When juxtaposed they may appear contradictory, yet are factual. As a British colony, the focus on agricultural development led the area to witness a boom, prima facie yet agricultural indebtedness was not far too seek. Recently, the Green Revolution made the economic statistics soar yet industrially it staggerred. Such perplexities can be clarified only when the pages of history are surveyed, of course, with the focus on its economy.

Punjab, etymologically the land of the five rivers, is a vital segment in the history and culture of South Asia, located at the entrance of the Indian subcontinent and an essential channel to the rest of the world. In the historic continuity of this region, over thousands of years, it has been variously referred to as 'Sapta Sindhu' (Rigveda), the land watered by the seven fold Indus, 'Pancananda' (Mahabharata) and 'Uttarapatha' as the north-western division of 'Bharatavarsha'.[1] Implements have been found, which reflect its historical moorings, as early as the first inter-glacial period and the beginning of the second age that is between six and five lakh years. Punjab, was also the cradle of the Chalcolithic cultures of India several sites in Sindh and Baluchistan, have revealed the existence of the Bronze Age culture, amidst

1. Singh, Ganda, Introducing the Punjab, *The Punjab Past and Present* Vol.V, Part I and II, April 1967 and October 1967, Edited by Singh, Ganda, Punjabi University, Patiala, p.28.

small townships and village settlements dating back to the pre-Harappan period.[2]

However, the apex of archaelogical finds was the Indus Valley Civilization, which put Punjab on the map of the ancient civilized world.[3] The antiquities found here are unique, among other contemporary civilizations of West Asia. Similar antiquities were found in various parts of North India, testifying a well-developed urban culture and civilization. Later Aryan settlements in Punjab, reflected a reversal to village culture. It is in these village settlements, that the priests developed the socio-religious ideology, which is called 'Vedism' or 'Brahmanism'. "The Punjab was thus the earliest part of India to be Aryanized or Brahminized, never completely though."[4] The Aryans established small republics and monarchies all over the Punjab.[5]

After Alexander's invasion, a virtually non-effectual Greek influence, the Punjab became an integral part of the Great Mauryan Empire.[6] After its downfall, the historical pageantry unravelled, the Kushan and Huna period followed by a Hindu revival under HarshaVardhana.[7] With the rise of Islam and the Muslim incursions towards India, Punjab was annexed to the Ghaznavid empire. The successors ruled over this area, for over 150 years and the last of them was

---

2. Handa, Devendra, The Pre-Harappan Settlements of Ancient Punjab, *The Punjab Past and Present* (Edited by Singh, Ganda), Punjabi University, Vol.V, Part I and II, Patiala, 1970, p.5.
3. Singh, Gurcharan, Indus Valley Civilization and Drama (28-30 October), Punjab History Conference, Proceedings; Punjabi University, Patiala, 1966, p.31.
4. Ibid., p.2.
5. Thapar, Romila, *A History of India*, Vol.I, Penguin 1966, p.33.
6. Hutchinson J., A Note on the Passage of the Hydaspes by Alexander, *The Punjab Past and Present*, Edited by Singh, Ganda, Vol.II, Part II, October 1968, Punjabi University, Patiala, p.28.
7. Ibid., Thapar, Romila, op.cit., p. 136.

ousted from Lahore by the new rulers of Afghanistan, the Ghurids before the end of the twelfth century. Under Muslim rule, Punjab received a cultural fillip since the Caliphs and other Islamic sovereigns of the time encouraged literature and the arts. The art industries from foreign countries attracted by the accumulated wealth of the capitals of the Muslim sovereigns, soon found their way to Punjab and merged with the Hindu manufacturers and established themselves.[8] Afterwards, Punjab was conquered by Mohammad Ghori and this became the stepping stone, for the establishment of the Delhi Sultanate. During the Sultanate period, the Punjab was industrially well organized, there were guilds and crafts in villages and towns which carried on widespread commerce, silk weaving was carried on at Samana, Sunam, Ghurham, Sirhind, Dipalpur, Jallandhar, Lahore and Multan.[9] Then came the Mughals under Babur, who occupied Punjab in the 1520s and for over two centuries, it remained a part of the Mughal Empire. During the reign of Akbar, in the late sixteenth century, Punjab was synonymous with the Province of Lahore and actually smaller than the area lying between the rivers Indus and Sutlej.[10]

One of the most momentous occurrences in the annals of Punjab's history, was the evolution of the new sect of Sikhism, which emanated as a reform movement of Hinduism and its adjunct. The history of the Sikhs can be

---

8. Hundal, Simran, *Small-Scale Industries in the Punjab, under the Raj:1901-1947,* M.Phil. Thesis, Punjab University, Chandigarh, 1993, p.4
9. Nijjar, Singh Bakshish, *Punjab under the Sultans* (1000-1526 AD) Sterling Publishers Pvt. Ltd., Delhi, 1968, pp.123-124.
10. Grover, B.R., Approach and Methodology to the Study of Medieval Punjab, 28-29 February, Punjab History Conference, Proceedings, Patiala, 1976, pp. 45-47.

traced to the late fifteenth century. The founder was Guru Nanak, who was born in the Rachna Doab in April 1469, when Bahlol Lodhi was ruling at Delhi. The 'Janamsakhis' are replete with the trade contacts of Punjab' particularly of the Khatri merchants with Central Asia and Afghanistan. In 1577 Guru Ram Das founded a new centre for Sikhism called Ramdaspur, this city eventually became Amritsar and gradually developed as an important cultural and commercial nucleus of North India, so he invited traders, artisans and craftsmen to settle in the town.[11] Sikhism, later branched out into its distinctive ethos, as the Khalsa was created by the tenth Guru, Guru Gobind Singh.[12] The Khalsa transformed the dramatis personae in the forefront of Punjab, as it fought with newly infused enthusiasm against the Mughal oppression, which failed to suppress them.[13] So gradually Mughal tyranny eased out, as their empire began to disintegrate only to be replaced by Afghan repression. The Sikhs moved onto the central stream of Punjab history, as the plains of Punjab during the eighteenth century remained a battle ground since the Afghans, Marathas and Sikhs marauded the region.[14] The Sikhs consolidated their power in Punjab, during the prevailing confusion and anarchy, which followed the invasions of Nadir Shah and Ahmad Shah Abdali. The resuscitated Sikhs, organized themselves into small fiefdoms called 'Misls' which

---

11. Narang, Gokul Chand, *The Transformation of Sikhism*, New Book Society of India, New Delhi, 5th edition, 1960, p.35.

12(a) Cunningham, J.D. - *A History of the Sikhs*, reprinted by S.Chand & Co. New Delhi, 1972, p.66.

(b) Banerjee, A.C., An Aspect of Guru Gobind Singh's Career, *Indian Historical Quarterly*, Vol.I, 1945.

13. Bannerjee Indu, Bhushan. *Evolution of the Khalsa*, Calcutta, 1962, p.115.

14. Singh, Khushwant, *History of the Sikhs*, Vol.II, Princeton University Press, Princeton, 1972, p.78

were frequently at war with each other.[15] During this period, owing to political instability, trade and manufacturing suffered. As Hamilton commented, "An open regular trade with Punjab from other parts of Hindustan has in a great measure ceased,"[16] the city of Lahore temporarily looked dissipated.[17] It is also significant that at this juncture, a large number of Khatris migrated to Uttar Pradesh, Delhi, Rajasthan, Hyderabad, Bengal and Gujarat by the end of the seventeenth and through the eighteenth century.[18]

During the Mughal period, there are numerous references to trade links that existed between the Punjab, Persia, Afghanistan and Central Asia. The major towns like Lahore and Multan functioned both as centres for the products of the hinterland, as well as bases for traffic with Central Asia and Afghanistan, in fact, Lahore was a major centre for inter and intra regional trade.[19] The exports from the latter were sugar, rice, indigo, wheat and white cotton cloth.[20] Multan was known as a mart for imported Arabian horses, its hinterland produced woollen and cotton carpets, chess pieces, chintz, calico and bows. The political turbulence of the eighteenth century saw the relative decline

---

15. Chopra, G.L., *Punjab as a Sovereign State* (1799-1839), Hoshiarpur, 1960, p.3.
16. Hamilton, W. A. *Geographical, Statistical and Historical Description of Hindostan and Adjacent Countries*, Vol. II, Oriental Publishers, Delhi, 1971, p.470.
17. Mason, Charles. *Narrative of Various Journeys in Baloochistan, Afghanistan and the Punjab*, A. Belney, London, 1848, p.408.
18. Datar, Kiran, The Traders of Punjab and Asian Trade, 17th to Early 19th Centuries, *The Punjab Past and Present*, Vol.XX, Serial No. 39 (Edited Singh Ganda), Punjabi University, April 1986, Patiala, p.87.
19. Bhandari, Sujan Rai, *Khulusat ut Jawarikh*, Ed. Zafar Hussain (Delhi 1918), p.65.
20. Forster, W., *English Factories in India*, 1637-47, Clarendon Press, Oxford 1912, p.314.

of some of the north Indian towns but it also witnessed the growth of new trading centres like Amritsar, which carried on an extensive trade with Bombay as well as Calcutta.

Maharaja Ranjit Singh carved out the kingdom of Punjab, out of war ravaged fiefdoms 'misls' which would unite, whenever there was an emergent and common foe.[21] His rule gave the region, a scope for rejuvenation, since, in spite of intermittent aggression, an administrative infrastructure had been laid, other spheres, like cultivation, trade and revenue collection, which had begun in the late eighteenth century reached a high watermark in his reign.

Ranjit Singh realized that he could not build a formidable state without giving it a strong economic base, so he recognized the importance of industries. Primarily, he was interested in industries like arms, ammunitions for the requirement of his court, administration and his forces. The government of the Maharaja took great care to manufacture weapons, industries which were a state enterprise, whereas workshops manufacturing arms were set up at Nakodar, Shahdara and Peshawar. These workshops manufactured cannons, matchlocks, carbines, guns, pistols, small fire arms, steel caps, helmets, spears and all types of ammunition powder required for arms. Other manufacturing towns were Amritsar, Shujabad and Multan.[22]

The Maharaja also encouraged private entrepreneurs. Private industries produced cotton, silver, woollen goods, utensils, ornaments and paper. Amritsar, Lahore, Multan and Srinagar were major industrial centres and so were Jullundur,

---

21. Singh, Fauja, *Some Aspects of Sikh Society under Ranjit Singh*, Master Publications, Patiala, 1982, p.372.
22. Steinbach, John, *The Punjab*, Punjabi University Press, Patiala, 1970 (reprint), p.50.

Batala, Hoshiarpur, Wazirabad, Dera Ghazi Khan and Peshawar, considerable assistance was given to the private industries, taxes were levied at moderate rates and the small craftsmen paid nominal taxes.[24] Trade within Punjab and outside was encouraged by the peace and stability during the Maharaja's reign. His impetus to urban development by encouraging trade and industry, led to the gradual expansion of towns into cities. Wazirabad became an important town known for boat manufacturing, hosiery and chenille,[25] was also an important centre for trade on the River Chenab. Gujranwala owes its flourishing position to the Maharaja, which later became a leading industrial town. He made Amritsar the summer capital. It began to flourish, and was transformed into the biggest commercial city, known for textile manufacturing and shawls, carpets, silk and cotton fabrics which began to be exported to other parts of India. Walter Hamilton, a European traveller regarded Amritsar as a "grand emporium of trade".[26]

Multan was another important town in importance about which Steinbach wrote,

> Its modern consequences arise from the great extent of commerce of which it is the seat, the banking transactions particularly, giving it a prominence over all other towns in Western India.[27]

---

23. *Maharaja Ranjit Singh's First Death Centenary Memorial Volume*, Singh, Ganda (Ed.), Khalsa College, Amritsar 1930 (reprint), pp.128-137.
24. Nayyar, Gurcharan Singh, The Dynamics of Maharaja Ranjit Singh's Policies, *The Punjab Past and Present*, Edited Singh, Ganda, Serial No. 43, Vol.XXII-I, April 1988, Punjabi University, Patiala, p.45.
25. Arora, F.C., *Commerce by River in the Panjab*, Punjab Government Record Office, Monograph No. 9, p.93.
26. Steinbach, op.cit., p.5.
27. Dutta, V.N. in Singh, Kirpal, op.cit.

Maharaja Ranjit Singh took special interest in encouraging the silk trade in Multan, as has been testified by Alexander Burnes who writes,

> Ranjit Singh has with much propriety encouraged this manufacture, since he captured the city and by giving no other cloth at his court, has greatly increased their consumption, they are worn as sashes and scarves by all Seik Sardars. They are exported to Khorasan and India and the duties levied are moderate.[28]

So Maharaja Ranjit Singh's reign reflects how political stability in the strife-ridden state led to infrastructural growth, which promoted trade and industry. The Maharaja's death in 1839, was followed by a phase of turbulence and internecine struggles among the Maharaja's sons and the emergence of the Khalsa army as an indomitable force.

The British who were always game to fish in troubled waters decided to step in. Moreover, the Sikh aristocracy invited them to settle their personal scores and they intervened, gladly, two Anglo-Sikh wars followed and the Sikhs were routed. After which, Lord Dalhousie annexed the state in 1849 and Maharaja Dalip Singh became a British pensioner. Soon after, the British colours were hoisted on the citadel of Lahore and "the Punjab every inch of it, was proclaimed to be a portion of the British Empire in India".[29] Punjab was the last state to lapse into the British colonial mosaic, they were well aware of its strategic topography, its

---

28. Burnes, Alexander, *Travels into Bukhara*, Volume I, John Murray, London 1834. pp. 94-98.
29. Baird, *Private Letters to Lord Dalhousie*, quoted in Yadav K.C., *British Policy towards Sikhs, 1849-57*, Punjab History Conference, Proceedings, 28-30 October 1966, Punjabi University, Patiala, p.162.

volatile human resource material, since they had subtly scrutinized Ranjit Singh's domain from across the Cis-Sutlej, while they had awaited annexation.[30] During this period, some occurrences took place in India which influenced British policies in India bringing their Punjab strategy into focus on enhancing agricultural production. In England, the Corn Laws had ceased to exist, which was indicative of the growing political power of the industrial class. Under the doctrines of free trade and laissez faire it demanded a larger share in the exploitation of colonial India, which meant on the one hand, an increasing import of cheap raw material (cotton standing first) and on the other hand, an enhanced export of manufactured goods (specially cotton textiles). The British manufacturers had, succeeded in abolishing all duties on cotton exported from India into England between 1836 and 1844. However, in order to:

> have both the raw material and the manufacture in her own hands, and be thus independent of America and thus cotton cultivation should be increased in India by reducing the revenue in cotton growing lands.[31]

In 1850, the short cotton crop in the United States caused a loss of 11 millions for the industrial class, which gave a fresh impetus to the struggle for a more satisfactory supply from India. At this time, the condition of the East India Company was also financially precarious.[32] Lord Dalhousie remarked on Punjab, "The incorporation of Punjab will add considerably to the available revenue.......

30. Kohli, Sita Ram, *Sunset of the Sikh Empire*, Manohar Publishers, Delhi, 1967.
31. Dutt, Romesh, *The Economic History of India in the Victorian Age 1837-1900*, Vol.II, reproduction Delhi, 1960, pp.95-96.
32. Government of India, Foreign Department, Political Consultation, File 8 December 1853.

The soil generally fertile, requires only moisture to bring it into rich cultivation; while as appears from reports already received, the character of the rivers which divides the country affords singular facilities for supplying readily the means of developing resources of the soil."[33]

Punjab at the time of annexation was regarded as a promising province, and after annexation investment was made for the improvement of cotton cultivation. The political strategy of pacification and generating support to British rule was interlinked with the preparation of the Punjab for colonial exploitation with the adoption of various projects.[34] The government surveyed the resources of the Punjab, this process of culling information started with the establishment of British rule. It was observed by the government that by judicious measures, the agricultural produce of Punjab may be increased in quantity and improved in quality to the immediate benefit of the people and the ultimate advantage of the government.[35] The expansion of canal irrigation was considered most important among the works for the development of the resources of the Punjab.[36] Throughout the period, the Government constructed large irrigation canals in the Punjab which were interpreted as the benevolence of the government, with the passage of time, the state income from canal irrigation

---

33. Edwin Arnold, *The Marquis of Dalhousie's Administration of British India,* Vol. I, London 1862, p.406.
34. "Resource of Revenue", Chandra, Bipin, Reinterpretation of Nineteenth Century Indian Economic History, *The Indian Economic and Social History Review,* Volume V, No. I, 1968, p.52.
35. Government of India, Home Department Proceedings: Public Consultation, 12 November 1852, No. 28-A.
36. Government of India, Foreign Political Proceedings: 4 August 1849, No. 87.

multiplied and came to be counted, as a major source of revenue.[37]

Annexation, of course, brought inevitably the benificence of Pax Britannica—the administrative framework with its mechanical procedures, missionary activity, a railway network, a postal network and exclusively for Punjab — a well laid out canal system. Trade was not their primary purpose here, as these motives were now being eclipsed by the rapacious and imperialistic desires of the Governor General, Lord Dalhousie.[38] Punjab had so far been significant, as a buffer state because of its frontier position to counter the Russophobia, which would erupt occasionally in Afghanistan, so it was imperative, to keep both these areas under their control, by keeping puppet monarchs with the strings in own hands. Once the Union Jack was planted on Punjab's soil, the child heir Dalip Singh was ousted to Christendom overseas.

As the British troops had marched into Punjab with their army of occupation of 6,000 soldiers, they found the immediate tasks to be taming a belligerent army trained on western lines, wooing a hostile, landed aristocracy and a traumatized population seething with discontent.[39] The Sikh soldiery, whom the British dreaded, were paid and disbanded immediately after annexation.[40] With the passage of time, British political sagacity enabled them to rule two years short

---

37. Ibid., Foreign Consultations, 29 December 1849, Numbers 78-79.
38. Suri, V.S. Political, Territorial and Administrative Changes in the Punjab, From Earliest Times upto 1947, in *The Punjab Past and Present,* (Ed.), Singh, Ganda, October 1967, Punjabi University, Patiala, Vol.I, p.196.
39. Report on the Administration of Punjab for the Year 1851-53, *Calcutta Gazette* of 1853, pp.41-42.
40. Lee Warner, Dalhousie's Administration I, 262, *Calcutta Review* 1856, Vol.XXVII, p.107.

of a century and transform Punjab from a pastoral savannah to a major centre of commercialized agriculture in South Asia. The British engineered many social and economic changes in the Punjab, the most notable being the development of agricultural colonization by introducing a remarkable system of irrigation.[41]

The British tried to overcome their initial problems by developing a semi-military despotic system of governance, built upon the indigenous administerial infrastructure systematized it and steered it out of its medieval moorings. "The paternal rule of the early decades was eventually replaced by the machine rule of laws, codes and procedures".[42] The region was placed under the control of a three men Board of Administration, which was dominated by the towering personalities of John Lawrence and Henry Lawrence. The most experienced civilian and military officers were despatched to assist them, they were given both administrative and judicial powers. A well organized judicial system evolved in Punjab, post 1897, changes and reforms were brought about in the judicial system but the basic structure remained the same.[43] In the army, the Punjab regiments were raised to assist the 8,000 strong military police force for the maintenance of law and order.[44]

---

41. Singh, Sukhwant, Canalization and Colonization in the Punjab 1849-1901, *Journal of Regional History*, Vol.IV, Guru Nanak Dev University, Amritsar, 1996, p.79.
42. Grewal, J.S., *The Sikhs of the Punjab*, Cambridge University Press, 1994, p.128.
43. Kumar, Pawan, *Judicial Administration in Punjab During 1897-1919*, Punjab History Conference Proceedings, 18-20 March 1994, Patiala, p.33.
44. Talbot, Ian, *The Punjab and the Raj 1847-1947,* Manohar Publications, New Delhi, 1988, p.34.

The Board of Administration in Punjab became proverbial, as it honed some of the best talent among British officialdom, who initiated a large number of economic reforms. It abolished internal customs' duties and improved the roads, thus removing barriers to the development of trade and commerce. In local administration, the British incorporated certain elements of customary flair, they adopted the Mughal pattern of subdividing the districts into tehsils and sub-tehsils and the major administrative divisions were under Commissioners.[45] However, to keep in direct touch with the grassroot level, they used the services of the Zaildar for liason. The latter was at the bottom of the administrative pyramid, a unit of ten or twenty villages, he supervised the village headmen and acted as an honorary police officer, in charge of the village police. Eventually, his position emerged as a vital mediator between government and society. The British ensured that it was held by local landowners, who had demonstrated unquestionable loyalty. The institution of the Zaildar was in fact, unique to the Punjab's local administration, it reflected the importance, which the British attached to securing the support of the rural notables.[46] Punjab gradually began to experience a rapid and extensive economic growth from the late nineteenth century onwards. Canal irrigation was developed in western parts, in areas, that eventually came to be known as 'canal colonies'. Cultivated lands, were confined to areas accessible to irrigation, which was derived either from ground water sources, through wells or from seasonal canals utilizing river water.[47]

---

45. Gilmartin, David, *Empire and Islam: Punjab and the Making of Pakistan,* Oxford University Press, New Delhi, 1989, pp.11-28.
46. Talbot, Ian, op.cit., pp. 34 and 35.
47. Singh, Sukhwant, op.cit., p.81.

The sizeable immigration from other parts of the Punjab, that followed upon canal construction and the ensuing extension in agricultural activity has made the canal colonies, a phenomenon of major importance in the recent history of the world.[48]

For the British, the canal colonies were the most spectacular benefit of their rule to the people of the province. This was their prime focus thus commerce and industry were sidelined.

They had annexed Punjab as a logical corollary to their moves towards the completion of their dominion, so they used all possible strategies to good governance. In fact, so as to win over the Sikhs, they even began a perusal of their scriptures, compiled, translated them and wrote their history.[49] Their rule brought stability to Punjab, which had been constantly on the warpath, their agricultural wand turned a belligerent people into a contented yet dynamic workforce. During the revolt of 1857, this partnership was augmented, when the Sikhs did not participate, the British attributed this loyalty to the ideals imbued by the Punjab School of Administration.[50] In fact, the Sikh army was mainly responsible for the reoccupation of Delhi for the British. These troops saved India for the British, and "bore the privations, the fatigues, the perils of the ridge before Delhi and shared in the final conflict within the City Walls."[51] Punjab had stood aloof and helped the British to re-

---

48. Ali, Imran, *The Punjab Under Imperialism, 1885-1947*, Oxford University Press, p.I.
49. Grewal, J.S., Essay on Cunningham in *Essays on Sikh History*, Amritsar, 1984, p.35. Also see Mcleod, W.H., *Who is a Sikh*?
50. *The Problem of Sikh Identity*, Clarendon Press, Oxford, 1966, pp.40.
51. Walia, Jagjivan Mohan, The Mutiny of 1857 and the Sikhs in *The Punjab Past and Present* (Ed.) Singh, Ganda, Volume XXI-II, Serial No. 42, October 1987, Punjabi University, Patiala, p.381.

establish their rule and Sir John Lawrence was hailed as a saviour of the state. In fact, the loyalty of the Punjabis was often quoted to disprove the view, that the uprising was a show of popular disaffection against the colonial government.[52]

Punjab continued contribuing manpower to satiate the British imperialistic appetite for conquering, as well, as policing far flung areas, it was an important recruiting ground for the British. In fact, by the First World War, three-fifths of the Indian army's troops came from the state.[53] Almost half the British army came to be recruited from this province, and in the course of time, the British cossetted them, calling them the "martial races of India and the sword arm of their empire".[54] Though Punjab's historiography, reflects, that it was the British who labelled the people of the region as being "martial", however, this epithet emerged from the region's turbulent history. The people instinctively, developed military prowess and martial values to meet the challenges their chequered region threw up, there existed a strong military tradition, on which the British could build. Towards the end of the nineteenth century, the region had replaced the Presidencies of Bombay, Madras and Bengal, as a major centre of recruitment to the Indian army.[55]

The British tackled the different sects among Punjab's population deftly. The loyalty of the peasantry was crucial because of their willingness to pay land revenue, since they drew the bulk of their recruits from here to ensure the solvency and military security of the Raj. It was equally necessary to win the support of the Muslim leaders and large

52. Ibid., p.386.
53. Ali, Imran, op.cit., p.4.
54. Talbot, Ian, op.cit., p.299.
55. Ibid., p.41.

landowners of West Punjab, who acted as the Raj's military contractors in the post-Mutiny period, the region's aristocracy was to be used as "the great bulwark for the state".[56]

After the British had established their administrative infrastructure, they undertook revenue settlements in each district, which became the most important source of income.[57] To begin with surveys were carried out to assess the revenue paying capacity of each area and then they eventually began to collect revenue. From 1885 onwards, the economy of Punjab began to be reshaped by the unprecedented extension in agricultural production brought about by canal colonization. By 1895-96, in British India, the total capital outlay on irrigation works amounted to Rs. 38.3 million, Punjab had emerged on top and the North Western Provinces had been relegated to third place.[58]

Agricultural development brought along with it, its own share of problems. The land tenure arrangements introduced by successive rulers of the Punjab were probably determinative of the rural class structure. Initial British policy, for example, aimed at levelling the agrarian class structure by eliminating large landlords and equalizing the rights of tenants and proprietors. The British began settling the land revenue, by determining, who should pay government charges on the land and thereby holding proprietary rights on peasant cultivation rather than rural magnates, who also claimed proprietary rights.[59] Their

---

56. Ibid.
57. Farmer, B.W., *Agricultural Colonization in India Since Independence,* London 1974, p.25.
58. Kumar, Dharma, *The Cambridge Economic History of India,* Volume II, 1757-1970, Cambridge University Press 1975, p.715.
59. Douie, James M., *Punjab Settlement Manual*, reproduced Superintendent Government Printing Press, Lahore, 1961, p.117.

purpose was to maximize government revenues by removing all intermediaries between the peasant proprietors, to enhance revenue collection.[60]

One of the greatest problems of rural Punjab had been rural indebtedness. It was not abating with military remittances nor protective irrigation works and the control over agrarian production by merchants and moneylenders was also increasing. The commercial forces fostered by the British themselves, namely the merchant class, originally threatened those very colonial interests. After the Mutiny, the British had realized that the continuance of their rule depended upon the support of the war like people of the province. The object could be attained only if the rural people, the landed class and the peasantry which formed 90 per cent of the population would remain loyal to the Raj.[61] So the Government wished to introduce remedies for the welfare of the peasantry.

Fearing a loss of army recruits, rural unrest and disaffection of indigenous troops from the 1870s onwards, the colonial administration passed legislation, the Land Alienation Act of 1900, that prevented cultivators from alienating their lands or mortgaging them for extended periods except to other cultivators.[62] The Act took away the zamindar's right to sell or mortgage his land, without prior approval of the district officer. These officers generally gave

60. General Report on the Administration of the Punjab Territories, 1854-1855, p.22, para 38.
61. Domin, Dolores, Dr. Some Aspects of British Land Policy in Punjab after its Annexation in 1849 in *The Punjab Past and Present*, Ed. Singh, Ganda, Volume VIII, Part I and II, Punjabi University, Patiala, October 1974, p.30.
62. Annual Report of the Working of the Punjab Alienation of Land Act XIII of 1900, Civil and Military Gazette Press, Lahore, 1907.

permission only when the recipient of the land could prove that he belonged to a tribe designated in the Government Gazette as agricultural. The Government of India, placed restrictions on land transfer to improve the peasants' plight, but this was a political manoeuvre, to hone support of the large body of the agricultural strata essential for the stability of the British Empire in India.[63] The repercussions of this, divided the Punjab population, between the so-called traditional agricultural and non-agricultural castes. The British bureaucracy used the provisions of this Act, to create a new class of agricultural usurers and middlemen to act as a bulwark of British rule in India by facilitating in certain respects, the means of expropriation of the cultivator.[64] Eventually, "the British purpose of cheap military recruits, legal landlords, contented soldiers and inexpensive rural policing could be maintained".[65]

If the British at all, self-consciously adopted a divide and rule policy in Punjab, it was not along the lines of religious communities, but in terms of rural-urban divisions. The agriculturist communities were to be safeguarded from the economic and political domination of the urban elite. David Gilmartin has adduced convincing evidence of British efforts to protect tribal identities and interests.[66] The British wanted to benefit the middle class zamindar at the cost of the cultivator, they were nervous by then, about the rising tide of nationalism in the rest of the country, so the measure was a calculated one to create a class of people loyal to them. They did ultimately succeed in their objective is proved by

---

63. Barrier, N.G., *The Punjab Alienation of Land Act 1900*, Duke University, Carolina 1966, p.34.
64. Singh, Gurcharan, The Punjab Alienation of Land Act 1900, its Background, Punjab History Conference, Proceedings, Ist Session, 12-14 November 1965, Punjabi University, Patiala, p.151.
65. Douie, James, op.cit., p.59.
66. Gilmartin, David, op. cit., p.32.

the subsequent historical events, where the agricultural community, i.e. the Jat Sikh became richer and steadfast loyalists of the British. As a matter of fact, this Act, cast its shadow on the political events, upto partition in 1947, the powerful Unionist Ministry of the Punjab, which remained loyal to the British may be regarded as an offshoot of the Act.[67]

The year 1907, saw the emergence of a new political consciousness and witnessed a stir, never seen before in the annals of Punjab, since British occupation. Though the causes of the movement stemmed from agrarian discontent, it widened into a political movement. This was despite the fact, that the Punjab Government had passed several paternal measures, which were calculated to improve the economic position and the standard of living among Punjabi agriculturists.[68] In 1907, its further attempts to help the agriculturists unexpectedly resulted in the alienation of the political support of the agrarian population in Central Punjab, this perturbed them since the area was the recruiting ground, for more than a third of the Indian army. There were some indications that Punjabi agriculturists had moved towards rebellion, as a reaction to the Punjab Colonization of Land Bill and the Bari Doab Canal rates.[69] The Chenab colony, had been mostly inhabited by ex-soldiers, who had been rewarded with lands, for their services to the British. As the size of each holding was being reduced by partition among heirs, the Government proposed to check further division by passing an act providing for inheritance by primogeniture. This and other regulations in this connection

67. Singh, Gurcharan, op.cit., p.150.
68. Report on the Administration of the Punjab and its Dependencies, 1921-1922, p.I.
69. Barrier, N.G., The Punjab Disturbances in 1907, *Modern Asian Studies*, 1967, pp. 455-58.

were resented by the people, as an unjustified interference in their time honoured practices and traditions.[70] Meanwhile, Punjab had been ravaged by famine and plague, and the Government remained insensitive to these calamities but increased the land revenue by 30 per cent, land became a valuable commodity and the small farmers could not resist the temptation of selling land to the moneylenders. Though the Land Alienation Act saved the agricultural land from passing into the hands of moneylenders, yet it failed to solve the problem of rural indebtedness.[71]

A significant repercussion of British rule in Punjab was the emergence of an educated middle class, which included government servants, teachers, doctors, as an offshoot of the formal education introduced by them. As a consequence of the Educational Despatch of 1854, there was to be a Department of Education in each province, this gave a fillip to education in Punjab. A cess amounting to one per cent of the land was attached to education and within two years, village schools were established and so was a University. English education was considered useful and expedient, as well as consistent with the political requirements of British rule in India, although, the basic policy of the Government was to widen its scope, but practical considerations demanded that it should be limited to the upper and middle classes of society.[72]

---

70. Wasti, Razi, The Punjab Colonization Act 1907 reprinted in the *Punjab Past and Present*, Volume I, Part I and II, (Ed.) Singh Ganda, Punjabi University, Patiala, 1967, p. 389.
71. Gajrani, S.D., Agrarian Unrest in British Punjab in the *Punjab Past and Present,* S.No.39, Vol.XX, April 1986, Ed. Singh, Ganda, Punjabi University, Patiala, p.170.
72. Bruce, J.F., *The Beginning of Western Education in Punjab, 1856-57*, Government Printing Press, Lahore, 1860, p.I.

The growing middle class wanted to maximize their share in political and economic power, hence communal sentiments began to be institutionalized[73], in fact the emergence of reform movements accentuated this divide, some Hindu against Muslims and Christians initially but gradually against Sikhism as well. The British writers added fuel to the fire by consistently projecting the Sikhs, as a separate entity. The advent of western education and the printing press had ideological implications as educated people were exposed to western religious and secular values, which had triggered off, reform movements like the Arya Samaj among Hindus, the Singh Sabha among the Sikhs and the Ahmediyah movement among the Muslims. These movements tried to modernize their religions, and struck a conciliatory path between modern western culture and their traditional customs.[74]

In India, during the early twentieth century, the freedom movement was picking up and Punjab could not remain unaffected. The rise of communalism in Punjab, was a major tragedy in the way of the rapid development of national and militant forces working for independence and the social transformation of society. The Unionist Party maintained a pro British, pro agriculturist stand, which actually nourished the interest of the landlords. On account of the peculiar geographical distribution of the population, the Unionist Party could build a stronghold in Western and Eastern Punjab, while Central Punjab remained the nerve centre of nationalist, militant and Akali politics. The

---

73. Sohal, Sukhdev Singh, Professional Middle Classes in the Punjab, *Journal of Regional History*, Vol.III, GNDU, Amritsar, 1982, pp.72-73.
74. Singh, Amandeep, Impact of the British Rule on the Social Scene of Punjab and the Rise of Communalism, Punjab History Conference Proceedings, Vol.XXVI, 1992, (Ed.) Singh, Ganda Punjabi University, Patiala, p.70.

communal leadership of all the three existing religious groups tried to use every forum, including the floor of local bodies and the legislative, to advance their own interests. Taking advantage of the communal dissension and class differences, the British bureaucracy tried to manipulate them for their own imperialist designs.[75]

However, the year 1919, brought the focus of the Freedom Movement onto Punjab and in fact, the Jallianwala Bagh episode, where 379 were killed and 1200 were wounded, boosted the anti British tirade and made it take an irretrievable turn. It had begun as an agitation, against the Rowlatt Act spearheaded by Congress leaders like Dr. Kitchlew and Satyapal. Hartals had taken place, which had demonstrated complete communal amity and coordination, this alarmed Michael O'Dwyer, the Governor, so the crowds which assembled to agitate against the Rowlatt Act, were fired at and it snowballed into a gruesome episode with national repercussions.[76] The Congress Enquiry Committee reported, that even the figure of 1000 persons killed would not be an exaggeration.[77] Meanwhile, the agrarian unrest blended with revivalist aspirations, found expression in regional parties like the Akalis a majority of whom were from among the Jat Sikh agriculturists. The Akalis, in the first two decades of the twentieth century, fervently

---

75. Rai, Satya M., The Structure of Regional Politics in Punjab, in *The Story of Punjab,* Volume II, Edited by Verinder Grover, Deep and Deep Publications, New Delhi, 1995, p.191.
76. Government of Punjab Memo, Disturbance in Punjab, 1919, 144, Z/2587, Punjab Archives, Chandigarh.
77. Kapoor, Satish, Punjab and the Freedom Struggle, *The Tribune*, 9 August 1997.
78. Wallia, Jagmohan, The Role of the Sikhs in the National Freedom Struggle, *The Punjab Past and Present,* Edited Singh, Ganda Volume XXIV, Serial No. 47, 1991, Punjabi University, Patiala, p.148.

participated in various anti-British tirades, particularly, the Gurdwara Reform Movement, in which they were strongly backed by the Congress.[78]

The Akali agitation culminated in the passing of the Gurdwara Reform Act of 1925 and the creation of the Shiromani Gurdwara Prabandak Committee, which was to play a pivotal role in Sikh politics. Religious reform in Punjab, eventually, took the shape of an anticolonial crusade in Punjab.[79] Meanwhile, the landlords protested against their oppression by organizing the Unionist Party to represent their interests. Punjab had played its role in the wider national context of the freedom struggle, however the Sikh homeland issue took precedence over others.[80]

As efforts for liberating the country began to fructify, the clouds of partition loomed large on Punjab's horizon. The communal tension, which had engulfed the whole of north India, affected Punjab the most, on account of the vital importance of the province to all three communities. As partition became inevitable, the leaders of political parties and officials were preoccupied with working out details of the division of assets and liabilities of the country, paying scarce attention to a planned exchange of population. A planned inter-migration between the two newly formed countries had not been envisaged by either government.[81]

The Muslim League leader, Muhammad Ali Jinnah had suggested an exchange of population on 10 December 1945 and again on the 15 November 1946 but it was not seriously considered by the Congress leaders. The election results of

79. Government of India File No. 459, Part II, 1922.
80. Singh, Mohinder, *The Akali Movement*, Macmillan Press, Delhi, 1978, p.178.
81. Rai, Satya M., *Partition of the Punjab*, Asia Publishing House, Bombay, 1965, p.42.

1946 had clearly indicated that the Muslims of Punjab were solidly behind the Muslim League and were aspiring to form Pakistan with Punjab as one of its provinces. In order to avoid this, the Sikhs and the Hindus insisted on the creation of a Province.[82] On the contrary, Mahatma Gandhi felt every province is Indian, be he Hindu or Muslim, it is his. It won't be otherwise, even if Pakistan came in full. For me any such thing will spell the bankruptcy of Indian wisdom or statesmanship, or both."[83]

There were a variety of opinions on the subject, the crux being, that the leaders, decided against a planned exchange of population, thinking that it would bring in its wake a number of problems. However, the unprecedented orgy of violence that erupted brought tremendous destruction, death and uprooted thousands of people. The Governments and leaders could not arrest the spread of communalism and with the establishment of the two dominions, communal frenzy occurred in its most brutal form.[84] Nearly a million persons perished, and over 13 million crossed the borders, over 4 million refugees from West Pakistan crossed into the Punjab and a large number of Muslims from the Indian side, crossed into Pakistan. In 1951, when the total population of the Indian Punjab was 12½ millions, there were nearly 2½ million refugees, forming a fifth of its population.[85]

The partition of Punjab brought about a drastic transformation in the life patterns of this region, since the

---

82. Singh, Giani Kartar, *The Case for a New Sikh Hindu Province in the Punjab*, Delhi, 1946, p.9.
83. Gandhi, M.K., *The Statesman*, Delhi, 12 December 1945.
84. Gandhi, M.K., Letter dated 24 September 1944, Gandhi Papers at Gandhi Memorial Museum and Library, Raj Ghat, New Delhi, To the Protagonists of Pakistan, Allahabad, 1947, p.264.
85. Grewal, J.S., op.cit., p.181.

collapse of the Sikh Empire and British annexation. The division of the state on communal lines, which affected every sphere of life — political, economic, social, linguistic, administrative and cultural. The Hindus who were a minority of 30 per cent, now became a majority with 70 per cent of the population, the Sikhs a small, though sizeable minority with 30 per cent of the population in East Punjab and Muslims, a majority in former Punjab now became a microscopic minority. It was within the strands of Punjab's history, that it was to be divided into two, this was only a beginning in its vivisection, which was to subsequently take place once again, each partitioning had repercusssions which reverberated within its body politic.

Chapter I

Pre-Independence Industrial Lag

A perusal of the entire gamut of Punjab's history is essential before bringing the focus onto the specific theme of industrialization, the British advent cannot be overlooked, as colonial ramifications offset vital trends in the culmination of the modern history of India in every sphere. In the eighteenth century prior to its colonization, India (or the congeries of states on the subcontinent) had been a great manufacturing, as well as a great agricultural sector and the products of the Indian loom supplied the markets of Asia and Europe. The advent of the East India Company and subsequently, the British Government followed a commercial policy discouraging the Indian manufactures in the early years of the British rule, so as to encourage the Indian manufactures of England.[1] Their policy was to make India subservient to the industries of Great Britain and to make the Indian people grow raw produce, solely in order to supply material for the looms and manufactures of Great Britain. This policy was implemented most harshly, "orders were sent out, to force Indian artisans to work in the Company's factories, commercial residents were legally vested with extensive powers over villages and communities of Indian weavers, prohibitive tariff excluded Indian silk and cotton goods from England, English goods were admitted into India free of duty or on payment of a nominal duty."[2] In England, owing to industrialization, a gradual change from a mercantile oriented ideology based on protectionism

---

1. Baron, Paul A., *The Political Economy of Growth*, New Age Printing Press, New Delhi, 1958, p.174.
2. Dutt, Ramesh Chandra., *The Economic History of British India in the Victorian Age*, VII Edition, 1960, Tribner Press, London, 1960, pp.VIII.

and geared to the goal of having a surplus balance of payments to free enterprise was made around the middle of the eighteenth century, this proved disastrous to Indian industrial development.[3]

Britain had never encouraged industrial development in India, if at all there was any industrial progress, it was only as a corollary to their own industrial needs. The determinant of growth of any industry in India was the need, which it could fulfil to provide for the production process of British industry.[4] Any indigenous industry, that could compete with the market of British finished goods, always saw a declining rate of growth with respect to its British counterpart. In fact, the British levied excise duty on the Indian industry, to make the indigenous industrial production more expensive, as compared to the inputs of their own goods.[5]

Contrary to the supposition, that whatever industrial development occurred in India in the past, occurred as a result of the integration of the Indian economy with the World Capitalist System through trade and capitalist investment is disproved by Bipan Chandra that:

> a very interesting historical phenomenon that the major spurts in Indian industrial development took place precisely, during those periods when India's colonial economic links with the world capitalist economy were temporarily weakened or disrupted.[6]

According to him, on the three occasions when the

---

3. Dutt, R.Palme, *The Problem of India*, International Publishers, New York, 1943, p.38.
4. Eric Hobsbawm, *Industry and Empire*, Pelican History of Britain, Vol.III, London, 1960, p.154.
5. Baron, op.cit., p.124.
6. Chandra, Bipan, *Nationalism and Colonialism in Modern India*, Orient Longman, New Delhi, 1979, p.81.

foreign capital inflow was interrupted during the two World Wars and the Great Depression 1929-34, industrial production improved. In the latter half of the nineteenth century, there was a rapid decline of indigenous cottage industries, especially cotton spinning, weaving, dyeing and tanning, owing to the import of cheap machine made goods from Britain, an inadvertent impact of the industrial revolution. Britain preferred,

> that India should remain predominantly agricultural. Whilst the government wished to avoid both the active encouragement of industries (like the cotton mill industries), which competed with powerful English interests and increased state expenditure.[7]

Punjab lagged behind other regions in the industrial field, whatever, limited industrial development had taken place in India, so far, it was generally confined to ports, which became prominent industrial nodes like Bombay and Calcutta. For instance, Bombay had major cotton textile mills, in which later Ahmedabad followed suit and Hooghly had five mills, so major industrial investment took place here in the pre-First World War period. The spread of industry had been aided by the relative cheapness of labour in the new centre, cheap hydroelectric power and coal.[8]

The enormous expansion in imports and exports corresponding with the increase in most of the transport and communication, had an important bearing on the problem of regional imbalances of industrial development

---

7. Anstay, Vera, *The Economic Development of India*, Longmans Green & Co., London, 1957, p.210.
8. Bagchi, Amiya Kumar, *Private Investment in India*, Cambridge University Press, Cambridge, 1972, p.433.

in India.[9] It was easier to carry industrial goods from areas around the ports, this gave an added advantage to the regions surrounding the ports. Moreover, the colonizing nature of the railway rate policy was so designed, so as to give preferential treatment to the transportation inwards of manufactured goods and outwards of raw materials. In Bombay, even the emergence of a class of commercial bourgeoisie accelerated the process of industrialization as compared to Punjab, where primarily, the population consisted of farmers or former soldiers.

The commercial bourgeoisie benefitted from the expansion of trade upon colonization for developing manufacturing industries, notwithstanding, the backwash effect of British industries. Commercial inclinations prevailed in the South, where too many communities which had earlier been in trade moved to industry, for instance the Chettiars. In Central Indian Provinces, the Jains and Marwaris became involved in industry in Gwalior, Bhopal and Indore.[10] By the time, Punjab was annexed, areas such as Bombay were well advanced in the process of cotton textile manufacturing because of the cotton boom of the 1860s, which provided the bourgeoisie opportunities to exploit.

The Indian Industrial Commission, 1918 (which had been set up during the First World War to speed up industrial home production) in discussing the possible reasons for the relative advancement of Bombay had this to say:

---

9. Khanna, J.S., "Lagging Industrial Development in Punjab: An Analysis," Edited by Johar R.S. and Khanna J.S., *Studies in Punjab Economy*, Punjab School of Economics, Guru Nanak Dev University, Amritsar, 1983, p.89.
10. Bagchi, op. cit., p.435.

if the causes be sought, some indication of it may be found in the fact, that Indians have held a large and important share in the trade of Bombay, since the city first came into English hands. The Muslims of the West Coast, especially, traded by sea with the Persian Gulf, Arabia and East Africa from much earlier times. The Parsees and Hindus from the Northern Bombay Coast districts are recorded, at the beginning of the British occupation as trading with the sects of Khojas, Memmons and Bohras.[11]

Alfred Marshall corroborates that an industrial culture is essential for industrial evolution. So when an industry has chosen a locality for itself, it is likely to stay there long, so great are the advantages, which people following the same skilled trade get from their close neighbourhood.[12]

On the contrary in Punjab, the people have been primarily agriculturally inclined even a Census of 1868 shows that a majority local Sikhs were in agricultural pursuits.[13] The same was corroborated by Abdul Latifi, an ICS officer in 1911, that 56 per cent of the people were agriculturists,[14] moreover, after annexation, the British priority was agricultural colonization to provide raw material to their growing industry and so industrial growth was sidetracked. However, they never regretted it, as Sir Malcolm Darling said that, "Punjab's only industry is

---

11. Government of India, Indian Industrial Commission Reports, Calcutta, 1918, p.72.
12. Marshall, Alfred, *Principles of Economics*, Oxford University Press, London, VIIIth edition, p.271.
13. Report on the Census of Punjab, 10 January1868, Indian Public Press, Lahore 1870.
14. Latifi, Abdul, *The Industrial Punjab, A Survey of Facts, Conditions and Possibilities*, Longmans Green & Company, London, 1911, Introduction.

agriculture".[15] Since Punjab was colonized later, its agricultural base had not been completely exhausted and devastated, as had been the case with Bengal.

The British, felt that agriculture would serve more than one purpose for the then volatile circumstances, so they maintained an agricultural focus in Punjab. The British wanted the state to be a supplier of agricultural produce and so they scarcely focussed on the development of industry in the state.[16] At a later date, Sir Michael O'Dwyer, the Governor of Punjab was to remark,

> Some captious critics try to belittle our agricultural prosperity and suggest that, it is a poor substitute for industrial expansion, we do not know who these captious critics are. Our own impression is that what the critics of official policy, do is to urge industrial development, not as a substitute but as being essentially complementary to agricultural development and in this, they are perfectly right.[17]

Agricultural colonization had undoubtedly brought forth peace and stability, facilitating for the British, an ideally suited recruiting ground for their peripatetic army. However, in the totality of economic development, the state like other colonized economies suffered from an acutely retarded industrial base. The seeds of an appropriate industrial infrastructure were not sown, so it never culminated in the right direction.[18] The British attitude towards Punjab's commercial development is evident from

---

15. Darling, Malcolm, *The Punjab Peasant in Prosperity and Debt*, Manohar Publishers, Delhi, 1977 reprint, p.5.
16. Malik, Ikram Ali, *The History of Punjab, 1799-1947*, Low Price Publications, New Delhi, 1993, p.229.
17. *The Tribune*, 28 April 1918, Lahore.
18. Ali, Imran, op.cit.

A.C. Badenoch, an ICS officer's remark, even though commercial education was virtually non-existent in Punjab. He felt that "the same scale of commercial education is not necessary as in Punjab in Bombay and Calcutta."[19]

Apart from its British legacy, which christened it as an agricultural state, there were various other reasons for its industrial lag. Primarily, the British had concentrated, whatever, minimal industrial growth in the port regions of Bombay and Calcutta, as the trading activities in these regions remained in the control of the East India Company.[20] In 1930, the factory workers of Punjab were 44,274 as against 3,81,349 in Bombay and 4,80,349 in Bengal.[21] Other areas where industry gained were Ahmedabad and Baroda, with an inflow of entrepreneurship from Bombay, Delhi, Cawnpore and Madras. By the Second World War, India became a major exporter of textiles, other new industries which came up were steel, cement, refined sugar and heavy chemicals. Though Punjab lacked emergent large-scale industry, there were cottage industries and small foundries. There was a dearth of industrial prerequisites like coal, water, cheap labour and no regional entrepreneurial group with the extensive connections, capital and experience comparable to these groups that existed in the Central, Southern and even Eastern India like the Tatas, Birlas, Narangs, Kamlapat and Dalmia Sahu Jains.[22]

---

19. Badenoch, A.C., *Punjab Industries 1911-17*, Punjab Government, Lahore, 1917, p.(vi)
20. Singh, Jaswinder, *Industrial Development of Punjab, Problems and Prospects*, M.Phil., Dissertation, Guru Nanak Dev University, Amritsar, 1981, p.5.
21. Josh, Bhagwan, *Communist Movement in Punjab, 1926-1947*, Anupma Publications, Delhi 1975, p.30.
22. Bagchi, A.K., op.cit., p.433

Historically, there was practically no large-scale industrial dispersal in the context of the macro perspective of economic growth, Punjab started getting viewed, as an agrarian appendix of the British metropolis and was incorporated into the world capitalist market because of its agricultural produce. In 1871, the Province received only 4 lakhs of rupees for its surplus grains, in 1912-13 it received Rs. 1448 lakhs and in 1918-19 no less than 2437 lakhs of rupees. In thirty years, the exports increased four fold.[23]

The colonial integration stimulated the production of export-oriented, agricultural raw materials and opened a new market for the consumption of manufactured goods.[24] The factors responsible for surplus produce, had been internal security, peace, periodic settlements, record of rights, rise in the prices of produce, the price of land, availability of capital, new means of communication and new means of irrigation. Calvert, an ICS officer had remarked that there was a relationship between railway development and the development of canal colonies: it may be assumed, that the great colonies would never have been a financial success, without the railways to serve their needs. (Table I) The two are complimentary, such a sudden increase in agricultural production was followed by opening of the great canals, it would have resulted in a disaster, if the only markets had been local ones and the fact, that the flow of commodities was originally to the sea. This shows that markets, within India were unable to absorb all that was offered.[25] (Table II)

---

23. Blyn, G., *Agricultural Trends in India, 1891-1947*, London, 1966, pp.136-137.
24. Johar and Ķhanna, op.,cit., p.126.
25. Calvert, H., op. cit., pp. 411-12.

Table I

Development of Rails, Roads and Irrigation Canals in Punjab

Year	Railway mileage	Road mileage (metalled)	Canal mileage
1872-73	410	1036	2744
1882-83	600	1467	4583
1892-93	1725	2142	12368
1902-03	-	-	16893
1922-23	4000	2614	16935
1932-33	5500	3904	19601

Table II

Percentage Distribution of Investment in Irrigation, 1898-1914

	Uttar Pradesh	Punjab	Bombay	Madras and Orissa	Other	Total
By the end of 1897-98	27	25	8	13	31	100
During 1898-1914	7	50	11	20	12	100*

* 54.62 crores

Source: H.Calvert, The Wealth and Welfare of the Punjab, Civil and Military Gazette, Punjab Civil Secretariat, Lahore, 1936, p.107.

As an aside, however, Calvert analysed, there were pitfalls in this situation of prosperity. The increasing acreage of land under share tenancy (batai), was an obstacle to agricultural improvement and production. The chance of tenants becoming owners were obviated by the high price of land, while mortgages and sales were steadily adding to the number of fields under tenant cultivation.[26]

A rapid and continuous rise in the price of agricultural land, was a conspicuous feature of British rule. It made the land attractive, as a source of investment but brought little advantage to the cause of agriculture.[27]

The investment of the surplus of the agricultural sector in more land, however, stunted the possibility of capital formation in the industrial sector. The smaller peasant became poorer due to the feudal system. He also got tied down to land due to indebtedness, and could not think of leaving the land and becoming a labourer, elsewhere. He had no surpluses, the surpluses were with landlords, who had at that point of time, absolutely, no industrial culture.

As Malcolm Darling had concluded that the bulk of cultivators "are born in debt, live in debt and die in debt".[28] The rapid increase of debt, deprived the cultivator of much of the benefit, that he would, otherwise have derived from the growing prosperity of the province. Debt was allied to prosperity and poverty alike; while its existence was due to poverty, and its volume was due to prosperity.[29] Over 80 per cent of the proprietors of Punjab were under debt and mortgage debt was about 40 per cent of the whole. In

---

26. Ibid., pp.109.
27. Ibid., pp. 196.
28. Darling, Malcolm, op.cit., p.36.
29. Hira, B. S., Agrarian Prosperity and Rural Poverty in the Upper Bari Doab (1849-1947), *The Punjab Past and Present*, Vol.XXVII, Part 11, October 1993, Punjabi University, Patiala, p.84.

1912, Calvert calculated the number of moneylenders at about 4,000[30] and the agricultural debt of Punjab amounted to Rs. 900 million in 1921 and Rs. 1,350 millions in 1929. (Table III).

Table III

Estimates of Total Agricultural Debt, Population, Value of Agricultural Produce, and Debt as Multiple of Land-Revenue in British Indian Provinces, Selected Years

Province	Agr.debt In 1929 (Rs.Crs.)	Total pop. in 1931 (Million)	Value of agr. Produce (Rs. Crs.)	Debt as mulitple of land revenue
1	2	3	4	5
1. Bihar & Orissa	155	37.5	120	-
2. Madras	150	46.5	165	19
3. Panjab	135	23.5	91.5	25.5
4. United Provinces	124	48.5	-	17
5. Bengal	100	50	244	18
6. Bombay81	22	152	15	
7. Burma	55	14.5	-	-
8. C.P. & Berar	36.5	15.5	79	12.5
9. Assam	22	9	-	21
10. N.W. Frontier	11	2.5	6.5	-
11. Delhi & Ajmer-Marwar	4.5	1.2	2	-
Total	874			

Source: M.L. Darling, op.cit.,p.18.

Despite problems allied with agriculture, Punjab strode

30. Calvert, op.cit., p.255.

ahead in it but continued to be industrially backward. Apart from various other causes, it was also deficient in mineral resources, a basic requisite for industry.[31] Whilst limestone and slate, were the only two significant minerals deposits, coal had to be imported. The state was completely landlocked and bereft of navigable rivers, industry seeded here could ideally be agro-based, since the agricultural base was well established.

Punjab evolved as a feudal society, composed of landlords (zamindars), rich peasants, tenants at will, agricultural labourers and servants. In fact, the rural society was divided between the rural rich and the rural poor tenants at will, agricultural labourers were at the lowest rung of stratification in rural Punjab. The latter two sections were the most oppressed and exploited sections of society, even though, the per capita income in Punjab was still higher than that of peasants in other parts of India, but from 1921-41 there was a decline in output by 13 per cent.[32] There was no homogeneity in the agrarian structure of Punjab, progress was made in areas where there was colonial interest, whereas other areas remained underdeveloped.[33]

Coming back to the theme of Punjab's industrial economy, when the First World War broke out, it brought about a realization of the danger of dependence on foreign supplies, even for daily necessities. In fact, the war was like a double - edged weapon. On the one hand, it caused some financial difficulties by restricting the supply of capital and certain necessary machinery, on the other, the war provided

---

31. Sidan, Meena, *Growth Performance of Industrial Sector in Punjab*, M.Phil. Dissertation, Guru Nanak Dev University, Amritsar, 1991, p.14.
32. G.Blyn, op.cit., p.102.
33. Gajrani, S.D., Agrarian Structure and Economic Condition of Peasantry in Punjab 1920-47, *Punjabi History Conference, Proceedings*, Punjabi University, Patiala, 15-17 March 1991, p.92.

Punjabis, with fresh opportunities. Since more than half the army was recruited from their land, certain local industries could make substantial profit by supplying the armed forces with their necessities. Besides, the Government, in order to keep the lines of communication open with the theatres of war had to pay attention to certain industries and transport system, so industry, trade and communication got a boost. In the post war period new factories opened up for the purpose of manufacturing cotton yarn, cloth, woollen yarn, carpets, pottery, iron work, surgical instruments, matches, engineering material, flour, ice, sugar, leather goods and oil.[34] The Indian Industrial Commission in 1919, as mentioned earlier, was to examine and report on the possibilities of the further industrial development of India and to submit recommendations for a permanent policy of industrial stimulation, with the passage of the Reform Act of 1919, industry became a provincial subject.[35] However, it was only in 1921, as a result of the recommendations of the fiscal commission, that a new era of industrial development began in Punjab, so the number of factories rose from 152 in 1901-2 to 296 in 1921, 673 in 1932-33 and 887 in 1939.[36]

During the Depression of 1929-34, when the international economy was temporarily disrupted, the British hold on the Indian economy weakened. India's foreign trade was sharply reduced and the domestic market, which was otherwise shrinking became available to India.[37] Consequently, as a result of the Depression, the sharp fall in

34. Report on the Administration of Punjab for 1923-1924, Superintendent, Government Printing, Lahore 1925, p.138.
35. Government of India, Proceedings of the Department of Commerce and Industry 1918-1919, Superintendent, Government Printing Press, Calcutta 1921.
36. Figures culled from the Annual Reports on the Working of the Indian Factories Act in Punjab, 1939.
37. Chandra, Bipin, op.cit., p.12.

agricultural prices and exports, commercialized agriculture was hit most severely. Among the peasantry, those who had any savings kept them in gold and silver ornaments, they parted with them, in order, to meet their cash commitments of various kinds. Simultaneously, came several legislative enactments which restricted the activities of the money lenders, gradually, moneylending, as an occupation began to decline. Depression in the world market brought a decline in income, so diversion of income to gold started instead of capital formation, on the other hand, the anti industry policy of the British, in Punjab was also responsible for discouraging people from investing in industry.[38]

As compared with the rest of British India, Punjab was industrially backward, though, there was some industrial activity. The existing large-scale industries in Punjab, consisted of textiles, cotton, silk, wool, hosiery, cotton seed oil, sports, leather, chemicals, oil, sugar, paper, iron and steel. Cotton spinning was the most important domestic industry of the province connected with agricultural produce, and coarse cotton cloth was being hand woven in every village. In 1881, there were 3,87,633 weavers in the Punjab and they formed the largest occupational group among the artisans. The estimated value of the turn over of the handloom weavers was nearly 3.23 crores of rupees, finer qualities were manufactured, as well but these included only long clothes and damasks, white or coloured with woven patterns.[39] The position of the industry was not satisfactory, due to the influx of foreign goods in the market.[40] The

38. Johar and Khanna, op.cit., p.106.
39. Report on the Administration of the Punjab and its Dependencies for 1872-73, Punjab Government Press, n.d., p.92.
40. Sharma, Harish C., Handloom Weavers of the Punjab under British Rule: A Study of Socio Economic Change – Punjabi University, *The Punjab Past and Present*, April 1989, Serial No. 45, Volume XXIII, p.38.

annexation of Punjab had taken place at a time, when the demand for raw cotton by the textile manufacturers of Lancashire and Manchester was increasing rapidly. The textile manufacturers, were eagerly looking for new areas for the procurement of raw cotton, which could at the same time, serve as a market for their products.[41]

The textile industry got a considerable stimulus, owing to the First World War and with the introduction of new varieties of cotton, in Punjab. Further, the government's patronage to the textile industry gave it an impetus and certain textile centres, like the one at Ludhiana, specialized in military uniforms, puggries and haversacks, and considerably met the demands of the war. The military requirements in cotton had grown, there was a shrinkage in Lancashire imports in India, due to preoccupation with war work, which led to an increase in production at home.[42] After this shortlived prosperity, the industry was soon faced with competition arising with the influx of Japanese fabric. In Punjab, there was tremendous scope, for this being one of the largest cotton producing provinces in India, yet they imported very large quantities of cotton yarn and piece goods Indian and foreign, though there were a number of obstacles to the rapid development of the cotton textile industry in Punjab, the locally grown cotton had a very short staple to be spun to fine counts. Moreover, the province was away from the great cotton markets.[43]

The attitude of the provincial government towards the artisans and the growth of cotton industry was not

---

41. Punjab Government, Monograph on Cotton Manufacturers in the Punjab, 1885, p.8.
42. Government of India, Indian Munition Board Industrial Handbook, Superintendent Government Printing, Calcutta, 1919, p.45.
43. Chhabra, G.S., *A Social and Economic History of the Punjab, 1849-1901,* S.Nagin & Co. Jullundur City, 1962, p.266.

encouraging, apparently they were not interested in the promotion of technical education since they did not try to promote the activities of the few government weaving schools that existed in the province at Lahore, Ludhiana, Kulu and Bushahar state.[44] The first symptoms of depression in the industry were visible after the Non-Cooperation Movement, as a measure of relief, the cotton excise duty was removed in December 1925, though the Japanese competition did not lessen. The duties on British piece goods were revised by appealing to the Tariff Board, the Indo-British Trade Agreement was signed in 1939, subsequently by which the duties on British goods were reduced to 17 per cent. The Act affected a conjunction between the British purchase of India's raw cotton and her sale of cotton goods to India. This arrangement was criticized for favouring Lancashire and sacrificing the interests of the indigenous industry.[45] Owing to the late induction in the Empire, the factory industry could not really develop in the province, and the network of railways, also, could not reach all parts of Punjab. The cotton textile industry in the Punjab under the British did survive, although, its development was effectively checked. The cotton spining and weaving industries were at Lahore, Amritsar, Lyallpur, Montgomery and Sind.[46]

Woollen textile manufacturing in Punjab, dates back to the Mughal rule, when shawls of a special texture were made at Lahore.[47] Later, during Maharaja Ranjit Singh's time, the vast regular and irregular forces, were supplied

---

44. Punjab Government, Monograph on Cotton Manufacturers in Punjab 1885, p.8.
45. Report of the Indian Tariff Board, Regarding Grant of Protection to the Cotton Textile Industry, 1932, I, pp. 13-16.
46. Council of State Debates 1939, I, March 30, pp.810-862.
47. Chatterton, Alfred, Handweaving in India, *Indian Review*, Vol..III, Calcutta, 1902, pp.104-106.

with winter uniforms and woollen manufactures were purchased to meet the needs of the royal households.[48] The states' woollen manufactures consisted of blankets, coarse woollen blankets, coir, flannels, pashmina and woollen rugs. The chief centres for the production of woollen cloth were Kashmir, Kullu, Kangra, Shimla, Dera Ghazi Khan, Dera Ismail Khan, Jalalpur Jaltan, Sialkot, Lahore, Dera Jat, Kohat, Amritsar, Ludhiana, Dinanagar, Kanjaur, Panipat and Hissar.[49]

The woollen mills in the Province, which undertook spinning, as well as weaving, by using canal water power for the first time, were such as the Egerton Woollen Mills Dhariwal, in Gurdaspur District, established by the British, for the first time in 1882. The factory produced broad cloth, blankets, lois, shawls, knitting yarns and many other goods. Coinciding with the beginnings of modern industry during the late nineteenth century, the laying of the Pathankot—Amritsar railway line in 1884, served as an incentive for the factory at Dhariwal.[50] In Ludhiana, in the first half of the nineteenth century, women had come with their families they were displaced by a famine from Kashmir, they began a commercialization of their knitting to earn their livelihood, this is how the industrial identity of Ludhiana began.[51] Hosiery can be traced back to the last century, when 25 units started functioning in the city, the First World War and the start of the Rachel loom gave a boost, by the Second World War, Ludhiana had placed 1900 machines for hosiery.[52] There were also a few hosiery factories mostly located at

---

48. Singh, Fauja, op.cit., pp.236-237.
49. Ibid.
50. Chhabra, op.cit., p.267, Report of the Indian Tariff Board on the Woollen Textile Industry II, 1936, p.348.
51. Census of India, District Census Handbook, 1961, Ludhiana, 1962.
52. *Encyclopedia of India,* Volume XXIII, Punjab, Manmohan, Kaur Rima Publishing House, New Delhi, 1994, p.89.

Ludhiana which manufactured woollen hosiery during the months of July to November. They numbered 62 in 1939, as against 16 in 1934 and 3 in 1928. The post partition period witnessed the modernization and phenomenal growth of the town and by the mid 1950s, the town had 800 concerns with 5,000 workers, subsequently, of course the town also became famous for bicycles and sewing machines.

Some obstacles to the growth of woollen industry, were the low quality of indigenous wool and competition with imported woollen goods. For instance, the 'pashmina' manufacturers of Amritsar had been ousted by power looms set up at the woollen mills. The industry, was practically finished with the import of shawls from France and Germany, which were cheaper and better in finish.[53] In fact, many Kashmiri manufacturers had migrated and settled in areas of Punjab like Lahore, Amritsar, Nurpur, Ludhiana, and plied their craft there. However, the shawls woven at Amritsar, were closest in quality to the ones, woven in the Kashmir valley.[54]

The wool industry in Gurdaspur had declined in the later years of 1914, in the face of the competition of cheap shoddy articles of European manufactures. Prior to British annexation, woollen manufactures had figured, as important export items of the province. The shawls of Amritsar and Gujarat were sold in London and in France in considerable numbers. In 1850, the annual value of shawls exported from Amritsar to Europe was 85,000 to 1,00,000 worth sterling.[55] At, this stage, Ludhiana emerged as a large centre of hoisery production. During the First World War, this industry too received a stimulus but in the 1920s, it got into difficulties

53. Powell, Baden, op.cit., pp.41-43.
54. Ibid.
55. *Punjab District Gazetteer*, Amritsar District, Vol.XXII, Lahore 1914, p.107.

as a result of the World Economic Depression and also suffered competition from Japan and Italy.[56] Till 1947, the major industry of East Punjab was woollen textiles which provided one third of the total output.

Table IV

Important Industries in (Erstwhile) Punjab

Name of Industries	Aug. 1947 No. of Factories	Aug. 1950 No. of Factories
Rice Milling	18	21
Fruits & Vegetables Processing	9	3
Sugar	1	1
Vegetable Oil	8	33
Cotton Textiles	10	9
Woollen Textiles	22	27
Chemicals	5	3
Aluminium & Copper	28	3
Iron & Steel	65	83
Bicycles (parts)	-	15
Sewing Machines (Parts)	1	4
General Engg.	69	319
Cotton Ginning & Pressing	115	66
Hosiery	53	66
Other	86	317
	490	1031

Source : Statistical Abstract of Punjab (1947-50).

Punjab proportionate to its area had a large animal population, as compared to other provinces, i.e. goats, sheep

56. Chhabra, op.cit., p.284.

and camels. With this large volume of cattle wealth, it was obvious, that Punjab had a surplus of hides and skins for export.[57] It exported the bulk of its best hides and raw skins and imported better quality leather, from small scale tanneries and mechanized ventures based at Lahore, Wazirabad and Rawalpindi. Many more were set up thereafter and their total number in 1929 was 53, which increased to 155 in 1939. However, there was leather goods factory and whatever shoemaking process existed it was confined to the cottage worker, while the educated middle class depended upon shoes either imported from other provinces or from abroad.[58] Some other deterrent were tanning methods, which had caused an enormous waste of raw material and a lack of capital.[59]

In Sialkot (now in West Punjab), a considerable sports industry developed, which began to export overseas. The aggregate output value was of lakhs of rupees in 1932. This industry required rubber, which was imported parts of the rubber goods, e.g. bladders, cycle tubes, washers, heels and soles were made in Sialkot. After partition, the Sports industry shifted to Jullundur and continues to thrive there .[60]

The first attempt to manufacture glassware was made in 1892, when a bottle making factory was started at Jhelum.[61] The factory was abandoned soon after, on account of a high cost of production and a lack of certain chemicals, which had to be imported. Two more relatively unknown major glass works existed at Ambala, known as the Upper

---

57. Ibid., p.285.
58. Anand R.L., Tanning Industry in the Punjab, Board of Economic Enquiry, 1939, Lahore.
59. Government of India, Labour Investigation Committee, Tanneries and Leather Goods Factories, 1946, p.2.
60. Singh, S.B., *Sports Industry in Punjab* – an unpublished M.Phil. Dissertation, Punjabi University, Patiala, 1979, p.42.
61. Monograph on the Pottery and Glass Industries of the Punjab 1892, p.23.

India Glass Works and the other Panipat Glass Works. During the First World War, Ambala Glass Works specialized in chimneys and supplied them to the whole of Punjab and the North West Frontier Province. However after the war, the industry got into difficulties due to the revival of foreign competition, the severest being offered by Japan, the United Kingdom, Austria and Belgium. The Glass factory at Amritsar had submitted to the Indian Tariff Board a memorandum which indicated that the industry needed a high tariff wall against foreign competition, decades later, a cut glass unit came up in Amritsar.[62] In 1918 ploughs, lathis, grinders, bandsaws began to be manufactured in Batala. Before 1927, the chief source of chaff cutting machines were imported from Germany and England. These were intially being manufactured at Goraya and subsequently by towns like Phillaur, Jullundur and Phagwara. Sewing machines were made in Bassi Pathana, followed by Jullundur and Ludhiana.[63]

The colonial rulers found a well established silk industry in Punjab, which was existent through the Misl period as well as in Maharaja Ranjit Singh's time, silk continued to be in popular demand as a form of apparel. The British wanted to continue with this industry, so as to give the people a purposeful employment as a means of destraction from their militant inclinations. An Agro Horticultural Society had been formed where research was encouraged in silk production and subsequently, overtures were sent to other areas of India. This industry consisted of two separate industries, sericulture or the growing and reeling of silk and its weaving.[64]

62. Report of the Indian Tariff Board on the Continuance of Protection to Glass Industry, 1950, p.7.
63. Government of Punjab, Board of Economic Enquiry, Iron Foundry Industry at Batala, 1941.
64. Dhanki, J.S., Presidential Address at the Punjab History Conference, Proceedings, 27 March 1999.

In the second half of the nineteenth century, there were many famines, so the manufacturing classes suffered, a later setback to sericulture was the wholesale death of silkworms. However, in the early twentieth century, fresh attempts were made to revive sericulture, by putting it under the purview of the Department of Agriculture.[65]

The Department of Agriculture imported pebrine free seed from France and distributed it among the rearers in Gurdaspur, Lyallpur, Pathankot, Kangra and Simla, nurseries were also set up in Sialkot, Campbellpur, Rawalpindi and Hoshiarpur.[66] By the time partition took place, even though a variety of silk cloth was manufactured at Multan, Lahore, Amritsar, Nabha, Nurpur and Patiala it was an industry on the wane.[67] Sericulture never assumed the form of a flourishing industry, the quantity of raw silk produced in 1938-39, was only maunds which was inadequate for the requirements of the silk weaver, who accordingly depended entirely on imports from China and Japan.[68] The silk industry was threatened by the influx of cheap rayon products from Japan, which captured the Indian markets. The weaver in Punjab also adopted artificial silk to meet the growing menace,[69] but the Customs Tariff Policy of the Government of India unwittingly made his position precarious. In 1934, the Indian Tariff Amendment Act, while giving effect to the decision of the Government of India on the recommendations of the Indian Tariff Board, 1933,

65. Report on the Exhibition of Silk, Department of Commerce and Industry, 7, No. 84.
66. Department of Commerce and Industry, Punjab, op.cit.
67. Powell, Baden, *Handbook of Manufactures and Arts of Punjab,* Vol.2, Punjab Printing Press, Lahore, 1872, p.64.
68. Ibid.
69. Lal Ram, Report on the Department of Industries, Punjab for the Year Ending 31 March 1933, Superintendent Government Printing, Punjab, Lahore, 1933, p.5.

appointed to investigate the claims of the sericulture industry to protection, imposed protective duties on raw silk, silk yarn, piece goods and mixtures as well as fabrics of artificial silk and mixtures. The Act, however, neither proved beneficial to the sericulture industry in the Punjab nor did it arrest foreign competition. Representations were made by the silk weavers to get the duties reduced on raw silk and artificial silk but in vain.[70] As a result, the silk weaving industry began to decline rapidly and many weavers gave up their hereditary occupation.

Paper mills were established in the United Provinces and Bengal during the latter half of the nineteenth century with an influx of cheap wood pulp paper from Europe.[71] It is surprising that though the Province had favourable conditions for the manufacture of paper as regards raw materials, there was no paper mill in it till as late as 1929 when the first mill was started at Jagadhri by the Punjab Paper Mills Company Ltd., and the mill in Lahore was established in 1923. The total production of different types of paper from April to December 1937 was 2,446 tons and the expenditure incurred on its production during the same period was Rs. 11,62,281.[72]

Certain other industries existed for instance, Nizamabad near Wazirabad was famous for a long time for its workers in iron; particularly, cutlery. However, this too faded out,

> In other parts of the country, one result of the orders of the Supreme Government, to the effect that cutlery of native make should be substituted in Government offices for that, hitherto, imported from England, has been a demonstration of the hopelessness of the

---

70. Indian Tariff Board written evidence on the Sericulture Industry, I, 1940, pp.599, 607.
71. Latifi, Abdul, op.cit., p.84.
72. Indian Tariff Board Paper and Pulp Industries I, Evidence 1939, pp. 431, 439.

competition between Indian and Sheffield cutlery. That the craft survives at all, shows that the country cutlery finds a place somewhere. A very rude form of pen knife with immoveable blade and turned up point in a wooden handle, seems to be the only article of Nizamabad production, that finds a large sale.[73]

Carpets were made in Punjab, mainly at Amritsar and Multan initially by jail inmates. The Indian carpet was first brought to the notice of Europe at the London International Exhibition of 1851, but it was not till 1862, that the exhibits of the Lahore Jail introduced this to the world market.[74] In the nineteenth century carpets were exported to America, they continued to be made in Amritsar District. Later, the Oriental Carpet Mills (OCM) was set up in 1924.

Despite all these industrial stirrings, Punjab remained industrially backward, even in comparison to the general industrial lag, prevalent all over the country. For administrative purposes on the recommendations of the Industrial Commission, the British had established a Department of Industries in 1920, which performed many functions like providing loans to industries needing financial assistance, establishing demonstration or model factories like a powerloom weaving demonstration factory built at Shahdara, mainly with the object of giving instructions in the art and practice of powerloom weaving to professional weavers of the Province and establishing various industrial schools at Lahore, Amritsar, Kasur, establishing cooperative societies and conducting industrial

---

73. Note by Mr. Kipling Lockwood, Principal of the Lahore School of Art, in the Gazetteer of the Gujranwala District 1883-4, p.12.
74. Latimer, A., *Monograph on Carpet Making in the Punjab*, Lahore, 1906 (1905-1906)

research on specific problems.[75] However, in spite, of the endeavours of the Department of Industries, the tariff policy of the British Government had adverse effects on Indian industry.

The tariff policy in India, was directed towards protecting the business interests of the British, which advocated free access to the Indian market. Till 1924, the Government had refused to impose custom duties on the import of foreign goods.[76] Even when they did impose low duties on some goods for the purposes of collecting revenue, they sought to neutralize their effects by imposing equivalent excise duties on goods of local origin. The Indian Government leaned heavily on British industry, for its large purchases of equipment for public utility in health and education, even simple machines and standard supplies were imported, whereas those orders could well have served to stimulate expansion for indigenous industry.[77]

When the Second World War began, the cessation of imports was total. There were serious import restrictions, and requirements to suit war exigency, so manufacturing got some impetus. Owing to the huge demand for war goods and the comparatively limited capacity of large-scale industries in the Punjab province, the War Supply Department placed an increasing reliance on the manufacture of small scale industries like cotton and woollen goods.[78] With Japan's entry, it seemed that India might become an

75. Sharma, S.C., op. cit.
76. Habib, Irfan, *Studying a Colonial Economy, Essays in Indian History, Towards a Marxist Perception* (Ed.) Irfan Habib, Tulika Publications, New Delhi, 1992, p.362.
77. Dutt, Ruddar and Sundaram K.P.N., *Indian Economy*. Manohar Publications, New Delhi, 1992, p.23.
78. Kulkarni, M.R., *Industrial Development*, National Book Trust, New Delhi, 1971, p.127.

active theatre of war. However, after a shortlived panic, the industry was quick to recover from the initial shock and to exploit the opportunities offered by war. The devastation caused by bombing to the British economy, enhanced the strategic role of the Indian economy. The Indian industrial structure recorded a substantial progress, during the inter war years but that was mainly in the direction of the production of certain consumer goods like textiles, sugar, paper, cement, matches, etc. The only basic industry which developed was iron and steel.[79] Some industrialization had taken place in Punjab, as a response to agricultural growth primarily agro-processing and agro-input machinery industries. The two world wars also gave a fillip to industries and a few towns like Lahore, Amritsar, Dhariwal, Sialkot,Gujranwala Wazirabad and Batala emerged as industrial centres in the state.[80]

In 1931 the Punjab Government set up an Industrial Research Laboratory to undertake experiments for ascertaining the possibilities of starting new industries or developing the existing one based on the raw materials available in the Province. This laboratory soon proved its usefulness and its scope gradually widened. After the war, industrial research received special attention, valuable research had also been done on examining tanning raw materials, fibres and reeds.[81] In fact, industrial research continued to be an important feature of the activities of the Department and the work was confined to determining their industrial uses.[82]

---

79. Ibid.
80. Bhalla, G.S., *Agricultural Growth and Industrial Development: A Case of Study of Punjab*; Paper presented at China 4 July 1990, Centre for Regional Studies, Jawaharlal Nehru University.
81. Lal, Ram, *Report on the Working of the Department of Industries, Punjab for the Year Ending 31 March 1940*, p.39.
82. Mahmood, M.H., *Report on the Working of the Department of Industries, Punjab for the Year Ending 31 March 1941*, p.45.

Similarly, in the year 1939, a scheme for systematic industrial surveys of the Province, as a preliminary step to a planned development of industries was launched.[83] In 1940, the industrial surveys of Ludhiana, Multan, Sialkot and Lahore districts were completed and reports were compiled. Simultaneously, provincial surveys of the oilseed industry, ceramic raw materials, pottery, industry and tanning industry were also completed.[84] War time conditions had enlarged the scope of the work of surveying and special enquiries had been instituted with a view to assess the impact of war on industrial development in the Province.[85]

In the post partition scenario, the industrial take off was dismal, since the Indian Punjab was economically backward. It had all the characteristics of economic backwardness, such as traditional agriculture, inadequate development of transport, communication and lacked the basic industrial infrastructure.[86] In any case, the British geared up Punjab, only to be a source of agricultural products and they had done little for the development of industry in the state. Most factories were only agro-based, producing raw material for factories in other parts of the country.

---

83. Lal, Ram, *Report on the Department of Industries, Punjab*, for the *Year Ending 31 March 1939*, p.I.
84. Ibid., 31 March 1940, p.9.
85. Mahmood, M.H., *Report on the Working of the Department of Industries, Punjab for the Year Ending 31 March 1941*, pp.11-12.
86. Ghosh, Ravindra Nath, *Agriculture in Economic Development with Special Reference to Punjab*, Vikas Publishing House, New Delhi, 1977, p.37.

Table V

Number of Factories Surveyed

Column 2 in the table below contains the number of factories located in border districts and established before partition, excluding those owned by the state. Column 3 gives the number of factories owned by Muslim evacuees, column 4 that of factories closed down or shifted since partition and column 6 the number of factories actually surveyed for the present inquiry.

Number of Factories in Border Districts

Sr. No.	Industry	Total No. of Factories	Owned by Evacuees	Shifted or Closed	Balance	Factories Surveyed
1.	Flour & Rice Mills	14	2	-	12	11
2.	Fruit Products	1	-	-	1	1
3.	Breakfast Food	1	-	-	1	1
4.	Cotton Ginning & Oils	20	1	2	17	16
5.	Hosiery	53	6	3	44	39
6.	Textiles	74	3	4	67	56
7.	Metal Works	17	1	5	11	9
8.	Mechanical Engineering	153	53	7	93	79
9.	Steel Re-rolling Mills	12	-	4	8	8
10.	Electrical Engineering	18	1	4	13	11
11.	Scientific Engineering	1	-	-	1	1
12.	Chemicals and Paints	7	-	3	4	4
13.	Printing Presses & Stat.	4	-	-	4	3
14.	Glassware	4	-	1	3	2
15.	Lime Grinding, etc.	2	1	-	1	1
16.	Woodworks	5	3	-	2	1
17.	Distillery	1	-	-	1	1

Contd........

18. Button Factories	3	-	2	1	1
19. Tanneries	2	1	-	1	-
20. Rubber Works	1	-	1	-	-
21.Tobacco	2	-	1	1	-
22.Tea Polishing	2	-	1	1	-
Total	397**	72	38	287	245

* Figures obtained from the register of factories maintained by Chief Inspector of Factories to East Punjab Government.

** Ice factories excluded.

Source: Luthra, K.L. Impact of Partition on Industries and Border Districts of East Punjab, The Board of Economic Inquiry, East Punjab Publication No. I, 1947.

The predominant form of industry in Punjab till partition was small-scale and it continued to be so in the post-partition period. (See Table VI). The number of important factories registered in August 1947, stood at 490. The cotton ginning and pressing industry accounted for the largest number of factories 115 or 23.5 per cent of the total factories. This group was followed by textiles, 85, i.e. 17.3 per cent of the total, this industry included — woollen textiles, cotton textiles and hosiery, the iron and steel smelting industries were only 65 in number and general engineering were 69. The rice milling, fruit and vegetable processing, sugar and vegetable oil industries were only 36 in number.[87]

87. Singh, Balbir, "Regional Dispersal of Punjab Industry since Independence," *The Punjab Past and Present*, Volume XXVII, Part II, Punjabi University, Patiala, October 1993.

Table VI

Small-Scale (Registered) Industrial Units

	By the End of 1950	
Industry	**Punjab**	**Haryana**
Food Products	40	6
Beverages	5	-
Hosiery	251	2
Wood Products	53	12
Leather Products	227	9
Chemicals	93	23
Metal & Alloy	85	14
Machinery & Parts	203	17
Transport Equipment & Parts	84	3
Electrical Machinery	19	3
Repair Services	58	20
Miscellaneous	29	18
Total	**1571**	**494**

Source: Statistical Abstract of Punjab – 1950.

Pepsu had been formed with the merger of the covenanting princely states of Punjab in 1948, there was not much industrial set up here the rulers had not encouraged large-scale industry, mainly to avoid any labour trouble.[88] However, the impact of the First World War and a shrinkage in imports led to the production of cycle parts.

88. Singh, Gursharan, "Industrial Development in Pepsu," Punjab History Conference, Proceedings, 17-18 March, Punjabi University, Patiala, 1989, p.339.

The Second World War large-scale factory came up for the manufacture of 50,000 bicycles in Rajpura.[89] The number of manufacturing centres were scattered at a number of places like Kapurthala, Phagwara, Patiala and the industry was mainly localized at Malerkotla and in some surrounding villages such as Gowara and Sarad.[90]

In fact, post Second World War, a number of factories sprang up as a biscuit factory at Rajpura, a distillery at Hamira, two cement factories at Dadri and Surajpur, two sugar factories at Hamira and Phagwara, a fruit juice and squash factory at Bahadurgarh, a tannery at Kapurthala, two flour mills at Patiala and Bhatinda, a glass factory at Faridkot, three starch factories at Rajpura, Faridkot and Phagwara bore the testimony of such industrial growth.[91] A further landmark in the industrial development in Pepsu was made with the switching to production in the year 1951-52 of a textile mill with an ultimate capacity of one thousand looms and forty thousand spindles at Phagwara, later well-known as the Jagjit Cotton Textiles (JCT).[92]

It was only after independence, that the era of proper planned industrial development began. In April 1948, for the first time the Government of India formulated a fairly comprehensive industrial policy covering large, medium, small-scale cottage and village industries.[93] The only

89. *The Statesman*, 13 June 1954 and *The Times of India* 5 February 1955.
90. Pepsu Government, Department of Industry 'Cycle Parts Industry – A War Baby (unpublished, Patiala, 1955, p.2).
91. Pepsu since Inauguration: Pepsu Government Patiala, 1951, p.58. "An assessement of the Level of Production and Development of the Industrial Sector in Pepsu under the First Five Year Plan and the Aim and Objects of the Second Five Year Plan for Industries," Patiala, 1956, p.I.
92. *The Statesman*, 15 July 1955.
93. Government of India, Ministry of Industries, State Policy 1948, New Delhi.

industries, which were developed in the state were small-scale, consumer goods industries, hosiery, handloom, spinning and weaving. Before partition, the industrial development had been sluggish and unsustained, though there existed a home market for various manufactured goods, which the state imported.[94] There were 572 registered factories with an employment of 37,486 workers in Punjab in August 1947. Among these factories, the largest number was that of the ginning and pressing factories followed respectively by general and electrical engineering, iron and steel, smelting, rolling, rerolling, hosiery, wheel flow and rice milling.[95]

Whatever limited industrial development, Punjab had at the time of independence, it was not geographically evenly distributed. Some areas had a concentration of industries, viz. Amritsar district housed 187 out of a total of 572 factories registered in the state in 1947. Ludhiana district stood second with 78 units, followed by Jullundur (63), Gurdaspur (58), Ambala (49) and so on.[96] As far as small-scale industrial units are concerned, Ludhiana and not Amritsar District had the largest concentration. In a survey of 1950, Ludhiana district had the maximum number of small industrial units (452) followed by Amritsar and Jullundur districts, which had 239.[97]

The despatch of the colonial masters was a matter of revelry in the rest of India, where new found independence brought hopes and aspirations as the process of

---

94. Bhatia, B.S., "Pattern of Industrial Development of Punjab since Independence," unpublished Ph.D. Thesis, Punjab University, Chandigarh, 1970, p.2.
95. Government of Punjab, *Statistical Abstract 1947-50*, Simla, 1958.
96. Ibid.
97. Government of Punjab, *Industrial Statistics of Punjab*,1952 Economic and Statistical Organization, Simla, 1953.

decolonization began after shackles of centuries. However, Punjab was decolonized in more ways than one. The problems escalated, as millions of bewildered men and women crossed the border on both sides.[98] Here was a state-truncated, its inhabitants suffering, bereft of brethren, hearth, vocation and property,[99] they left behind, not only their cultural heritage but fertile agricultural land, a vast network of colonies and agricultural prosperity.[100] The mass exodus of people from West to East Punjab of Hindus and Sikhs, threw up multitudinous problems before the Punjab Government in India. These people left behind 5,700,000 acres of colonized land in West Punjab and they were to be settled on 4,500,000 acres left by Muslim landowners in East Punjab. The Government evolved a scheme of graded cuts, by which the refugees lost land in increasing proportion to the size of landholdings.[101]

The rural population of about 350,000 peasant cultivator families from West Pakistan were moved straight to Muslim evacuee villages by the East Punjab Government, leaving behind two million acres of land more than the evacuees of East Punjab. Those families who had gone to West Punjab as colonists, now returned to their ancestral villages as refugees. The Governments of India and East Punjab had risen to the occasion. The liasion officer and MEO personnel rendered yeoman service in evacuation. However, the refugees had to face problems, owing to the vacillating policy of the Government regarding planned mass migration, practices of corruption and bribery in the administration.[102] The East Punjab Government had to

98. Rai, Satya M., *Punjab since Partition*, Durga Publications, Delhi, 1986, p.164.
99. Hasan, Mushir-ul, *India's Partition, Process, Strategy and Mobilization*, Oxford University Press, Delhi 1994, p.2.
100. *The Tribune*, 10 December 1997.
101. Randhawa, M.L., *Out of the Ashes*, Chandigarh 1954, pp. 81-82.
102. Nanda, Inder, *Punjab Uprooted*, Bombay, 1948, p.67

spend huge sums on refugee resettlement, though competent Punjab officials had been appointed in the Ministry of Relief and Rehabilitation.[103]

As a part of the process of rehabilitation, East Punjab began searching for its industrial moorings, even though natural resources were meagre, coffers were bare and banking facilities were dislocated. The first budget was presented in 1947, in which large sums were allotted for rehabilitation, Rs. 5 crores to be precise but there was no mention of industry specifically.[104] The prepartition industrial development in East Punjab had been negligible with just a few factories, which had mainly sprung up during the Second World War. Non-Muslims had left behind more than 4,000 industrial establishments valued at over Rs. 40 crores, against this only about 1,000 industrial units and that too in a poor shape were left behind in East Punjab by the migrating population.[105] Major industrial areas Lahore, Gujranwala, Sialkot and Wazirabad were left in West Punjab. Some of the important factories left behind in Pakistan were cotton spinning at Lahore, Lyallpur, Montgomery and Sind and the cotton ginning was at Multan. There was a cement factory at Hasan Abdal in Attock District, a woollen handloom industry at Dera Ghazi Khan and woollen hosieries at Sialkot and Lahore, and the tanneries were at Lahore, Wazirabad and Rawalpindi. Iron safes and steel trunks were made at Gujranwala and Sialkot, surgical instruments at Sialkot, Wazirabad and Nizamabad, which was also known for its excellent cutlery. Sialkot had a thriving sports goods industry from where they were exporting items. Rubber goods were also made here as well

103. *The Tribune*, 6 October 1947, Simla, p.I.
104. *The Tribune*, I November. 1947.
105. Government of Punjab, "Industrial Statistics," Economic and Statistical Organization, Simla, 1953, p.I.

as at Wazirabad and Lahore.[106] The major large-scale industries in Punjab consisted of textile industries, cotton, silk, wool, hosiery, cotton seed oil, sports goods, leather industry, chemicals, salt, oils, sugar, paper and iron and steel.[107] The newly formed state was poor in minerals, and the areas which supplied agricultural raw materials for industry such as cotton oil seeds fell to the share of Pakistan, with the result, the small-scale hosiery and textile industry were badly affected.[108]

The industrial backwardness of the region is also indicated by the sectoral distribution of population though the mainstay of the state's economy lay on agriculture. In the accompanying table 17.7 per cent families were engaged in agriculture and 35.8 per cent in trade and business comprised, largely of cloth merchants, commission agents, etc. with very few families in the industrial sector, barely 0.008 per cent (see Table VII).

Table VII

Occupational Distribution of Refugee Families from Areas of West Punjab

Occupation	Number of Families
Agriculture	17118 (17.7)
Trade and Business	34531 (35.8)
Industrial (owners)	2109 (0.08)
Services	18231 (18.9)
Liberal Profession	4779 (4.9)
Labour	13374 (13.8)
Others	6312 (6.5)
Total	**96454**

Source: Punjab Government, Statistical Abstract, 1947-50

106. (a) Punjab Government, *Monograph on Cotton Manufacturers in the Punjab 1885*, p.8. (b) Shah, K.T. *Industrialization of the Punjab*, *1941*, p.205 (c) Saini, B.S. *The Social and Economic History of India 1901-1939,* Ess Ess Publications, Delhi, 1975, p.287.
107. Shah, K.T. op.cit., p.203.
108. Kapoor, T.N., *Industrial Development in the States of India*, Sterling Publishers, Delhi, 1967, p.353.

The bulk of the departing urban Muslim population of East Punjab, consisted of artisans, mechanics, craftsmen, blacksmiths, potters and a large number of skilled workers, while the vast majority of urban Hindu and Sikh refugees from West Pakistan belonged to the trading classes. These people could not take the jobs left by Muslims, as they lacked the requisite expertise. Flour, rice milling, cotton ginning and oil, hosiery, textiles, metal engineering and glass were some of the industries having more than half of their skilled labour consisting of Muslim workers. About 54.8 per cent of the skilled labour in Amritsar textiles and 61.1 per cent of skilled labour in Ludhiana hosiery came from the Muslim community. There was quite a deficiency caused in carders, spinners, weavers and so were foremen and machine supervisors in short supply. The dyeing and finishing departments were adversely affected by the immigration of skilled Muslim workers. So was the mechanical engineering industry in Gurdaspur district badly in need of moulders after partition. Similarly, there was a shortage of tongsmen and cutters in the Ludhiana mechanical engineering. In Jullundur city, iron and steel fabricating were also adversely affected, so did tinsmiths, blacksmiths, gas and electric welders, moulders, filters and machinemen employed in metal works before partition belong largely to the Muslim community.

At this stage, the Government had to find fresh avenues of employment and resettle nearly 84 per cent of the urban refugee population in the economy of the state, in such a way, that it would not only meet this objective but also resuscitate the economic life. The average number of skilled workers fell from 15,022 to 9,784, i.e. by 34.9 per cent during the period. The fall in numbers employed being heaviest in Gurdaspur and the least in Ludhiana, out of the overall 15,022 skilled workers employed during 1946-47, as many as 8,101 came from the Muslim community (53.9

per cent) which emigrated after partition. As the industries remained understaffed during 1947-48, the capital employed per unit of labour rose from Rs. 3,200 to Rs. 4,800 which shows the way investment suffered.

The main task of administrators, immediately after partition was to take (i) stock of the changed industrial structure caused by partition (ii) to rehabilitate dislodged entrepreneurs, who carried the necessary skills with them but lacked investment funds (iii) to initiate industrial training to supplement the existing state of knowledge and to train new entrepreneurs.[109] Reputed training institutions like the Craig Technical Institute, the Dyeing and the Calico Printing Institute, the Weaving Demonstration Factory, the Central Pottery Agency and the Mayo School of Arts went to the share of Western Punjab.[110]

A few months preceding partition and immediately afterwards, economic activity in the Punjab was virtually at a standstill because of the collapse of the administrative machinery. The worst sufferers were the towns and villages, which were once located in the heart of the province, but now happened to fall on the borders of the newly created states. The business and industrial activity of these towns was totally paralyzed.[111] The economic life of the border areas was completely dislocated, since labour and capital fled to safety zones, they were still apprehensive having witnessed communal clashes just recently.[112] A large number of affluent displaced industrialists migrated to Delhi and other parts of India, where they boosted the economic life of those cities

---

109. Rai, op. cit.
110. Government of Punjab, *Industrial Statistics of Punjab 1952* Economic and Statistical Organization, Punjab, Simla, 1952, p.(I).
111. Luthra, K.L., op.cit., p.42.
112. Ibid., p.181.

by virtue of their enterprise and investments. However, border towns were left poor and a number of factories, previously located there, were either closed or shifted to other areas.[113]

The gross value output of all the industries surveyed by the Economic Enquiry Committee worked out to Rs. 1014.96 lakhs during 1947-48 as compared to Rs. 1245.82 lakhs during 1946-47. Thus it registered a fall of Rs. 230.86 lakhs or 18.5 per cent of the total value of output. The reduction in the labour force and the contraction of output reacted heavily on the economic life of province.[114]

The Table (VIII) below gives the average monthly gross value of output for each industry during the years 1946-47 and 1947-48 and also during the first quarter of the year 1948-49.

Table VIII
Average Monthly Gross Value of Output
(In Thousands of Rupees)

S.No.	Industry	Average Monthly Gross Value of Output		
		1946-47	1947-48	First Quarter of 1948-49
1.	Flour & Rice Mills	17,32	24,61	24,61
2.	Fruit Products	36	13	13
3.	Breakfast Food	25	8	10
4.	Cotton Ginning & Oils	11,02	9,78	10,50
5.	Hosiery	6,21	4,94	4,94
6.	Textiles	37,49	26,67	26,09
7.	Metal Works etc.	4,31	1,39	1,56
8.	Mechanical Engineering	9,09	7,32	7,63

Contd........

113. Mehra, Diwan C., *Note from Textile Manufacturers Association*, Amritsar 1948.

114. *Statistical Abstract of Punjab*, *1947-1950*, p.48.

9.	Steel Rerolling Mills	1,62	54	57
10.	Electrical Engineering	2,85	1,27	1,30
11.	Scientific Engineering	25	-	-
12.	Chemicals and Paints	2,30	2,10	2,10
13.	Distillery	7,96	4,59	4,59
14.	Printing Presses and Stationery	1,33	75	75
15.	Glass Wares	86	-	-
16.	Lime Grinding	32	25	25
17.	Wood Works	13	1	2
18.	Button Factory	15	15	15
	All Industries	**1,03,82**	**84,58**	**85,29**

Source: *K.L. Luthra, op.cit., p.42.*

A comparison of figures in columns III, IV and V would reveal that average monthly output during the first quarter of the year 1948-49 registered, on the whole, very little improvement as compared with the average output during the year 1947-48. The average output in the textile industry, on the other hand, had fallen by a small margin.

Table IX
Variations in Gross Value of Output

S.No.	Industry	Gross Value of Output		Increase (+) or Decrease (-) during 1947-48 over 1946-47	
		1946-47	1947-48	**Amount**	**Percentage**
		Rs. lakhs	Rs. lakhs	Rs. lakhs	Rs.lakhs
1.	Flour & Rice Mills	207.87	295.34	+87.47	+ 42.1
2.	Fruit Products	4.32	1.54	- 2.7	- 64.3
3.	Breakfast Food	3.00	0.90	- 2.10	- 70.0
4.	Cotton Ginning & Oils	132.21	117.36	- 14.85	- 11.2
5.	Hosiery	74.53	59.22	- 15.31	- 20.5
6.	Textiles	449.94	320.03	-129.91	- 28.9

Contd........

7.	Metal Works etc.	51.70	16.73	- 34.97	- 67.6
8.	Mechanical Engineering	109.17	87.79	- 21.38	- 19.6
9.	Steel Re-rolling Mills	19.52	6.51	- 13.01	- 66.6
10.	Electrical Engineering	34.17	15.27	- 18.90	- 55.3
11.	Scientific Engineering	3.00	-	- 3.00	-100.0
12.	Chemicals and Paints	27.51	25.21	- 2.30	- 8.4
13.	Distillery	95.52	55.06	- 40.46	- 42.43
14.	Printing Presses, etc.	15.90	9.00	- 6.90	- 43.4
15.	Glass Wares	10.32	-	- 10.32	-100.0
16.	Lime Grinding	3.84	3.00	- 0.84	- 21.8
17.	Woodworks	1.50	0.15	- 1.35	- 90.0
18.	Button Factory	1.80	1.85	+ 0.05	+ 2.8
	All Industries	**1245.82**	**1014.96**	**-230.86**	**- 18.5**

Source: K.L. Luthra, op.cit., p.43.

There was a big void in the industrial structure of border towns by the emigration of Muslim workers, which was not even partially filled up from these and other available sources. Some non-Muslim workers in Amritsar shifted to safer places where conditions were less disturbed. Most of the workers immigrating to East Punjab after partition had a tendency to settle at places far inside the border and they preferred to move towards Delhi. There was a lack of initiative on the part of the industrialists to train their labour, the reasons being the all round dislocation of the economy of the province and grave uncertainties about the future of industries.[115]

There was a dislocation of sources of raw material as well as markets. It was well nigh impossible for industrialists to tap new sources in order to make up for those lost in Pakistan. Some rice mills used to get paddy from Sheikhupura and Gujranwala, cotton ginning factories in Amritsar also used to get cotton from the canal colonies of Punjab and Bahawalpur State. One or two woollen textile

115. Luthra, K.L., op.cit., p.59.

mills purchased a part of their requirement of wool from Lahore and NWFP was seriously affected, as wool from Bahawalpur ceased to be marketed at Fazilka after partition.

The textile industry in Amritsar used to get some chemicals from Karachi and was in short supply of these for a few months after partition. The chemical industry depended upon Pakistan rock and salt-petre. The dislocation of certain raw materials under normal circumstances would have had no pronounced effect on industrial output. However, during this period even the transport system had collapsed.[116]

Industry suffered heavily due to the dislocation of markets for disposal of their turnover after partition. About over three-fourths of the total turnover of the textile industry of Amritsar used to be consumed in markets now located in Pakistan in areas such as the North Western Frontier Province, British Baluchistan and Bahawalpur State. This industry was completely cut off from most of these markets as a result of partition, cotton ginning and oil factories used to sell over 69 per cent of their turnover in West Punjab. About one-third of the turnover of the hosiery industry and over half each of metal works, mechanical engineering, electrical engineering, fruit products and stationery were consumed before partition in the markets left in Pakistan. Chemical concerns, too, used to sell over 60 per cent of their turnover in towns of West Punjab and the North West Fronter Province. The major output of the glassware industry was supplied to markets left in Pakistan.[117]

For a few months after partition, even the existing markets in India and East Punjab remained inaccessible to

116. Satya, M.Rai., p.61.
117. Luthra, K.L., p.61.

industries located in border towns. There were numerous other hardships, dealers from all over India did not find it convenient or safe to book orders with manufacturers in the border towns of East Punjab. Orders could not be executed because of the non-availability of transport facilities moreover even banks refused to finance trade with border towns, they had suffered heavily as a result of partition, while deposits of the public with them were mostly transferred to India. The assets of these banks which stood invested in immovable forms could not be transferred, nor could the loans due from business and industry be realized. So the banks in East Punjab had reason to be jittery since uncertainty loomed large over the already much dislocated economic structure of the province. The banks which survived from the tremendous shock of partition,

> shifted from the Punjab towns not merely their head offices but also their main spheres of activity, particularly, so far as their investment was concerned. They virtually stopped financing trade in East Punjab.[118]

However, the massive migration due to partition was a major factor in the urbanization of Punjab. Most migrants, who were involved in commercial activities from across the border, preferred to settle in the cities and towns. Model Towns had been set up to rehabilitate the refugee population in the peripheral areas of some selected towns like Jullundur, Ludhiana and Patiala. Under the scheme of the Ministry of Rehabilitation, a large number of people from Bahawalpur were settled in Rajpura. Here the government provided incentives for industry, through special schemes and it eventually emerged as an industrial town. Similarly, Mandi Gobindgarh after partition emerged as the "Steel and Iron Town of Punjab", Amritsar also became the hub of

118. Rai, Satya M., p.181.

industrial, trade and commercial activity of Punjab after partition. The refugees who came from Sialkot, established the sports industry in Jullundur, whereas hosiery was firmly established in Ludhiana and Dhariwal. Therefore, the establishment of small and medium scale industrial units after partition led to the growth of urban centres.[119]

In the post partition period, attention was given to the various schemes of irrigation. For instance, the Madhopur-Beas link was completed in two years by 1955, the Bhakra Dam had been originally conceived as a water storage scheme, there was no proposal to generate hydroelectric power from it. The idea was probably conceived, during the years 1914-15 or 1916-18. The Indian Industrial Commission had suggested that the Government should immediately undertake a hydrographic survey, in order, to ascertain the hydroelectric resources of the country.[120]

In united Punjab, the only important source of electric power was the Uhl River Hydroelectric scheme with an effective capacity of 36,000 kw. As needs increased, the whole scheme was revived in the light of the upto date needs for irrigation and power and some preliminary work commenced in 1945. However, the progress was withheld by the turbulent conditions of 1947. Post partition, the demands for power rose sharply, because new townships and industrial estates were envisaged to settle the displaced population from West Pakistan. So in 1948, regular work started for the construction of the Bhakra Dam.[121]

---

119. Walia, Jaspreet, Growth of Urbanization in Punjab 1951-1991, *Punjab History Conference, Proceedings,* 26 Session, 18-20 March, Punjabi University, Patiala, 1994, p.295.
120. *Souvenir Bhakra Nangal Power House (Patiala)*, Punjab Government, Publication, 1963.
121. Bajaj, Y.P., Genesis of the Bhakra Dam Scheme, 1914-1948, *Punjab Past and Present* Vol.XI, Part I and II, Punjabi University, 1993, p.149, Patiala.

By 1948, as the wounds of partition were begining to heal and the nascent state began to grope around for its survival and success. In the budget of 1948, delineated by Chief Minister Gopi Chand Bhargava, in spite of a deficit of 6.69 crores, new schemes were outlined in the sphere of Industries, Labour, Agriculture and Education.[122] Besides, there was a keen desire of the Government to make Punjab prosperous by building new projects, which would enhance the supply of more water and electricity to the Province, since partition, had taken away the biggest component of their canal network. The Chief Minister was also cheered, when he announced the plan to exploit the rich reserves of minerals in the Simla Hills and in Kangra district. There was also,

> a desire for providing better facilities to the labour, getting them a better wage and re-establishing them in East Punjab; the industries which were ours in West Punjab, were either destroyed or taken over.[123]

On the political front, after partition, there was a switch of the ruling political parties from the Unionist party to Congress, the first Chief Minister was Gopi Chand Bhargava as mentioned earlier and Sir Chandu Lal Trivedi took over as Governor from Sir Evan Jenkins. The Government Secretariat had been scattered in various parts of the East Punjab. In Punjab politics, in what was to become a tradition later, a tussle ensued between two political stalwarts, Bhim Sen Sachar and Dr. Gopi Chand Bhargava. The former and Pratap Singh Kairon joined hands in ousting their rival, the latter from office. This had then resulted in the promulgation of the President's Rule in the state in 1951. *The Hindustan Times* in its editorial "Storm in a tea cup" recounted how

122. Government of India, *Census of India*, New Delhi, 1951.
123. *The Tribune*, 9 March 1948.

Punjab had earned the uneviable distinction of being the first state of the Union to suffer the application of Article 356 of the Constitution. A tradition which was to be followed three decades later during the phase of terrorism in the state.[124] After the first general elections in 1952, the chief minister was Bhim Sen Sachar, who resigned in 1956, after differences with Pandit Nehru. Nehru felt that Kairon was indispensable for Punjab and got him elected in place of Sachar.[125]

In the infant state, there was political instability at this juncture, particularly, when it was beset with massive social and political problems and the economy was seriously impaired. The Indian Punjab received a small share of irrigation (20 per cent) and 34 per cent of the area, while it inherited 47 per cent of the population. During this period, other states got a massive industrial fillip by way of investments, Punjab was ignored, due to the historic turbulence, and resultant instability, even though infrastructural investments were made in the First Five Year Plan. The emergent problems had been the reclamation of wastelands to settle refugees and acceleration of food production, so obviously the emphasis was on agricultural expenditure.[126]

One of the major constraints on Punjab's industrial development, had been the disadvantage of a late start. Under the impact of the colonial transformation of the Indian economy, several other states got the 'momentum of an early start'. Some port town states because of infrastructural facilities started as early centres of production.

124. *The Hindustan Times*, 21 June 1951, New Delhi.
125. Arora, A.C., *Turmoil in Punjab Politics*, Mittal Publications, New Delhi, 1980, p.83.
126. Government of Punjab, *First Five Year Plan – A Summary*, Simla, 1953, pp. 42-45.

Through a 'process of cumulative causation', according to Gunnar Myrdal, Punjab was confined to a state of industrial backwardness.[127] The remoteness and the absence of mineral resources ruled out the establishment of mineral-based industries especially, those requiring large markets.[128] At partition, in East Punjab, the main industries were as follows:

1. Cotton textiles and spinning at Amritsar.
2. Foundry and machine tools at Batala (Gurdaspur).
3. Sports industry, water pipe fittings and transport equipment at Jullundur.
4. Forging foundry and agricultural implements at Goraya (Jullundur district).
5. Electrical goods at Kapurthala.
6. Woollen and hosiery industry, cycle and cycle parts industry, sewing machines and parts and machine tools and agricultural implements at Ludhiana.
7. Cycle and cycle parts industry at Malerkotla (District Sangrur).
8. Steel re-rolling at Sirhind (District Patiala).
9. Food industries at Rajpura (District Patiala).[129]

Despite all these unfortunate twists, such as partition so typical of Punjab's history, the people reflected a remarkable sense of resilience. Punjab's destiny was impacted by its geography, now in its truncated form, it became a border district. Punjab's industrial activity was barely

---

127. Myrdal, Gunnar, *Economic Theory and Underdeveloped Regions*, Indian Edition, New Delhi, 1978, pp.26-27.
128. Sahota, G.S., *Industrial Development, the Growth of Punjab Economy*, Souvenir presented to Joint Session of All India Economic Conference, Department of Economics, Punjab University, Chandigarh, 1960, pp.IV-11's.
129. Sandhu, J. S. and Singh, Ajit, *Industrial Development in Punjab : Some Features* (Edited) Johar and Khanna, op.cit., p.138.

evolving, when Indo-Pakistan relations deteriorated and there was juction in Kashmir in 1949, which resonated in the border region trade and commercial activities were the first casualties, as routes were sealed.[130] The prevalent and prescent tension between the two neighbours, was a major obstacle to future economic growth and stability in the state, inhibiting large- scale industrial investment and growth.

Table X

Number of Factories, Productive Capital Employed, Persons Employed, Value of Products, and By-products and Value Added by Manufacture, Punjab and Other States in India, 1948-50

States	No. of Regd. Factories in existence			Factories from which returns were received No. and (percentage)		
	1948	1949	1950	1948	1949	1950
1. Bengal (West)	1408	1484	1444	1351 (96)	1407 (94)	1360 (94)
2. Bombay	1237	1596	1736	1126 (91)	1376 (86)	1575 (91)
3. Madras	1465	1473	1471	1408 (96)	1458 (99)	1446 (98)
4. Uttar Pradesh	623	623	605	523 (84)	540 (87)	512 (85)
5. Bihar	393	403	383	333 (85)	368 (91)	370 (97)
6. Punjab	322	341	468	291 (90)	321 (95)	416 (89)
7. Madhya Pradesh	276	308	300	258 (93)	287 (93)	298 (99)
8. Orissa	109	126	135	106 (98)	124 (98)	129 (96)
9. Assam	75	79	89	73 (97)	77 (97)	88 (99)
10. Delhi	144	147	177	133 (93)	139 (94)	167 (94)

Cont.....

11. Ajmer	8	10	9	8	9	9
				(100)	(90)	(100)
12. Vindhya Pradesh	6	9	10	6	7	7
				(100)	(78)	(70)
13. Travancore	62	77	74	59	68	67
(Cochin) (Cochin only)				(95)	(87)	(91)
14. Pepsu	7	79	103	6	72	103
				(86)	(91)	(100)
15. Himachal Pradesh	9	3	4	9	3	3
				(100)	(100)	(75)
16. Rajasthan	-	-	88	-	-	52
						(59)
17. Kutch	-	-	3	-	-	3
						(100)
Total	6144	6758	7099	5690	6250	6605
				(93)	(92)	(93)

Source: R.S.Johar and J.S.Khanna (Edited) Studies in Punjab's Economy, Punjab School of Economics, Guru Nanak Dev University, Amritsar, p.118.

Chapter II

Speed Breakers in Industrial Growth: Punjabi Suba Agitation and Militancy

The wounds of partition were just beginning to heal, and the state was on the path of resurrection, as the utilization of funds at its disposal began. However, this respite was shortlived, as the injection of the language issue created a crisis in Punjab's body politic.[1] An inadvertent impact of British colonialism had been the emergence of a search for communal identity among the Sikhs.

To consolidate their position in India, the British engendered an awareness of religious, regional, linguistic and caste disparities in Punjab. They spurred research on ethnic disparity which they later exploited.[2] The criteria for representation in governmental bodies and services was on the basis of communal identity. Therefore a competition began among the three major communities on religious lines, which led to the growth of communal organizations among the three entities, as these communities became conscious of their distinct identities and political aspirations. In the new state of Indian Punjab, along with reconstruction, there began a simultaneous yearning for a specific ethnic identity, of course, within the format of India.[3] As a large number of Sikhs migrated from Western to Eastern Punjab, their concentration led to an increase in their numerical strength, which placed the Sikhs in a position, where they could demand political concessions from the newly formed Government of India.[4] The years following partition, saw

---

1. Gopal, Krishan, "Inception of Punjabi Suba Movement," Punjab History Conference, Proceedings, Punjabi University, Part I, 18-20 March, Patiala, 1994.
2. Macauliffe, M.A., *The Sikh Religion*, Delhi, Vol. I and II, p.7.
3. *The Tribune*, Ambala, 20 October 1949.
4. Lall, Shiv, *Dateline Punjab, Lifeline Sikhs,* Election Archives, New Delhi, 1994, p. 122.

ethnic aspirations and linguistic friction, emerge under the auspices of the Punjabi Suba Movement, which eventually reflected strong political overtones. The state, which was barely recuperating from the sutures of one surgical incision, was again embroiled in renewed political rumblings, hardly conducive to the welfare of an infant state's infrastructural rehabilitation, essential for progress. It could have been on the basis of this infrastructure, that industrial growth could be augmented.

The saga of linguistic aspirations of the Sikhs was rooted in their fear psychosis of being submerged by the other majority communities. In colonial Punjab, they had felt threatened by Muslim submersion so a quest for representation culminated with the Gurdwara Reform Movement and the formation of the Shiromani Gurdwara Prabandhak Committee under the able stewardship of Master Tara Singh.[5] His main aim was that as the National Movement progressed to ensure that no constitutional arrangement was foisted on the Sikhs, which would lead to their dominance by either community. As the Gurdwara problem was sorted out they began to concentrate on the major political developments occurring. In 1921, after the Montford Reforms, the Sikhs were given 19.1 per cent seats and this failed to satisfy them, as had the Lucknow Pact (1916).[6] At the All Parties Conference (1928), they were assured of an adequate weightage in Punjab, though the Nehru Committee Report did not given them the minarity status accorded to muslims in majority areas,[7] even Mahatma Gandhi was convinced that the Sikhs were justified in their objections.[8]

---

5. Singh, Teja, *Gurdwara Reform Movement and the Sikh Awakening*, Jullundur, 1922, p. 236.
6. *The Tribune*, Lahore, 11 October 1927.
7. *Report of the Indian National Congress,* Madras Session, 1927.
8. *Collected Works of Mahatma Gandhi*, Vol.LXV, p.399.

At the First Round Table Conference in 1930, they reiterated the demand for 30 per cent representation in Punjab, like the Muslims. After the Gandhi - Irwin Pact, the Congress and the Central Sikh League decided to participate in the Second Round Table Conference, later Master Tara Singh met Gandhi with a charter of seventeen demands.[9] The Sikhs wanted the Congress to reject the Communal Award.[10] When the Second World War broke out, the former then demanded a protection of their interests in return for the martial services rendered by them. This created a controversy between Master Tara Singh and the Congress. At this juncture, the Cripps Mission was announced, proposing India as a federal state with the right of units to secede, if they so desired. Master Tara Singh put forward his "Azad Punjab" scheme, since he was disillusioned with the Congress.[11] The following years saw enough turmoil and the "Azad Punjab" scheme died down as a counterblast to Pakistan. Before partition, the Sikh leaders, Baldev Singh and Giani Kartar Singh had met Lord Mountbatten to suggest that, either the Constituent Assembly should give weightage to the Sikhs in the new constitution or the Hindi- speaking areas of East Punjab should be separated from its Punjabi-speaking areas. However, to a suggestion by Mountbatten, this was brushed aside by Pandit Nehru as "a fundamentally wrong principle."[12]

From the Sikh point of view they had been hoping, that, after independence, they would be able to get those parts of Punjab, which had a socio-historic significance for them. It was with such aspirations, that the Sikh leadership had

---

9. *The Tribune*, 22 March 1931, Lahore.
10. Home Department (Political File) Government of India File 41/32, 1921.
11. Correspondence between Master Singh Tara and Stafford Cripps Stafford vide letters dated 31 March 1942, 30 May 1942. Budwood, C.B. *A Continental Experiment*, London, 1945.
12. *Jawaharlal Nehru's Speeches,* Ministry of Information and Broadcasting, New Delhi 1954, p.37.

spurned Jinnah's offer to them to join a Confederation of Pakistan, with one autonomous Sikh State, therein and they threw in their lot with the Indian Union.[13] However, the acceptance of the Radcliffe award, coupled with the suffering of partition and the massacre of Sikh refugees, disappointed them. They felt that, they had been let down and given a raw deal in the distribution of territories between Hindus and the Muslims. Master Tara Singh gave expression to Sikh sentiments in these words: "Every minority, except the Sikhs had been given justice. The Muslim demand was Pakistan, they got it and the Scheduled Castes wanted representation and they got it. The Sikhs demanded, that, they would not like to be dominated by any single community and they were being discriminated against, for repeating the same demand, as the Hindus had supported before partition and with which the Congress sympathized".[14]

It was in this situation, that the Akali Dal began to chalk out alternative strategies for protecting Sikh rights. The issues that came handy to them was the reorganization of the state on a linguistic basis. The Akalis felt that there should be a facility for the development of the language, so that their separate identity and culture could be protected. Jawaharlal Nehru tried to assuage the feelings of the Sikhs, by promising them one such area, in the new and free India, which they could call their homeland, "a separate state in the North of India, where the Sikhs could enjoy the glow of freedom."[15]

After partition, once the initial trauma of being uprooted, seeped in, people had to come to terms, so as to carve a life for themselves.[16] Both the Hindus and Sikhs of

13. Singh, Kirpal, "Partition of the Punjab, 1947," *The Punjab Past and Present*, Volume XXII, Punjabi University, Patiala, October 1986, No. 42.
14. *The Tribune*, 20 October 1949, Ambala.
15. *The Statesman*, 7 July 1946.

Eastern Punjab, viewed both communities from Western Punjab with suspicion. An example of this is, that, even today in Haryana, which is erstwhile Punjab, the Hindus who came from Pakistan are referred to as 'refugees' and the Sikhs in the present Punjab who came from West Pakistan are referred to as 'Bhapas'.[17]

After partition, the Hindus became a majority community with 61 per cent of the population. The Sikhs became a sizeable minority with 33 per cent of the population within six districts.[18] The Akali leaders started raising apprehensions, that in an overwhelmingly Hindu dominated state, with no special safeguards, the Sikhs as a separate entity would disappear. On the other hand, the demand for Punjabi Suba was interpreted by the Hindus, as a step towards Sikh hegemony. Instead of the two communities settling down and cementing the process of rehabilitation, linguistic issues with underlying apprehensions took precedence for them. During the Census of 1951, the Hindus by and large, declared Hindi as their mother tongue, thus disowning Punjabi. The Akalis interpreted this move, as an attempt on the part of the Hindus to gain a position of superiority in the Punjab, but the Hindu communal press and organizations argued that by declaring Gurmukhi as the only script for Punjabi, the Government had denied them their right to name Punjabi, as their mother tongue.[19]

In Punjab, two social reform movements had gained strength, widening the chasm between the Hindus and Sikhs. The Arya Samaj had struck roots among the Hindu urban population and propagated the use of Hindi in Devanagri

---

16. Singh, Gursharan, "Rehabilitation of Refugees in Pepsu," *The Punjab Past and Present*, Volume XXII, Serial No. 40, Punjabi University, Patiala, October 1986, p.382.
17. Ibid.
18. Census of India 1951, Volume VIII, Part IIB, pp.298-300.
19. *Akali Patrika*, 18 January 1951, Jullundur.

script. Whereas the cause of Punjabi, was taken up by the Chief Khalsa Diwan, a religious organization of the Sikhs, during the same period.[20] This organization gave a religious overtone to Punjabi, despite the fact, that it was spoken by all the people living in the province, though the language and medium of instruction had been Urdu.[21]

The Punjabi Sikhs felt that they had ultimately become the successors and custodians of Punjab's heritage, which had first seen its political identity during Maharaja Ranjit Singh's period.[22] After partition, most of the territories of the erstwhile empire had gone to Pakistan. The West Punjabi Muslim adopted Urdu and a Persian script for Punjabi, the migrant Hindu adopted Hindi, whereas the migrant Sikh, who did not settle in Punjab, in any case lost touch with Punjabi. So they continued to advocate the cause for Punjabi making it synonymous with a search for communal identity.[23] The Punjabi Sikh began to talk of Punjabi (it was the language used in the Adigranth) as a means of survival of his ethnicity and religious tradition, with subsequent political bolstering for the cause by the Akalis.[24]

At independence, the Dar Commission had first recommended the state's reorganization on a linguistic basis,

---

20. Singh, Teja, *Essays in Sikhism*, Siddharth Publications, New Delhi, 1989, p.97.
21. See Gopal, Krishan, Reaction of Hindus towards the Punjabi Suba Movement in *The Punjab Past and Present,* Volume XXVII, Part II, Serial No. 54, Punjabi University, Patiala, October 1993, p.186.
22. Singh, Harbans, *The Heritage of the Sikhs*, Manohar Publications, New Delhi, 1983, p.302.
23. Narang, A.S., Movement for Punjabi-Speaking State (Edited), Indu Banga, op. cit., p. 243.
24. Nayyar, Baldev Raj, *Minority Politics in Punjab*, Princeton University Press, Princeton 1966, p. 334.

which was not acceptable to the Congress Committee.[25] It recommended that contiguity, financial efficiency, administrative convenience, capacity for future development and a large measure of agreement, among the people speaking a language should be the criteria for reorganization.[26]

The Sachar Formula had evolved in 1949, with the combined efforts of Bhim Sen Sachar, the Chief Minister and Giani Kartar Singh. They proposed a zone in which Punjabi in Gurmukhi script was to be the medium of instruction upto matriculation and Hindi in Devanagri script was to be taught from the last year of the primary school. A parent could opt for Hindi, as the medium, if the number of such scholars was not less than ten at the primary stage; even so, a boy had to take up Punjabi as a compulsory language from the fourth class and a girl from the sixth. Accordingly there would be a Punjabi zone and a Hindi zone. Though the Akalis objected to the option given to parents to choose between Hindi or Punjabi, they welcomed the Sachar formula. However, the Arya Samajists, Jan Sangha and the Hindu Mahasabha opposed it.[27]

By the time the first General Elections took place in 1952, the Akali Dal and the Hindu organizations like the Jan Sangh and the Arya Samaj had become distrustful of each other and appealed to the religious and linguistic sentiments of the voters. However, in the elections the Congress was able to mobilize political support in the rural areas and came out successful even in the Sikh majority areas.

---

25. Singh, Khushwant, *History of the Sikhs*, Volume II, 1839-1988, Oxford University Press, 1991, p.295.
26. Dar Commission Report, p.120.
27. Singh, Narain, "Papers Relating to the Hindu Agitation in Punjab," Department of Public Relations, Punjab Government, 1957, p.11.

So till 1952, the Akali Dal could not claim to be the sole representative of the Sikhs.

The linguistic issue rose again in 1953, when Pandit Nehru set up the States Reorganization Commission, which submitted its report in 1955, in order, to consider the demands from various parts of India, that the state's boundaries, should be redrawn on a linguistic basis.[28] Some linguistic groups were satisfied, but not the Akalis. The Commission rejected the Sikh claim for a Punjabi Suba and recommended the merger of Punjab, Pepsu and Himachal Pradesh. The language issue took a communal tinge after the Census of 1951.[29] In the 1951 Census, many Punjabi-speaking Hindus declared Hindi as their mother tongue. Consequently, the records showed 11 million Hindi-speaking people and 8 million Punjabi speakers in Punjab.[30]

In the subsequent period, various formulae were propounded to solve this linguistic tussle. However, this escalated, bringing in its wake morchas, agitations and propagandas bearing pernicious communal flavours. "The language and communal issues have got so mixed up, that it is difficult to disentangle one from the other".[31] The supporters of each group tried to whip up communalism on their respective sides by identifying language with religiosity. The Congress, in order to accommodate the communalists of both types, worked out a Regional Formula in 1956. This divided the state into two regions, namely

---

28. Report of the States Reorganization Commission, Manager, Government of India Press, New Delhi, 1955, p.14.
29. Indian Election Commission Report on the First General Elections in India, 1951-52, Volume II, New Delhi, Manager of Publications, 1956.
30. Census of India, 1951, VIII, The Army Press, Simla, 1953, Part II.
31. *The Times of India*, 12 June 1957.

Punjabi-speaking and Hindi-speaking regions.[32] The Formula provided for one legislature for the whole state, which would be the sole law-making body and one Governor aided and advised by a Council of Ministers responsible to the State Legislative Assembly for the entire field of administration. There was a proposal to make a Punjabi and Hindi zone in Punjab, having different regional councils, which would have powers, excluding those of law and administration, tax and finances, and the decisions of these councils, would be binding on the Cabinet. Any dispute would be settled by the Governor, the language of the Punjabi region would be Punjabi and the script would be applicable to the Punjab zone and the Sachar Formula in the Hindi zone. There would be no difference between Hindu and Sikh scheduled castes.[33] The Punjab Government would establish two separate departments for developing the two languages. The general safeguards proposed for linguistic minorities would be applicable to Punjab like those in other states. In accordance with a furtherance of its policy, to promote the growth of all regional languages, the Central Government would encourage the development of the Punjabi language.[34]

The Regional Formula was accepted by the Akalis. Master Tara Singh, while explaining the reasons for accepting it said that it fulfilled the aspirations of the Sikhs to an extent and at the same time did not give them any opportunity to

---

32. Singh, Hukum, "The States Reorganization in the North," Paper with Shiromani Akali Dal, Publication Sikh Reference Library, Amritsar, 1956.
33. Tiwana, S.S., The Issue of Linguistic Reorganization in Punjab 1947-1966, A Study of Administration Strategies in *The Panjab Past and Present*, Volume XXVII-Part 5, Serial No. 53, Punjabi University, Patiala, April 1993, p.78.
34. Government of India, Parliamentary Committee Report on the Demand for Punjabi Suba, Appendix VB, Lok Sabha Secretariat Library 1966, p.362.

dominate others, a power which if given, might make them undemocratic and narrow minded.[35] It was on the basis of this Formula, that the Akalis gave up their demand for a separate Punjabi Suba and decided to eschew politics. The legislative wing of the Akalis joined the Congress in 1957 and fought the elections jointly in the forthcoming General Elections.[36]

The Regional Plan was not accepted by a certain section of Hindus and the people of Haryana. The Hindu Mahasabha at a Conference held at Karnal on 25 June 1956 resolved that the scheme of the Regional Formula was no solution to the Punjab problem and was no solution either to the peculiar backwardness of Haryana.[37] In April, 1957, after the formation of the new Ministry, the Hindu Raksha Samiti started demonstrations against the Regional Formula. The Hindi press played a major role in fanning agitation, on the other hand, Giani Kartar Singh warned that if the Regional Formula failed, the Punjabi Suba Morcha would be revived.[38]

A common programme (fight for freedom) and a common enemy (the British Government) had kept the Akalis close to the Indian National Congress, during the pre-partition phase, though gradually strains developed in the Akali-Congress friendship after the country got independence. The Akali anxiety to capture political power at the provincial level and the Congress' unwillingness to concede and accommodate the Akalis' claim, often resulted in mutual quarrels and led to Akali agitation against the Congress Government.[39] The Centre's refusal to re-organize

---

35. *The Tribune*, 16 March, Ambala, 1956.
36. Tiwana, S.S., op.cit., p.83.
37. Singh, Naranjan, op.cit., p.11.
38. Tiwana, S.S., op.cit., p.84.

Punjab on a linguistic basis, after the acceptance of the principle of other linguistic states provided the Akali leadership with a strong argument to agitate for the creation of a Punjabi-speaking state. The failure of the two experiments at coalition with the Congress, in forming the Government in Punjab, further heightened among Akali leadership, a sense of alienation.[40]

After parting company with the Congress, the Akali Dal launched another massive campaign in May 1960 in which over 57,000 people were arrested. It was during this struggle for the creation of a Punjabi Suba, that Sant Fateh Singh appeared on the political scene.[41] Master Tara Singh, who felt let down by Nehru and the Congress, undertook a fast unto death on 15 August 1961 to press the demand for a Punjabi Suba. The Prime Minister in his appeal to the nation on independence day, made a special appeal to the people of Punjab not to be carried away by parochial feelings, mere emotions or wrong sentiments and reminded them that even a good thing becomes bad, if wrong means are used to achieve it.[42] On 31 October 1961, the Government passed a resolution appointing a Commission to solve this tangle. This Commission gave its report on 9 January 1962, and found that there was no basis for any charge of discrimination against the Sikhs and came to the conclusion that the Punjabi Suba was a camouflage for the demand of a Sikh state.[43] The failure to coerce the Government led to mutual recriminations among Akali leaders and division

---

39. Singh, Fauja, "Akalis and the Indian National Congress (1920-1947)," *The Punjab Past and Present*, Volume XV-II, Serial No. 30, Punjabi University, Patiala, October 1981, p.453.
40. Ibid.
41. Singh Harbir, "Sant Fateh Singh's Role in the Creation of the Punjabi Suba" in Verinder Grover, op.cit., p. 173.
42. *The Spokesman*, 6 January 1961.
43. Gazette of India, 4 November 1961, New Delhi, Government Press, 1961.

within the Akali Dal. They even lost some electoral support in the third General Elections. The division within the Akali Dal now deepened and finally in 1962, Sant Fateh Singh set up a rival Akali Dal against that of Master Tara Singh.[44]

The Master Akali Dal faction convened a conference at Ludhiana on 4 July 1965, which recalled and discussed the issue, that the Sikhs had agreed to merge in the common Indian nationality, on the explicit understanding of being accorded a constitutional status of co-sharers in the Indian sovereignty, along with the majority community and that solemn undertaking, now stood cynically repudiated by the Congress Government.[45]

In successive years, Sant Fateh Singh was successful in building a new coalition, among the Akalis and defeated Master Tara Singh in the SGPC elections in early 1965. He now pressed with great vigour, the Punjabi Suba demand, but he and his lieutenants increasingly emphasized that they, in contradiction to Master Tara Singh and his followers, were interested in a linguistic state, as an integral part of the Indian Union.[46] On account of the Chinese aggression in 1962, the Punjabi Suba demand went into the background. In March 1963, the Punjabi Himachal Jana Sangh working Committee demanded that the Provincial Assembly be dissolved and the Punjab be made a centrally administrated state.[47]

Jawaharlal Nehru died on 27 May 1964, in the same year Partap Singh Kairon had to quit following strictures passed against him by the Das Commission. Both these leaders were against the creation of the Punjabi Suba. After the death of Nehru, Lal Bahadur Shastri became the Prime

---

44. *The Indian Express*, 12 August 1962.
45. Shiromani Akali Dal, Punjabi Suba, Panthic Tract Society, Amritsar, 1965.
46. Singh, Fateh Sant, Our Stand on Punjabi Suba, Shiromani Akali Dal, Amritsar, 1963.
47. Government of India, Report of Punjab Commission, Delhi Manager, Government of India Press, New Delhi, 1963.

Minister and held talks with Sant Fateh Singh. He took the stand, that the Government was ready to do anything for the advancement of the Punjabi language and to look into any Sikh grievances but felt that the issue of Punjabi Suba had been thoroughly examined before and there was no basis for its' establishment. Then in August 1965, Sant Fateh Singh issued an ultimatum to the Government, to accept the Suba demand within twenty five days, otherwise, he would go on a fast unto death, effective from September 10, for fifteen days and, in case he survived the fast, he would then resort to self-immolation by burning himself.[48] From amongst the opponents of Punjabi Suba, there came threats of counter-fasts if the Government conceded the demand. The Sikh leaders in the Congress party were themselves divided over the issue, some fifteen Congress Sikh MLAs met to urge the Government to accept the Punjabi Suba demand, while other Sikh MLAs dissociated themselves from this stand[49]. Meanwhile, in 1965 India went to war with Pakistan and it intensified in early September 1965. The Akali leaders asked Sant Fateh Singh to give up the idea of his proposed fast, in view of the emergency facing the nation.[50] The Union Home Minister, Gulzari Lal Nanda also announced that "the whole question could be examined afresh". The Sant finally withdrew his threat of self-immolation and called upon the Punjabis in general and the Sikhs in particular, to rise in the defence of the Country.[51] However, by this time, the movement for a separate Haryana Prant and Himachal Pradesh was also in full swing, which the Akali Party supported.[52]

The decade of the 1950s was one of resettlement of the ravages of partition, the unprecedented transfer of

48. *The Tribune*, 17 August 1965, Ambala.
49. Ibid., I September 1965.
50. Ibid., 3 September 1965.
51. Ibid., 10 September 1965.
52. Sharma, P. K., *The Reorganization of Punjab*, Verinder Grover, op. cit., p.163.

population, a total derailment of economy and a dislocation of administrative machinery. While in 1952, the First Five Year Plan did start but the state was still struggling with the contingencies of refugee settlement. The administrative machinery was yet to put into action plans to address the claims of the refugees for rehabilitation. East Punjab had no strong infrastructure in agriculture, while the need to focus on food scarcity was staring them in the face. The industry had yet to take shape to meet the demand for higher employment on account of refugee influx because except for some small-scale industries which were already there in places like Ludhiana, Phagwara, Amritsar (Chheharta), there was no prominent industry in the state. Despite the imminent need, in the First Five Year Plan, there was hardly any discernable outlay for industry. By the time the plan had reached its mid-term review, the complexion of the state got altered with the merger of the Pepsu. This once again unsettled the administrative machinery within the state. By 1956, the demand for the Punjabi-Suba started raising its head, though there was no immediate effect of this demand on the installation of industry because the state had still not reached the level of capital availability with which larger industry could have developed here. However, prospective entrepreneurs who had migrated from Pakistan and the fortunate ones who could bring their capital, started reflecting whether to give in to the apprehensions created by the vernacular press or not. The result of all this was, that quite a few refugees chose to migrate across the Yamuna to Delhi and beyond.

In the second half of the 1950s, Partap Singh Kairon did accord importance to industry as well as initiate many schemes of industrial development, most industrial development centres were set up in rural areas. These centres were established to provide facilities to rural and small-scale industries for their needs for tools and implements. By the

Second Plan, some investment of the Union Government was also planned by way of Nangal Fertilizers, Heavy water plant at Nangal and the Hindustan Machine Tools factory in Pinjore. In the context of the slow speed of industrial development, it is worth mentioning, that the havoc caused by the massive floods of late 1955, dampened the spirit of development as well.

Towards the end of the decade, even though there was no major investment in the industry apart from the one mentioned above, yet industries like hosiery, machine tools, cycle parts, hand tools, woollen and cotton textiles did start developing on their own with the enterprise and capital of the refugee population. In fact, the demand increase as a result of the influx of refugees gave some impetus to investments in the existing industries, as would be seen from the expansion of industrial houses like the Oswals for instance, in Ludhiana during this period. Government assistance, in this period was in the shape of grants of small loans under the State Aid to the Industries Act and Khadi and Village Industries Board schemes. In 1962, after the Chinese aggression the industry got an impetus owing to the increased demand of the Defence sector, especially for hosiery goods and woollen textiles for the army. In fact, the post 1965 Indo-Pakistan war period was a boom period for the industry. By this time, the industry started standing on its own feet. The effect of the Punjabi-Suba agitation during the ten years, was that, it slowed down the decision-making process of the individuals to make any new investment because they were not prepared to suffer the results of another dislocation in case of partition of the state. This apprehension was the result of the propaganda of the vernacular press, more than anything else. There are no bench marking statistics available because the entire process of industrialization was starting from scratch after partition. The completion of the Bhakra Dam and hydro-electric power projects made energy available in abundance. This gave some impetus to industry in the first half of the 1960s, as the table below indicates. However, no large-scale industrial investment took place.

In fact, during this period, there was no spectacular industrial development in the national context. In 1956, the Secondary sector (comprising small-scale and large-scale industry) was less important in the economy of the state than the All India figure contributory 11.3 per cent of the net output and 8.3 per cent of employment in the state as against the 17.5 per cent and 10 per cent respectively in India as a whole. Both in factory employment and the industrial consumption of power, Punjab, although superior to Orissa, was far behind the more industrial states, namely Maharashtra, West Bengal and Madras. (See Table XI)

Table XI

Factory Employment per 1,000 of Population (1956)

State	Total Factory Employment (Per 1,000 of Population)	Power (Million kWh)
India	7.36 (100)	3,511.36 (100)
Bombay	18.77	1,325.04 (37.74)
West Bengal	22.90	797.04 (22.7)
Madras	9.31	319.60 (9.1)
Orissa	1.39	19.52 (0.56)
Punjab	4.80	154.00 (4.3)

Table XII

Growth of Industries in Punjab

Group	Percentage Increase During 1951-56	Percentage Increase During 1956-58	Percentage Increase During 1951-58 (Annual)
Agricultural Processing	12.1	13.4	3.9
Textile Industries	43.8	8.5	8.0
Forest-based Industries	31.8	26.4	9.5
Mineral-based Industries	(-) 27.4	17.2	(-) 2.1
Engineering Industries	62.8	24.7	14.7
Chemical Industries	76.1	6.0	12.4
Miscellaneous	38.3	8.3	5.6

Source: NCAER, Techno Economic Survey of Punjab, New Delhi, 1962, p.77.

This period coincided with the span of the first two Five Year Plans. In the First Plan, there was only 0.92 per cent of total expenditure on industry. The significant development of this period was: (a) completion of an industrial survey of Punjab and (b) establishment of an Intelligence Bureau for the collection and dissemination of technical and commercial information. There was an emphasis on the development of road transport necessary for industrial development. However, it was low in view of the needs, it was Rs. 8.17 crores. At the end of the First Plan, Punjab had a smaller road ratio both on the basis of population and area compared to all India averages.

53. Ibid., p.107.

The Second Plan was formulated with the objective of stabilizing agriculture further but with a decisive shift towards industry. There was also a central provision of Rs. 20 crores for Nangal Fertilizers to meet these twin objectives.[53] Though this gave an increase of 31 per cent in the file outlay yet it compared unfavourably with India as a whole, where the increase was 124 per cent. Though the State Plan showed an increase of outlay to 9.34 crores from Rs. 1.3 crores of the First Plan, yet the actual expenditure was 4.67 crores (50 per cent of the outlay). The financing of the the First Plan had been far from satisfactory. Both in Pepsu and Punjab, there was a large gap in resources needed for the First Plan outlay. The state contributed only 19 per cent for industry of the total outlay as against an average of 56 per cent for all states.[54]

The NCAER study had suggested constituting an Industrial Development Board as a wing of the Industries Department for creating a climate conducive to rapid industrial development, but it was not set up. Figures reflect that during this period, there was no large-scale industry set up, no infrastructural provisions for it which is the responsibility of the state. There was no planned effort to provide an impetus for technological and organizational improvement in industry. In the year 1962, as compared to the All India figures of the industrial net output of 17.5 per cent and 10 per cent of industrial employment, Punjab contributed 11.3 per cent and 8.5 per cent respectively. The main industries were engineering industries linked with agriculture, which was the most important sector of the Punjab economy (14.7 per cent).

54. Ibid., p.110.

During this period, with the exception of large-scale units engaged in the manufacture of cotton textiles, woollen textiles, sugar, cement, paper, cycles most of the registered units in Punjab came under the category of small-scale industries.

A major obstacle to industrial development had been the lack of capital. Industrial finance was to flow either from institutions within the state or from the Centre, whatever financial assistance had been given by the State Government it was for small-scale industries. There was also an inadequacy of technical education and training, whereas other states had a larger number of technical institutions. All these factors arose out a lack of political stability, a major deterrent to decision-making and implementation.

Table XIII

Sector al Distribution

	Net Output			Percentage		
	1956	1960-61	1970-71*	1956	1960-61	1970-71
Primary	237	268	838.21	47	45	58.37
Secondary	57	80	219.94	11	13	15.31
Tertiary	211	264	378.01	42	42	26.32

* Economic Adviser to Government of Punjab: *Statistical Abstract of Punjab*, 1985, p.89.

---

55. Tully, Mark and Jacob, Satish, *Amritsar, Mrs. Gandhi's Last Battle*, Rupa Publications, New Delhi, 1985, p.42.
56. *The Tribune*, 12 June 1966.

Table XIV

(At 1980-81 Prices) Figures in

S. No.	Sector	1980-81	1981-82	1982-83	1983-84	1984-85	1985-86	1986-87	1987-88	1988-89	1989-90
1.	Primary	2.44	10.96	3.12	(-)0.82	11.17	8.41	(-) 0.61	4.73	3.20	10.84
2.	Secondary	3.12	8.67	2.51	6.26	2\3.23	12,93	7.12	5.14	11.36	6.77
3.	Tertiary	10.32	3.59	4.44	4.04	3.66	3.38	7.99	5.57	4.38	4.78
	Overall State Income	4.39	8.22	3.30	2.09	7.19	7.88	3.48	5.47	5.39	8.11

(At 1993-94 Prices) Figures in

S. No.	Sector	1990-91	1991-92	1992-93	1993-94	1994-95	1995-96	1996-97	1997-98	1989-99	1999-2000
1.	Primary	(-) 1.32	8.07	2.25	3.89	2.12	(-)0.55	9.12	(-) 4.52	2.54	8.30
2.	Secondary	3.39	3.05	9.87	8.80	7.82	8.22	6.77	9.21	7.31	6.21
3.	Tertiary	3.36	1.54	4.62	3.53	5.37	6.78	7.46	8.84	4.14	5.69
	Overall State Income	1.11	4.72	5.01	4.48	3.18	8.00	2.92	4.24	5.47	6.86

In the year 1965, Mrs. Indira Gandhi wanted to reward the gallantry of the Sikh troops who had fought, in the war against Pakistan in 1965, so she consented to the formation of a Punjabi-speaking state.[55] In her broadcast to the nation on 12 June 1966, the Prime Minister Mrs. Gandhi referred to the decision of the Union Government on Chandigarh.

> This may not be an ideal arrangement. But given a measure of goodwill on all sides, it does offer a workable solution. Punjab and Haryana will have so much in common, that a common capital should assist in developing cooperative relations. In the initial period, this would certainly be invaluable.[56]

Though the political quarters may have been satisfied with reorganization but it proved to be industrially disadvantageous to Punjab. The developing industrial complex around Delhi fell to the share of Haryana and whatever mineral and forest resources were available went to Himachal Pradesh. Haryana had the advantage of being on the national highway and the proximity to a metropolis like Delhi, so this helped important industrial conglomeration to emerge. Whereas in Punjab, the wars with Pakistan reinforced an apprehension for investment on the border areas like Amritsar and Ferozepur, so the major capital growth was centred around Delhi. This was reflected in state domestic products in Haryana with a relatively larger share of registered manufacturing units there as compared to Punjab. The tables reflects a visible slump 1966-1967 to 1967-68 in the post-reorganization phase.

The industrial drain from Haryana to Punjab is reflected in the tables which show the rate of growth from 1970 to 1980 in both states, comparatively Haryana had a marked industrial growth as compared to Punjab.*

Table XV

Nature of Industries and Workers Employed (Haryana) Year 1970

Industry	No. of Factories	No. of Workers
Processing Allied to Agriculture	130	NA
Food Products	210	-
Beverages, Tobacco	10	-
Cotton Textile	83	-
Leather Products	1	-
Chemical Products	49	-
Non-Metallic Mineral Products	74	-
Basic Metal & Alloy Industry	77	-
Electrical Machinery, Apparatus, etc.	46	-
Transport Equipment & Parts	48	-
Other Manufacturing Industries	69	-
Total	797	

Source: *Statistical Abstract of Haryana, 1971-72.*

Table XVI
Nature of Industries and Workers Employed (Haryana)
Year 1980

Industry	No. of Factories	No. of Workers
Agriculture Processes	-	-
Livestock Production	-	-
Manufacture of Food Products	322	8912
Cotton Textile	622	21199
Manufacture of Beverages Tobacco, etc.	-	-
Manufacture of Wool & Synthetic Fibre, etc.	81	479
Leather Products	10	413
Chemical Products	165	4135
Non-Metallic Mineral Products	82	9389
Basic Metal & Alloy Industries	220	14618
Manufacture of Metal Products & Parts	437	12482
Manufacture of Machinery Machine Tools & Parts	283	17488
Manufacture of Electrical Machinery, Apparatus, etc.	86	13190
Manufacture of Transport Equipment & Parts	53	9503
Repair Services	39	6585
Other Manufacturing Industries	55	120
Total	2456	13100

Source: Statistical Abstract Haryana – 1981.

Table XVII
Nature of Industries and Workers Employed (Punjab)
Year 1980

Industry	No. of Factories	No. of Workers
Agriculture Services	-	-
Livestock Production	3	166
Manufacture of Food Products	889	8912
Cotton Textiles	230	22529
Manufacture of Beverages Tobacco etc.	15	2649
Manufacture of Wool & Synthetic Fibre, etc.	820	26712
Leather Products	9	413
Chemical Products	120	3581
Non-Metallic Mineral Products	221	5476
Basic Metal & Alloy Industries	410	18543
Manufacture of Metal Products & Parts	679	14177
Manufacture of Machinery	820	18900
Machine Tools & Parts		
Manufacture of Electrical	197	4552
Machinery, Apparatus, etc.		
Manufacture of Transport	641	21699
Equipment & Parts		
Repair Services	89	4936
Other Manufacturing Industries	44	2692
Total	5187	13100

Source: Statistical Abstract, Punjab – 1981.

Table XVIII
Nature of Industries and Workers Employed (Punjab)
Year 1970

Industry	No. of Factories	No. of Workers
Agriculture Services	135	5663
Manufacture of Food Products	236	10153
Manufacture of Beverages	1	3062
Cotton Textiles	645	23507
Manufacture of Wool, Silk & Synthetic Fibre Textile	-	-
Manufacture of Leather	6	256
Manufacture of Chemical & Chemical Products	38	3186
Manufacture of Non-Metallic Products	148	3617
Basic Metal & Alloy Industries	246	7643
Manufacture of Metal Products	306	7196
Manufacture of Machinery, Machine Tools & Parts	1049	21696
Manufacture of Electrical Machinery, Appliances, etc.	77	3668
Manufacture of Transport Equipment & Parts	218	10197
Other Manufacturing Industries	63	1540
Total	3168	101457

Source: Statistical Abstract Punjab – 1970.

Table XIX

Development of Important Industries in Punjab

Name of Industry	1960-61	1965-66	1966-67	1967-68
1. Textile Cotton*				
(i) No. of Units	3	7	6	7
(ii) Production (Lakh metre)	N.A.	313	295	373
(iii) Employment (No.)	4,345	7,138	7,990	7,490
2. Textile Woollen				
(i) No. of Units	30	35	37	29
(ii) Production (Lakh metre)	1123	1262	1546	1624
(iii) Employment (No.)	7,628	9,928	9,123	9,329
3. Sugar				
(i) No. of Units	3	5	5	5
(ii) Production (000 tonnes)	33.95	69.75	39.57	26.74
(iii) Employment (No.)	2,522	4,134	3,815	4,411
4. Sewing Machine				
(i) No. of Units	256	307	333	347
(ii) Production (No.)	N.A.	73,289	75,670	66,428
(iii) Employment (No.)	2,973	3,776**	4,056	3,102
5. Agricultural Implements and Machine Tools				
(i) No. of Units	2,062	7,237	6,983	6,610
(ii) Production (Lakh Rs.)	520	1205	1456	1615
(iii) Employment (No.)	2,716	23,942	25,936	23,462
6. Steel Re-rolling				
(i) No. of Units	73	102	136	136
(ii) Production (000 tonnes)	105.76	165.43	194.41	1,747.73(b)
(iii) Employment (No.)	6,763	5,283	5,526	5,057
7. Hosiery				
(i) No. of Units	991	1,970	2,085	2,202
(ii) Production (Lakh Rs.)	4,69	7,32	8,33	9,03
(iii) Employment (No.)	8,790	25,566	14,061	14,754

Contd........

Development of Important Industries in Punjab

Name of Industry	1960-61	1965-66	1966-67	1967-68
8. Cotton Ginning and Pressing				
(i) No. of Units	153	175	173	207
(ii) Production (000 bales)	553	872	1,039	2,587
(iii) Employment (No.)	7,327	12,661	11,691	12,714
9. Sports				
(i) No. of Units	249	340	340	340
(ii) Production (Lakh Rs.)	1,04	145	200	214
(iii) Employment (No.)	5,410	5,238	5,511	5,610

* Excludes yarn produced.

** Includes labour employment in sewing machine parts

(b) Lakh rupees.

Source: Government of Punjab, Economic and Statistical Organization Publication No. 170, Socio Economic Review of Punjab 1970-71, Government Press, Chandigarh, 1972, p.54.

The other changes during reorganization were that the capital Chandigarh was to be a Union Territory and serve as a capital for both states. The Bhakra Dam Complex and Pong Dam were also to be administered by a central board. As a consequence, the new Punjab had 41 per cent of the area and 55 per cent of the population, but in reorganized Punjab, Sikhs constituted 60.22 per cent share of the population.[57]

The other major watershed in Punjab's scenario, had been the onset of the Green Revolution, so crucial for balancing the growth process of the Indian economy. However, when reorganization came into the implementation stage, through the Punjab Reorganization Act 1966, on 1 November 1966, many distortions had crept in.[58] The effect

57. Government of India, Punjab Boundary Commission Report, Manager of Publications, Government of India, 1966.
58. Danewallia, H.S., *Police and Politics in the Twentieth Century Punjab*, Ajanta Publications, New Delhi, 1997, p.312.

of these distortions became more glaring because the new state comprised a demographic balance in favour of the Sikhs, forming almost 80 per cent of the population.[59] The underlying antipathy between the two major ethnic communities, one primarily rural Sikh and the other primarily urban Hindu had been skilfully exploited by the Congress Party and the Akalis. Subsequently, unhealthy political manipulation and the whipping up of religious communalism embroiled Punjab in a simmering cauldron reeking of bloodshed.

The Reorganization Act left many lacunae in it; by keeping many common links between the two (the new state entity, which emerged from this reorganization). Even the delimitation of the boundaries between Punjab and Haryana, became a contentious issue from the start, because it was based on the 1961 Census, in which Punjabi Hindus reeling under the prevalent fear psychosis had declared Hindi as their mother tongue, enmasse. When the Akalis objected to this fundamental premise of reorganization, their objectives were brushed aside, resulting in their boycott of the Boundary Commission's proceedings.[60] In subsequent years, other controversial issues cropped up, which gained more complexity; the common capital: Chandigarh, transfer control of Bhakra Dam to a centrally controlled body Bhakra Beas Management Board, water sharing formulae between Punjab and Haryana, in which later, even Rajasthan was introduced as a co-sharer of Punjab waters.[61]

These potential distortions inevitably led to a reoccurrence of hiccups, so typical to Punjab's history and

59. Wallace, Paul, "Religious and Secular Politics in Punjab" in Grover Verinder, op.cit., p.210.
60. Government of India, Punjab Reorganization Act 1966, Also Boundary Commission Report, op.cit.
61. *The Statesman*, 22 March 1966, New Delhi, p.I.

politics. The subsequent two decades saw inter-party, and intra-community ramifications, which were of a grevious dimension. Though Punjab, did witness an era of comparative calm in the early 1970s, after a state of political flux, in which frequent political changes had occurred between 1966 and 1972. However, the National Emergency of 1975, declared by Mrs. Indira Gandhi created some fresh political waves in the state, when the Akali party, in power emerged as the only party in the country to resist the Emergency by launching a daily morcha of arrest by volunteers from the Akal Takht at Amritsar.[62]

On the political front, during the period 1967-71, the Akali Dal party came to power in 1969. In June 1971, Prakash Singh Badal, through the then Chief Minister, who still had a majority in the Vidhan Sabha, ordered the dissolution of the Assembly, within just about 2 years of its election, basically to forestall his rival in the party, Gurnam Singh (an ex-Chief Minister), Governor D.C. Pavate found it a good opportunity to play the tune of Indira Gandhi, for the install ation of a Congress Government in Punjab.[63]

On the industrial scene, the Punjab Government after reorganization, initiated the industrial ization by setting up focal points at Dhandarikalan, Mohali and Rajpura. However, industries in the state received a serious setback due to the Pakistani aggression in 1971. Large stocks of manufactured goods such as bicycles, sewing machines, hosiery, machine tools and auto parts worth crores of rupees accumulated within the factories on account of a sudden fall in demand and transport bottlenecks during the war and prewar days, the hostilities adversely affected the availability of required industrial credit. The industrial atmosphere was

62. Narang, Singh Amarjit, *The Spokesman,* Vol.27, No. 19, January 1978, pp.6-7.
63. Pavate, D.C., *My Days as Governor*, Vikas Publications, New Delhi, 1974, p.33.

vitiated by the tense border situation created a few months earlier than the start of war, and the industrial units located in the border towns of the state remained closed for some time. Some of these units also suffered damage owing to the enemy shelling.[64]

Politically, things continued to ferment with the Akalis reiterating their stance, that there was an 'anti-Sikh prejudice' towards them. However, to increase their political clout amidst the Sikh masses, the Party took recourse to fervent anti-Centre stances, radical declarations, a new conceptual agenda for the party's survival and from this surcharged atmosphere culminated the Anandpur Sahib Resolution.[65] It was prepared first in December 1972, by a group of leaders including Mohan Singh Tur, Surjit Singh Barnala, G.S. Tohra, Jivan Singh Umranangal, Balwant Singh, Gian Singh Rarewala, Jasvinder Singh Brar and Kapur Singh, a former ICS officer, it was adopted by the Working Committee of the Akali Dal in October 1973. This resolution spoke of the subjects, which were to be in the Central list only of Defence, External Affairs, Commonwealth and Currency, even Taxation was to be a state subject, with the states passing on a share to the Centre.[66] Though in its objective form, it was nothing more than a new statement of the concept of Federal polity, yet in its various forms and sometimes distortions, made by various politicians, it became the favourite dictum of secessionists. They had suggested that all key industries should be brought under the Public Sector, the basic consumer industries should be immediately

---

64. Government of Punjab, Socio-Economic Review of Punjab 1970-1971, op.cit., p.59.
65. The Text of the Anandpur Sahib Resolution adopted at the Open Session of the 18th All India Akali Conference at Ludhiana on 28-29 October 1978, Shiromani Akali Dal Tract, Amritsar, 1978.
66. Ibid.

nationalized to stabilize the prices of the consumer goods and to save the poor consumer at the hands of the industrialist and the middleman.[67]

Every militant group, in its' effort to appear more radical than the other, flaunted its' own version of the Anandpur Sahib Resolution, as a dominant philosophy during the phase of militancy in the 1980s. In the political arena, the Anandpur Sahib Resolution, however, became a basic policy programme for the Akalis and any opposition to it, from any quarter became an excuse to flog the opponents, as anti Sikh. While for the opponents of the Akali Party, it became an excuse to label them, as a communal and a separatist party.[68]

Political parties of various hues, even the Congress used communalism in an opportunistic manner. Giani Zail Singh who became the Chief Minister in 1972, pioneered a policy of tackling communalism with its patent formulae. He was aware that the Akalis were popular with the Jat Sikhs because of their religious appeal and the only dent into their sphere of influence, could be made by using the magic wand of religion.[69] The first half of the 1970s, thus saw a peculiar situation, where the Government (with Giani Zail Singh as Chief Minister) was participating in religious ceremonies of the Sikhs, more keenly, instead of enunciating Government reforms. They were organizing religious functions, like a march on Guru Gobind Singh Marg, while the Akalis were delineating the cause of religious discrimination against the Sikhs, to whip up political support. This was a period, when the ruling party and the

---

67. Ibid., p.319.
68. Tully, Mark and Jacob, Satish, op.cit., p.45.
69. Kumar, Pramod, Sharma N., Sood A., Handa A., *Punjab Crisis, Context and Trends*, CRRID Publications, Chandigarh, 1984, p.70.

opposition parties were vying with each other, to incite the religious proclivities of the masses for their respective political gains by exacerbating religious issues full throttle.[70]

In the wake of the popular anti emergency upsurge through North India, the Akali-Janata coalition came to power in 1977, though the interests and priorities of the two parties were quite dissimilar. The Akali Dal drew its support from the rural peasantry and concentrated on the problems and concessions to the agricultural classes. The Janata Party unit in Punjab, on the other hand was more concerned about promoting the interests of the urban industrial trading sections. Of course, they did compromise on issuing clearance for the construction of the Thein Dam, launch a 30 crore Integrated Rural Development Programme and various other concessions to the farmer.[71] The Akali legislators were always keen for concessions to agriculturists. The debates in the Vidhan Sabha indicate that the Janata legislators had a preference for the urban sections of society.[72] They alleged that the industry had been deprived of required supply of power and facilities were disproportionately given to favour the agricultural sector. The Janata legislators resented that whereas the flat electricity rate on tubewells had been decreased by 33 per cent, no relief was given to industry. These were some of the differences in priorities since one party represented the urban segment of Punjab and the other rural.[73] Meanwhile, the efforts of Zail Singh were on to destabilize the Government of Badal, as he continued with his old philosophy of playing the Pied Piper

---

70. Ibid.
71. Punjab – A Profile of Planned Progress: One Year of Akali Janata Administration, *The Tribune*, 20 June 1978.
72. Punjab Vidhan Sabha Debates, I; n 52 March 1979, p.(5). 74.
73. Ibid., 2, nI 21 March 1978, p.(11), 65.

of religion more rabidly than the Akalis.[74] During the Baisakhi festival of 1978, there was a clash between the Nirankaris and Sikhs, under the command of Jarnail Singh Bhindranwala — a self-styled saint, who subsequently rallied a sizeable mass following in rural Punjab.[75]

In August 1978, a press conference was arranged, at Chandigarh. Har Simran of Punjab University, a protege of Giani Zail Singh announced the formulation of the Dal Khalsa, with the specific aim of establishing Khalistan. This new bogey aimed at alienating the Jan Sangh from the Akalis, thus creating new dilemmas and intra-party problems for the Akali Dal. Giani Zail Singh strategically mobilized the second rank leadership and extremists to suit his narrow, personal, political interests.[76]

In 1980, Badal's Akali Government was routed in the elections and Indira Gandhi returned to power at the Centre. This was the beginning of an era of bloody battles in the state, leading to terrorism — the origin of which still remains obscure.[77] The Darbara Singh Government came to power in 1980. He changed the Congress policy of appeasement of extremists to one of confrontation with extremists as well as the Akali moderates. Consequently, factionalism sharpened within the Congress. He was removed after the first bus-massacre at Dhilwan of Hindu passengers, by accusing him of having failed to curb the advent of terrorism. The period upto 1992, was of political turmoil. Followed by a span of violence and gory bloodshed of one particular community by certain supporters of the self-proclaimed Saint Bhindranwale, some of who started

---

74. *The Spokesman,* Vol.27, 18, 26 December 1977, p.2.
75. Kumar, Pramod, etc. op. cit., p.27.
76. Ibid., p.71.
77. Wallace, Paul, op.cit., p.227.

going to Pakistan for training and bolstering the attainment of Khalistan.[78] Unfortunately, as a consequence of this policy of the appeasement of communal forces, "The logic of politics that had developed in Punjab, led a large number of Hindu leaders in the Congress (I) to take a Hindu communal — the so-called pro-Hindu-posture."[79]

The period of the 1980s, thus became a period of a political confusion and instability. Some foreign powers found it as an opportunity to fish in troubled waters. Communal politics were exacerbated by economic tensions, generated by the Green Revolution, which was basically perceived to have helped the middle and elite strata.[80] The impact of the revolution, created fissures in the social fabric by widening the chasm between the rural Sikh majority and the urban Hindu majority.[81] The Sikh farmers earned good profits by adopting new techniques in agriculture, while the urban economic environment continued to be the stronghold of urban Hindus. This experience in Punjab of disparate growth, created strong lobbies based on sectional interests, which exploded into economic movements with a fundamentalist extremist face.[82]

When the Green Revolution swept over Punjab between 1967-68 and 1979-80, it helped the state to increase the production of wheat and paddy by 136 per cent to 634 per

---

78. Ibid.
79. Kumar, Pramod, op.cit., p.71.
80. Ibid., Introduction
81. Kumar, Pramod, "Violence in Retrospect" in Grewal, J.S. and Banga Indu (Ed.), op.cit., p.130.
82. Gujral, I.K., The Economic Dimensions in Singh Amrik (Edited), *Punjab in Indian Politics, Issues and Trends*, Ajanta Publications, New Delhi, 1985, p.14.

cent respectively, the spread of agricultural development in Punjab was phenomenal.[83] The society in Punjab, therefore, could not remain untouched from the resultant sociological changes, as Neil J. Smelser has observed: "The technological development in any society is always accompanied by changes in social structure, such as differentiation, integrating (coordination) and social disturbances (social tension). Although, the impact may vary according to the level of development and the given social and cultural matrix."[84] In this very context, the onset of the Green Revolution has also created "severe ripples, not all of these pleasant, in the serene waters of rural life in Punjab"[85]

The active role of the market in the production and distribution mechanism of agricultural produce; the regulation of these processes in the larger natural interests of increasing food productivity and ensuring distribution, justice and efforts to bring the agricultural sector at par with the industrial sector, further created political conflicts in the people belonging to different sectors. Resultantly, during the post Green Revolution period, the policy of farmers was, no longer confined to village panchayat elections. They had realized the need for farmers' organizations to fight for their rights. Paradoxically, the Green Revolution had pushed the farming community into heavy debts while at the same time, raising per capita income,[86] increased crop intensity, more than offset the introduction of higher technology and the

---

83. Ladejinksi, Wolf, Green Revolution in Punjab: A Field Trip, *Economic and Political Weekly*, Bombay, 28 June 1969, p.33.
84. Smelser J, Neil, *The Sociology of Economic Life*, Prentice Hall, New Delhi, 1965, p.2.
85. Dosanj, S.S., "Socio-Economic Tensions as a Result of the Green Revolution" in *The Punjab Past and Present*, Vol.XVI-II, Serial No. 32, Punjabi University, Patiala, October 1982.
86. Ibid.

demand for labour increased.[87] On the other hand, the labour market, became more competitive with the influx of migratory labour from earlier UP and Bihar, where wage levels are very low. This competition for jobs, had also brought tension between the local and migratory labour. In fact, the local ruling artisan classes, had been displaced by technology, as well as cheap migratory labour.[88]

> In the wake of the Green Revolution in Punjab, the traditional agrarian system has changed to the capitalist agro-industrial one, resulting in a cut-throat competition in this profession. The operational holdings of those, who can survive in the profession are constantly increasing, but the marginal, small and even medium farmers are gradually being eliminated from the profession. The displaced farmers and allied workers are posing a great challenge to the set village life, as they are not finding any suitable alternative to earn their living. The Industrial sector is not developed enough to absorb the surplus of village population...........under these circumstances, the Green Revolution has posed a serious problem of placement of disabled peasantry. The frustration in the agricultural sector is a clear symptom of the serious problem the state will have to face in the near future.[89]

There was a division of land, the marginal farmer went into debt because the Green Revolution made agriculture, capital intensive. The tractor became a status symbol, every farmer wanted one, so consequently, the marginal farmers were in debt. The boys from these debt-ridden families, particularly from the Amritsar and Gurdaspur districts

---

87. Gill, M.S., op.cit.
88. Oberoi, A.S. and Singh, Manmohan, Singh H.K., Migration Flows in Punjab's Green Revolution Belt, *Economic and Political Weekly*, Volume 15, No. 13, 29 March 1980, pp.2-12.
89. Singh, Jasbir, *The Green Revolution in India, How Green is this*? Vishal Publications, Kurukshetra, New Delhi, 1995, p.75.

(which were comparatively less prosperous) eventually formed the militants' ranks. They were the first post Green Revolution generation, with the benefit of school and college education, they had not grown up in the erstwhile harmonious, rural Punjab but had witnessed economic and political tension. The mechanization of agriculture had forced them off the fields and the state had no jobs for them. The traditional Akali leadership was in the hands of rich farmers, these boys found Bhindranwale as a rallying point, as he was a marginal farmer.[90] These were the problems of skewed development, which aggravated the socio-economic difficulties in a predominantly agricultural society.

As is universally visible, the sudden escalation in agricultural productivity, should have led to the investment of agricultural surpluses into production channels of the secondary and tertiary sectors. However, if we look at both the indices of industrial growth for the two decades following 1975, we find that the political uncertainty caused by militancy had subsumed the industrial growth, in quite a substantial manner. The index patterns of agricultural growth and industrial growth, during 1975-76 to 1991-92, show that growth in industrial prodution was not upto the expected levels.

90. Singh, Gurmukh, "Rise and Fall of Punjab Militancy," Grover Verinder, Ed. op.cit., pp.603- 604.

Table XX

	Agricultural Production Indices	Industrial Growth Indices
1975-76	144.80	100
1976-77	110.11	—
1980-81	171.52	177.57
1985-86	236.04	228.86
1990-91	269.55	341.61
1991-92	290.11	356.11
1992-93	291.04	395.83
1993-94	286.19	430.11

Source: Figures taken from the Directorate of Industries, Punjab, Chandigarh.

Even compared to the all India industrial figures, Punjab lagged behind.

The period of militancy saw the killings of many innocent youth by the police and was followed by Operation Blue Star in 1984, which aggravated the feelings of communal differences in the state.[91] As a reprisal Mrs. Indira Gandhi was assassinated.[92] In 1985, the Moderate Sikhs signed an agreement with the Congress government, i.e. the Rajeev-Longowal Accord, which further led to the formation of an Akali Government under Surjeet Singh Barnala. However, this was not to be the end of terrorism yet and the Government at the Centre was still suspicious of the bonafides of the Akalis in Punjab. The Prime Minister, Rajeev Gandhi under the influence of S.S.Ray dismissed the Barnala Government, before the completion of its tenure of

91. Singh, Khushwant, "In the Aftermath of Operation Blue Star", *The Indian Express*, 25 October 1984.
92. Singh, Shaukin, "Punjab in Pain", *Link,* XXVII-2, 19 August 1984.

about 21 months. This action instead of curbing terrorism, aggravated the malaise besides antagonizing the local population. The life of the common man became one of anxiety and tension.[93]

Since 1982, the economy started deteriorating, industrial investments had stopped coming in to the state. Instead, there was capital flight from Punjab. The major expenditure of the state government was siphoned to law and order, maintenance and payment to the Central forces. In fact, discontent was increasing due to the rising unemployment during the 1980s. It is a universally acknowledged historical phenomenon, that an agricultural revolution is followed by an industrial revolution. However the Green Revolution in Punjab did not have the desired impact, even though, it brought prosperity but it did not lead to large- scale industrialization. This anomalous situation, became one of the major causes of terrorism.[94] Therefore, the amalgam of economic policies had not merely to view liberalization but this was to be utilized as a panacea for political stability, which was the essential prerequisite for any sort of initiative, as the state's history testifies.

A brief reference to the unemployment scenario between 1980-1992, would approximately quantify the magnitude of the problem, afflicting the state. It was a major issue for addressal. The Green Revolution, the progressive nature of the Punjabi, his cultural ethos, the constant interaction of the Punjabi farmer with foreign lands (through a large number of NRI population) and a lack of diversification in the agricultural sector increased the twin

93. Gupta, Shekhar, Punjab: The Rule of the Gun, *India Today* 16(1), I January 1991, pp.24-32.
94. Krishan, Gopal, Jobless in Punjab in *The Economic Times*, New Delhi, 21 May 1995.

problems of underemployment and unemployment.[95] Sociological factors played a role here, that, while the Punjabi population found itself unemployed, the migrant labour always got work in Punjab in the agricultural sector, as well as the industrial sector. This was because the Punjabi population was keen for employment at the higher end of the spectrum.[96]

Other extraneous factors had also built pressures on the demand for jobs, while the Green Revolution did not create enough opportunities in the matter of employment generation.[97] The demand for agricultural migration to other states for reclaiming unreclaimed lands had almost come to a halt, because of the political aspirations of the local population. The last straw for the Punjabis, was the population linked recruitment quota for the Defence Services, which adversely affected the cherished ambition of rural youth to join the Armed Forces, while a large number of ex-servicemen returned to the state, to look for newer avenues of employment.[98] Overall, the unemployment rate, witnessed a sustained increase from 3 per cent in 1973 to 3.5 per cent in 1979-81 rising to 4 per cent in 1987-88.[99]

Unemployment in Punjab had another peculiar aspect that almost 80 per cent of the unemployed youth are matriculates; 1/6th graduates; 1/8th post-graduates and 1 among 8

---

95. Bhushan, Bharat, Punjab Politics and the Farmers, *Business India*, 165, 22 July 1984, Bombay, pp.70-79.
96. Doosanj, S.S., op.cit., p.312.
97. Singh, Chauhan, Strained Economy of the Punjab, *Link,* XXVII, 37, 28 April 1985, p.41.
98. Brass, Paul, R., Socio-Economic Aspects of the Punjab Crisis in Grover Verinder (Edited), op.cit., p.80.
99. Government of India, Ministry of Labour, Annual Reports of the Department of Labour and Employment 1979-81, Volume II, Government of India Press, 1972, pp.56-57, Report 1987-88, Vol.II, pp.57-58.

professionally trained. Moreover, 1/4th of the unemployed workforce consisted of women, which would mean a rising demand for jobs in the organized sector. At this point, therefore, it was relevant, to take stock of the structure of its economy and the pattern of investment in the state.[100] Traditionally, agriculture occupied the key position, because of which the structural changes in the economy remained rather slow. From 1980-81 to 1992-93, the contribution of agriculture to the GDP of the state declined from 49.1 per cent to only 47.4 per cent. The population witnessed a growth rate of almost 2 per cent, while the rate of economic growth hovered around 5 per cent, thus leading to a backlog of unemployment.[101] By the rule of thumb, to tide over the crisis of unemployment, the state would have required a growth of 6 per cent, which could be possible only if some basic structural changes came into the economy.

One of the major setbacks to Punjab's economy had been militancy, that not only stifled the state machinery but paralyzed the normal lifestyle of people in every walk of life, much has been said regarding the economic effects of these disturbances on industry. There was a specific study of the impact of disturbed conditions on industrial development. This study is based on the information collected from randomly selected industrial units, it was carried out by Dr. Raghbir Singh and Mr. V. K. Sharma entitled "Impact of Disturbances on Small Scale Engineering Industry in Punjab"[102] The industrial development in Punjab in terms of acknowledged indicators was satisfactory till 1983-84, but owing to immensely disturbed conditions in the state

100. Krishan, Gopal, op.cit.
101. PHDCCI, Pamphlet – Industrial Development in Punjab: New Realities, 22 June 1995.
102. Deptt. of Economics , Guru Nanak Dev University, Amritsar, 1998.

especially after 1983-84, the pace of industrial development slowed down and the share of the Primary sector increased while the Secondary sector declined. In the latter sector, the share of registered manufacturing declined by 1983-84. The primary sector contributed, 52.74 per cent of the state income while the secondary sector's contribution to the state's income was only 15.26 per cent.[103]

Though, the adverse effects were felt in the whole of the Punjab State but the border districts including Amritsar, Gurdaspur and Ferozepur were worst affected. Industrial units from these districts shifted to other states and even the skilled workers migrated to other regions. The expansion activities of the existing industrial units came to a standstill, as the entrepreneurs were terrified and did not like to take the risk of investing more funds in the state. Ferozepur suffered even more with the uncertain future of Fazilka and Abohar sub-divisions, after the Shah Committee report on the reorganization of 1966. The controversy once again resurfaced in 1986 with the Kandu Khara Census and Mathew Commission.

Amongst the border districts, Amritsar district suffered the most in terms of industrial development because it was the most sensitive area. By the end of the 1970s, the common expectation was that the industrial units would come up along the Grand Trunk Road in such a big way, that Amritsar and Jullundur districts would seem to be totally interlinked and no vacant space would be available along the G.T.Road, but this expectation soon became a distant dream, because of the disturbed conditions in the state. In the study cited below statements were formulated, in order, to ascertain the level of agreement of the respondents units, regarding the impact of disturbances on the arrival of customers from other

---

103. *Statistical Abstract*, Punjab, 1985.

states, terms and conditions of sales, credit facilities for supply of raw-materials, capacity utilization, labour and further expansion of business. The response received in this respect are presented in the following table:-

Table XXI
Impact of Disturbances on Industrial Development
(Level of Agreement)

Statements	Strongly Agree (%)	Agree	Neither Not Disagree (%)	Disagree (%)	Strongly Disagree (%)
1. Customers do not come for purchase due to the sense of insecurity rather the manufactures have to contact them.	70.80	3.10	1.77	2.21	22.12
2. As the manufacturers have to visit the customers, therefore customers dictate their terms and conditons.	53.54	13.27	3.98	2.21	26.99
3. Suppliers of raw materials have reduced the credit facility due to uncertainty.	53.54	5.31	1.77	2.65	36.73
4. Capacity utilization has been adversely affected due to curfew, riots, etc.	53.10	16.81	2.21	4.87	23.00
5. There is serious labour problem as migrant labourers have gone back to their parent states.	32.30	9.29	3.54	5.75	49.12
6. Entrepreneurs are investing their money in other states rather than expanding their business in Punjab.	30.09	2.21	7.08	7.52	53.10
7. A strange type of fear psychosis exists, which deters the development of Industry.	48.23	4.87	4.53	5.31	38.05

Table XXI reveals that over 70 per cent of the unit strongly agreed that the 'customers do not come for purchase due to a sense of insecurity, rather the manufacturers have to visit them for selling the products. Further, 66 per cent agreed that 'the manufacturers have to visit the customers, therefore, the customers dictate their terms and conditions'. About 58.85 per cent of the units believed that 'the suppliers of raw material have reduced the credit facilities due to uncertainity'. With regard to capacity utilization, 69.91 per cent of the units felt that 'their capacity utilization has been adversely affected due to the restrictions on the movements during odd hours, curfew and riots etc. Over 50 per cent of the units surveyed disagreed that 'there is a serious labour problem as the large number of the migrant labourers have gone back to their parent states'. About 60.62 per cent of the units disagreed that 'entrepreneurs are investing their money in other states rather than expanding their business in Punjab'. However, most of the units (53.10 per cent) believed that 'a strange type of fear psychosis exists, which deters the development of industry'.[104]

From the overall analysis, it can be concluded that the majority of the units had been seriously affected because of the disturbances in Punjab, particularly in attracting the customers from other states, terms and conditions of sales, credit facilities and capacity utilization. Though, it has been seen that a large number of entrepreneurs were not investing their money in business in other states. Yet most of the entrepreneurs had that a strange type of fear psychosis existed, which determined the development of expressed business in Punjab.[105]

During discussions, many entrepreneurs had said that disturbed condition prevailed, it was not possible for them to market their products in villages. On the other hand, the

104. Survey carried out by Dr. Singh Raghbir and Sharma V. K., GNDU Amritsar, 1998.
105. Ibid.

farmers avoided investing money in heavy agricultural machinery and tried to manage their work by following the alternative means, so the units dealing in agricultural products were facing marketing problems. Many entrepreneurs reported that their working hours had been reduced because the police compelled them to shut down their shutters by 6 p.m. Some entrepreneurs mentioned that they had stopped advertising their products because of the prevailing conditions in Punjab. Thus, from the foregoing discussion, we can say that the working of the units in the border districts had been impaired seriously in comparison to the units from the other districts during militancy. The impact of the disturbances on the units from Amritsar had been very grave with regard to the arrival of the customers, terms and conditions of sale and capacity utilization. This was the unanimous view of all the entrepreneurs of Amritsar because of a 'strange type of fear psychosis, the development of industry had been severely impaired."[106]

Punjab had earned the distinction of being the most prosperous state in the sense that its per capita income is the highest among all the other states of the country, but 52.74 per cent of the state's income was contributed by the Primary sector, while the contribution of the Secondary sector to the state's income was only 15.26 per cent. [107] Even in the primary sector, the economy is dominated by agriculture, but much reliance cannot be placed on agriculture, as growth in the latter seems to have reached a plateau. In order to sustain Punjab's rate of growth and its prime position among the Indian states in terms of per capita domestic product, its economy needs orientation towards industrialization. Further, industrialization is also required

---

106. Ibid.
107. *Statistical Abstract of Punjab, 1984-85*.

to sustain the existing rate of agricultural growth and to solve the problem of unemployment, especially of educated unemployment, which was the root cause of the Punjab problem.

The industrial development in Punjab in terms of the acknowledged indicators was satisfactory till 1985-86. But due to disturbed conditions, especially after 1985-86, the pace of industrial development slowed down and the share of the primary sector increased and that of the secondary sector declined in 1989-90. Even in the secondary sector, the share of registered manufacturing declined since 1984-85 (see figures of 1989-90). Though, the adverse effect was felt in the whole state but the border districts including Amritsar, Gurdaspur and Ferozepur were the worst affected. Industrial units from these districts showed a tendency to shift to other states and even the skilled workers migrated to other regions. Even the neighbouring states of Haryana and Himachal Pradesh promoted specific industrial complexes with an eye on migrating Punjab entrepreneurs, though the later success of these new ventures is debatable. Haryana promoted an industrial focal point at Panipat To lune on the woollen textile industry of Amritsar and Ludhiana, while Himachal promoted industrial estates at Baddi and Parwanoo for the light engineering sector, as well as chemical and textile units. Subsequent developments, however, do not indicate a large-scale migration of industry but they do indicate that many units attempted to develop an alternate base, outside Punjab. This had the effect of fragmenting the capital because of which, the growth of mother units in Punjab slowed down, the growth of new units could not take off properly, as indicated by many entrepreneurs such as (Tarlok Chand of Jay Jay Wollen, Ludhiana, Rakesh Dumra of Greatways, Ludhiana, Samir Mehra of Essma, Amritsar). The expansion activities of the existing industrial units came to a standstill, as the entrepreneurs were apprehensive of the future and did not wish to take the risk of investing more funds in the state.

Table XXII
Growth Rate of GSDP (Manufacturing) 1980-81 Prices Since 1980-81

Year	Percentage
1981-82	19.97
1982-83	2.59
1983-84	8.04
1984-85	8.85
1985-86	14.38
1986-87	6.41
1987-88	6.71
1988-89	14.16
1989-90	6.54
1992-93	9.30
1993-94	9.35
1994-95	10.30
1995-96	8.09
1996-97	8.20
1997-98	9.05

Source: Department of Industries, Punjab.

As would be noticed from this Table XXII, the rate of growth of industry which was 19.97 per cent in 1981-82, came down steeply in 1982-83 (the first year of beginning of the wave of militancy) and then it picked up only marginally for the next two years. Suddenly in 1985-86, when the hopes of political settlements emerged and the Surjit Singh Barnala led Govt. came in place after the 1985 elections, industrial growth rose to 14.38 per cent indicating the pent up development potential. This again was short-lived: Barnala's government was dismissed in May

1987. The next spurt came in 1988-89, when in the last year of Rajiv Gandhi's Government at the Centre, new initiatives about Punjab were being planned. Mr. S.S. Ray, the Governor of Punjab released a new industrial policy with the Rail Coach Factory at Kapurthala. As a central sop the Goindwal Rail line was given a clearance, there was a gush of optimism and the rate of growth of stock markets spurted to 14.16 per cent. The next year, however, there was a downward slant with the general uncertainty and instablility at the Centre. However, in 1991 there was stability at the Centre and the return of an elected Government of Beant Singh in the state. This brought a definite shift in the graph upward, when in its third year, Punjab had a rate of growth of 10.30 per cent in 1994-95 which staggered in the next two years after Beant Singh's assassination.

Recounting Punjab's history from one major milestone, i.e. partition, in entirety the narrative upto the onset of terrorism in the 1980s is in a constant state of flux . There have been scanty spells of stability, which could augment its infrastructural development. The Punjabi Suba movement injected social dichotomy between the two major communities. The two major political parties, the urban oriented Congress and the rural repres entation of the Akalis persisted with their tussles. Eventually, terrorism which was aggravated by the unemployment situation, gripped the state, making the security of the people a priority of the Government. As the state's volatile history gave scarce respite industrial activity remained far behind expectations and staggerred in statistical graphs, nationally.

Nature of Industries and Workers Employed in Erstwhile Punjab

Industry	Years 1951 Workers	No. of Factories	1956 Workers	No. of Factories	1961 Workers	No. of Factories	1965 Workers	No. of Factories
Agriculture Processing	3785	105	9460	233	9703	217	9256	206
Food Products	3494	109	6039	179	9249	239	10387	300
Textiles	17810	275	25114	549	34830	1043	45470	1087
Leather Products	175	1	732	11	2778	11	4410	13
Chemical Products	499	19	787	38	3135	43	2350	54
Basic Metal Industry	944	50	2986	109	5474	171	6342	207

Manufacture of Metal Products	5958	109	5320	156	8938	292	11290	334
Manufacture of Mechanical Machinery	7912	323	9988	424	21362	313	29023	360
Non-Metallic Mineral Products	1828	106	2455	25	3772	39	5742	52
Electrical Machinery	427	21	1143	26	3887	89	7983	112
Transport Equipment	670	31	2375	50	4393	104	6321	143
Miscellaneous Industries	343	55	233	86	3087	116	4320	129
Total	43845	1204	66632	1891	110608	2677	139894	2977

Source: *Statistical Abstract of Punjab for Various Years.*

Chapter III

Green Revolution : Impact on the Industrial Sector

The inter-temporal study of the growth process of a particular region, can be aptly described as a process of transformation, which is usually strewn with exclusive oddities and incongruities. Wading through these, economic historians have chalked out developmental theories of stages, through which economies must pass to evolve. This historical process, has sometimes been metaphorically compared with the evolutionary phases of human life, which culminate in a maturity followed by decadence. However, some economic historians, such as Collin Clark highlight the predominance of various sectors at variant temporal and structural stages of an economy. Clark, in fact, concluded that historical development becomes a process of the successive domination of the primary sector (agriculture), the secondary sector (manufacturing or industry) and tertiary sectors (trades and services).[1]

The American economist W. W. Rostow, reached similar conclusions and propounded the thesis, that growth starts from a traditional or primitive society to a transitional society, when the foundations for growth are laid. The next stage is one of take-off, when development accelerates taking the economy to a stage of maturation. Any historical analysis, of these processes reflects that entrepreneurship and investment in respective sectors, are the two key factors for transition from one stage to the other stage.[2]

---

1. Clark, Collin, *The Conditions of Economic Progress*, Macmillan & Co., London, 1951, pp.11-13.
2. Rostow, W. W., *The Process of Economic Growth*, W. Norton & Co., New York, 1952, p.32.

Somewhat similar conclusions, have been derived in empirical studies based upon a long-term history of various economies. In the deliberations of a conference, it was observed that while the first stage, may be a stage of low agricultural productivity, the second stage, would be brought about by improved agricultural productivity, through changes in technology, crops and infrastructure, like irrigation and roads. The developments of the second stage, thereafter, proceed to set the conditions for a major transformation in the economy. The rising agricultural production and income, generate demand for agricultural inputs, consumer goods and various services. This sets in motion, the process of development of agricultural input supply — industries, consumer goods industries and an extension of the services sector. The integration of the rural economy with other sectors, thereafter, leads to the fourth stage, when labour intensity in agriculture declines and agriculture, also starts following the patterns of industrial methods of production and gets integrated into the overall mature industrial economy.[3]

For a study of the linkage of the development and growth of Punjab's economy and its subsequent industrialization, it is necessary to trace the history of agriculture in the state. It is to understand economic relationships, social stratifications and political aspirations of the people of Punjab, which delineate its history. While in the immediate past, the history of industrialization of Punjab, shall point out to the Green Revolution, as a major factor responsible for the industrialization yet it followed definite social, historical and

3. Chadha, G.K., Off Farm Economic Structure of Agricultural Growth, A Study of Indian Punjab, Paper read at the International Conference on Off Farm Employment in Rural Asia, Chiang Mai, Thailand, 23-26 July 1983.

political trends for more than a century that seeded in the state to bring about the visible economic development.[4]

In recent economic history, the agricultural dominance of Punjab's economy was reinforced since 1849, when the British annexed Punjab. The British sensed the simmering discontent, which could disturb the nascent and fragile fabric of the British dominion in India and so, they decided to channelize this potential energy of the Punjabis towards building the economic prosperity of the province.[5] They initiated a definite agricultural orientation in Punjab, keeping industry and trade on the back-burners, because they felt that agriculture would be the ideal panacea to appease the restless peasantry, the dissatisfied landed gentry, and the Khalsa army seething with discontent and vengeance.[6] Their Punjab experience was exclusive. They proposed it, as an essentially agricultural province and bequeathed to it a well developed canal network, as they colonized tens of thousands of acres of wasteland. Punjab's history was influenced by its geographical location on the border. It was a buffer for British animosities, so the colonial interaction was exclusive here. The colonists were satiated, wiser with experience, so they were "less pernicious in form and less exploitative in operation".[7]

The century-old British policy of accent on agriculture in the Province continued in the post independence and post partition period. Pre-partition Punjab, bore the fruits of

---

4. Bhalla, G.S., Agricultural Growth and Industrial Development in Punjab in (Ed.) by J.W.Mellor, *Agriculture towards Industrialization*, John Hopkins Press, New York, p.79.
5. Ladejinski, Wolf, Green Revolution in Punjab: A Field Trip, *Economic and Political Weekly,* Bombay, 1961, 28 June.
6. Ali, Imran, op.cit., p.186.
7. Chadha, G.K., *The State and Rural Transformation*, *The Case of Punjab*, Sage Publications, Delhi, 1986, p.26.

British colonization and it supplied some 10 lakh tons of foodgrains for other parts of the country. The British had made large investments in canal irrigation in the state, capital outlay on productive irrigation canals was 40 per cent of the total sum made by the British Government in India upto the years 1919/1920. Consequently, the share of irrigated acreage in Punjab was 50 per cent for agricultural acreage.[8]

In 1947, Punjab was deprived of its prosperous areas. There was a loss in cotton crops primarily, and other agro products, which the canal colonies produced in large quantities.[9] The Hindu and Sikh landowners left behind an area of 6,700,000 acres in West Punjab (Pakistan), while in East Punjab (India) only 4,700,000 acres were available out of which only 1,300,000 were irrigated. This vast gap of available irrigated cultivable area and the land left behind in West Pakistan was met by a scheme of graded cuts.[10] Every landholder, irrespective of his holdings, was subjected to a cut of 25 per cent and in the case of large landowners, it was as much as 95 per cent. The rich canal colonies Lyallpur, Montgomery and Sargodha had remained in Pakistan. The percentage of cropped areas, receiving irrigation was about 33 per cent in East Punjab, as compared with 61 per cent in West Punjab of government irrigated land, 80 per cent in the West Punjab and only 20 per cent on the East Punjab side was well irrigated: the division of land resources was 62 per cent and 38 per cent respectively between the West and East Punjab. The West Punjab and East Punjab governments came to an agreement, to prepare copies of revenue records in their possession for the use of the other provinces to enable each other to allot the lands to the

---

8. Bhalla, G.S. (Ed. J.W. Mellor), op.cit., p.70.
9. Singh, Tarlok, Rural Resettlement in Punjab, The Background, A Transfer in Population, *The Statesman*, New Delhi, 6 July 1950.
10. Randhawa, M.S., *Green Revolution*: *A Case Study of Punjab*, Vikas Publishing House, 1974, p.8.

migrant populations. The exchange of records was started by the end of November 1948 and was completed during the winter.[11] The joint province of Punjab had a fairly accurate system of land records, because of which the process of verification of claims was completed, as early as April 1949. The cuts on big landholders were very heavy, so there was a considerable levelling down of land ownership at higher levels, and as a consequence distribution was concentrated at the middle rung landowners, as compared to other states.[12] In fact, this system of land-distribution automatically ensured the process of land-reforms and balanced distribution of landholdings.

> "This unique, agrarian feature of Punjab has lent great dynamism to the process of agricultural modernization, in due course of time".[13]

In spite of various setbacks, the newly carved state of Punjab pursued its historical moorings towards agriculture and reached its zenith with the famed Green Revolution which eventually became synonymous with the state.[14] The people who had crossed the border brought with them agricultural enterprise and tradition, and the wherewithal to pursue new pastures successfully, as the subsequent years were to prove.

The canal colonies of Lyallpur, Montgomery and Sargodha were colonized by the farmers of Punjab and became models of agricultural development and the active granary of the

---

11. An Encyclopedia of Laws Relating to Evacuees Property & Displaced Persons in India & Pakistan, Lal, Bhiwani, Claims Officer, Punjab & Mittal, Harbans Lal, Advocate, Second Edition 1951, Federal Law Depot, Delhi, Evacuation of Evacuee Property Act 1950, p.I.
12. Singh, Tarlok, op.cit.
13. Chadha, G.K., op.cit., p.27.
14. Sharma, T.R., Political Implications of the Green Revolution in Grover Verinder (Edited), op.cit., p.2.

province. It was in these colonies that farmers had mastered the art of farming. The migrant farmers from these areas played an important role, in developing the agriculture of present Punjab as well, as also parts of Haryana, Rajasthan and Uttar Pradesh. Kusum Nair, during extensive tours of the state, found that refugee farmers were progressive and superior in techniques of cultivation as compared to the local farmers of East Punjab.[15]

The process of modernization of agriculture in Punjab began in 1950, with rehabilitation programmes for the refugees. Owing to the combined efforts of the state machinery and the people themselves, the rural economy was back on the rails. Twenty-seven garden colonies for the cultivation of fruit plants were developed on an area of 20,000 acres. Loans were provided for the sinking of tubewells, purchase of tractors and other agricultural implements, irrigation by means of tubewells was powered by electricity for the first time. The use of tractors for cultivation was another innovation, and the process of land allotment, a large number of holdings were consolidated. As migrant landowners had more substantial holdings, as compared to the landowners of East Punjab, they were naturally more experienced farmers, and were ready to accept innovation. So it was they, who in due course, spearheaded the Green Revolution.[16]

As everywhere else, a key factor in development is human capital for which Punjab is the requisite reservoir. Punjabis were always receptive to new ideas and opportunities. The farmers were ready to adopt new

---

15. Nair, Kusum, *Blossoms in the Dust: The Human Element in Indian Development*, Gerald Duckworth & Co., London 1961, pp.112-115.
16. Randhawa, M.S., op. cit., p.4.

techniques, despite the element of risk.[17] Commenting on the entrepreneurship of the Punjabi farmer as compared to his counterparts in other parts of the country, Jasbir Singh has said,

"In Punjab, the human element has played an important part in the Green Revolution. The Sikh farmers....are entrepreneurial farmers having almost a mystical love for their holding. The most prosperous among them are the refugees from the Canal colonies of Pakistan".[18]

At the Centre, in India's First Five Year Plan top priority had been accorded to Punjab, which it deserved because this was the only state, which had suffered the maximum destruction caused by partition and the largest ever mobilization of population unprecedented in history. In the post independence period, the National Extension Programme, the Panchayati Raj and the Community Development Programme introduced a cadre of trained agricultural extension workers. Like all other states, when the nation-wide process of planning commenced in 1952. Punjab, too had to formulate for itself a development strategy. They chose to develop agriculture for the migrant, rural population and small-scale industries for the urban migrant, situating all the requisite props for triggering off the agricultural revolution.[19] In Punjab, the laws of succession pertaining to land had been, such that when the father died, the land was divided equally among all the sons.

---

17. Barnala, S.S., Policy Statement on Science and Technology and Industrial Development in Punjab in *Technology for Development on Northern India,* Volume I, Editors Ragnekar S.B. and Malhotra R., CRRID, p. 23.
18. Singh, Jasbir, *The Green Revolution in India, How Green is it* ? Vishal Publications, New Delhi, 1974, p.40.
19. Chadha, G.K., Planning Implications of Transformation of Agriculture in a Developing Area, A Case Study of Punjabi India, Paper read at Berlin, 1976, p.I.

Each successor insisted on having a share from each location, which resulted in further fragmentation. The disadvantages of fragmented and scattered holdings are well known, a wasteful method of land utilization and many improved agricultural practices cannot be adopted.[20]

The work of consolidation of holdings in Punjab began during the British period in 1920, through Cooperative Consolidation Societies. Since consolidation was voluntary, the progress of the work was very slow and from 1920 to 1951 only 280,000 acres could be consolidated. After independence, the necessity of consolidation of holdings was realized by the Punjab Government and the East Punjab Consolidation of Holdings and Fragmentation Act was enacted in 1948. An element of compulsion was introduced at the time of fresh allotment to the migrants and hence the progress was rapid.[21] According to this Act, village advisory committees were formed to advise the staff on all matters concerning the consolidation of land and in particular, in the classification and valuation of fields and preparation of village consolidation schemes. Apart from consolidating the holdings of farmers, the scheme provided a unique opportunity for replanning the countryside, which included planning the location of schools, hospitals and roads. Land was also reserved for community buildings such as Panchayat-ghars, community centres, government and institutional offices like Patwarkhanas and cooperative societies, places of worship and playgrounds. Above all, straight roads were provided to the village settlement, as

---

20. Mann, T.S., Punjab Socio Economic Conditions after Land Reforms, Verinder Grover (Ed.), op.cit., p.113.
21. Punjab Government, Legislative Department, The East Punjab Holdings (Consolidation and Prevention of Fragmentation Act 1948, Printed by Controller Printing, and Stationery, Punjab, Chandigarh, 1961, pp.2-3, upto 1961.

well as to the entire cultivated area. Circular roads around the villages and roads linking one village with another and with the main roads were also demarcated.[22]

The most beneficial effect of the scheme of consolidation, was that the farmers were able to sink tubewells. In 1950, there were no tubewells and in 1975 there were 4,27,000.[23] Besides, there was a considerable reduction in land leased out. There was an increase in cultivated area lost in embankments: yet the increase in agricultural production due to consolidation was 25 per cent.[24] The passage of various acts for tenancy reforms and ceiling on holdings placed a large number of cultivators in direct relationship with the state. Punjab now had the perfect backdrop conducive for agricultural progress. Various other factors were responsible for triggerring off the Green Revolution, which changed the Punjab scenario from one of deficit to an agricultural boom, further siphoning surpluses to other facets of the economy. There was a gradual realization that, the country should be self-sufficient in food. On the other hand, with the various land reforms, which had taken place, particularly the abolition of landlordism and removal of intermediaries, the cultivators developed a personal stake in augmenting production through investments in new technology.[25]

---

22. Randhawa, M.S., op.cit., p.9.
23. Sohal, K.S. Evolution of Well and Tubewell Irrigation in Punjab 1950-1951 to 1990-91, Punjab History Conference, Proceedings, 18-20 March 1994, Patiala, p.317.
24. Gill, M.S., Pakistani Punjab vs Indian Punjab in *The Illustrated Weekly of India* 10 August 1975.
25. Bhalla, G.S. and Chadha, G.K., Agricultural Growth and the Structural Changes in the Punjab Economy: An Input and Output Analysis, Research Report No. 82, Centre for Regional Development, Jawaharlal Nehru University, New Delhi, 1980, p.43.

There were two other external factors which facilitated the Green Revolution.

> "One of the most significant factors in the development of agriculture in Punjab, was the establishment of the Punjab Agricultural University in place of the Lyallpur Agricultural College. It was organized on the model of Land Grant Universities of the USA, where land has proved to be a powerful engine of change. This boosted agricultural research and technology, moreover, an awareness was created amongst rural areas of the various scientific strides made in agriculture. The main distinguishing feature of this university, was that it combined teaching, research and extension, in such a way that it benefited the University as well as the farmer".[26]

The second major factor was the arrival of the high yielding seed from Mexico, thus the stage was set for the Green Revolution, which was being visualized by Partap Singh Kairon since the mid-1950s. Over the years, one fact cannot be overlooked that the agricultural price policy helped Punjab farmers to sustain and develop new technology. The Agricultural Prices Commission and the Food Corporation of India created in 1966, played crucial roles in augmenting agricultural output by ensuring highly remunerative prices to farmers, which encouraged large investments in tubewells, pumpsets and other farm assets.

The state government, also focussed on agricultural development by starting departments, various bodies and cooperatives like the Punjab State Cooperative Supply and

---

26. Randhawa, M.S., A Case Study of the Green Revolution in Punjab, *The Punjab Past and Present*, Volume XVI-II, October 1982, Serial No. 32, Punjabi University, Patiala, p.288.

Marketing Federation and the Agro Industries Corporation, which supplied fertilizers, tractors and other farm machinery to farmers and helped them market their products. Cooperatives have played an important role in the supply of finance, in crop production, and in the development of land and water resources.[27] However, the technological breakthrough in agriculture, which came with the advent of the Borlaug Seed fertilizer technology in the mid 1960s was, perhaps, the most important determinant of rapid agricultural growth in Punjab.[28]

Overall in agriculture, there was an increase in the production of rice, potato and cotton due to an increase in productivity and area. The average yield of wheat increased from 1236 kg. and maize from 1653 kg. to 1722 kg. of rice from 1000 kg. to 2606 kg. per hectare in the time span of 1965-1966 to 1979 -80. Due to high yield of rice and wheat, Punjab was now recognized as the food-basket of India.[29] This spurt in agricultural growth would inevitably result, in the higher growth of the secondary, as well as the tertiary sectors. The impact of agricultural growth was felt at various levels : the wage rates had more than doubled in the subsequent six or seven years, the total earnings of the labourers had increased nearly four fold because employment had become steadier, due to multiple cropping and more supplementary employment opportunities. The prosperity of labour was also reflected in their usage of consumer items like bicycles and radio.[30]

---

27. Gill, M.S., The Green Revolution : Success in the Indian Punjab, Centenary Celebrations, Birmingham University, 1975.
28. Frankel, Francine R., India's *Green Revolution, Economic Costs and Political Costs*, Princeton University Press, New Jersey, 1971, p.41.
29. Government of Punjab, *Statistical Abstract* 1966, 1979 and 1980, Chandigarh.
30. Chadha, G.K., op. cit., p.337.

The Revolution gave a thrust to the production of farm machinery. Originally, in the early part of the century the artisans, mostly Ramgarhia Sikhs had started in their one room workshops, manufacturing items like Persian wheels, steel ploughs and cane crushers.[31] This has played a vital role in the regeneration of the agro industry in Punjab. Genetically, they were experts in engineering machinery techniques they played a commendable role in the indigenization of machinery requirements for the agricultural sector. By studying the designs of various tools, implements and even vehicles they provided chaff cutters, threshers, sprayers and seed-cum-fertilizer drills to suit local conditions. They were pioneers in manufacturing electric motors and diesel pumps and they did not stop here. They even domestically fabricated a combine-harvester, when it otherwise could be procured only by a few rich farmers by importing it from abroad. Bhadson in Patiala District is famous for this engineering feat as families of small-scale mechanics turned manufacturers, some of the locals even fabricated an automobile commonly known in Punjab as "Maruta", by joining a rubber tyred wooden cast with a diesel engine and home-fabricated steering to enable small farmers to graduate to automobiles from bullock-carts. The farm machinery industry of the state owes its development substantially to the initiative and hard work of this caste.[32] These enterprising men eventually began to make farm machinery on a large scale, in Phagwara, Batala, Bhadson and Gobindgarh areas. This success even led them to manufacture sophisticated automobile-parts some of

31. Bal, Gurpreet, op. cit., p.39.
32. Ibid., p.40.

which are original equipment manufactures for farmers' automobile brands globally.[33]

Simultaneously, urbanization increased and agricultural marketing-cum-trading led to[34] the emergence of large marketing surpluses which provided a stimulus for urban marketing and trade. The agro-processing, agro-input and consumer goods' industries, also, got a boost because of the increased agricultural population.[35] Agriculture induced industrialization remains the main motive force for urbanization. The state is dominated by a large number of small and medium towns, which mainly specialize in trade, marketing, processing of agricultural produce, provision of agricultural implements and other inputs.[36] In Punjab, agricultural development is equitably distributed all over the state, this has led to a fairly dispersed development of agro-processing, agro-engineering and agro-input industries and the distribution of small and medium market towns all over the state. However, on the other hand, large industries and also some small-scale industries tended to get clustered in large cities, which lie on the Delhi-Amritsar Grand Trunk Road. Punjab is, therefore, one state, where the rapid process of industriali-zation, during the past two decades has been primarily induced by rapid growth in agriculture owing to the Green Revolution, which has further snow-balled into

33. Ibid., p.65, also Johar, R.S. and Kumar P., Aspects of Growth in the Small Scale Engineering Industry at Batala – A Note in Punjab School of Economic Analyst, Volume III, No. 2, December 1982, Guru Nanak Dev University, Amritsar, p.203.
34. Bawa, R.S. and Sharma, Manoj Kumar, Urbanization in Punjab, A Causal Analysis, Edited by Mishra S.N., Urbanization and Urban Development in Punjab, Guru Ram Das School of Planning, Amritsar, 1985, p.33.
35. Ibid.
36. Bhalla, G.S., The Role of Small and Intermediate Towns in Regional Development of India, Paper presented at The Indian Institute of Advanced Studies, Simla, May 1992.

urbanization often unplanned and sporadic.[37]

A great deal of public investment, took place in rural and urban infrastructure, particularly, in power, roads and communications, thereby fostering the growth rate of small-scale industries, in both the consumer goods sector, as well as in agro-processing and agro-input industries. Simultaneously with the increased capital investment in agriculture, there was a rapid increase in the demand for capital goods like electric motors, diesel engines, threshers, tractors and construction materials. To begin with these demands were largely met through imports but the increasing demands and controls on imports gave a fillip to local industries.[38]

Recent studies suggest that there is indirect evidence to support the view, that financial resources were flowing out of agriculture. The first piece of evidence is major increases in savings out of which a large part came from rural households. The second, is the fact, during the late 1970s and 1980s the terms of trade moved against agriculture, the existing literature on flow of funds analysis is highly inadequate and does not enable one to draw definite conclusions about inter-sectoral resource flows in Punjab, while there is some indirect evidence to suggest, that resource flows out of agriculture are being used for industrial investment.[39] An analysis of the backgrounds of some of the entrepreneurs upto medium scale, in many of the agro-processing industries like food-processing, oil-mills, cotton-textiles, paper industry and even sugar industry

---

37. Reserve Bank of India, Industrialization in Punjab with a focus on Agro- Industries, Paper presented at New Delhi, June 1997.
38. Bhalla, G.S. in Mellor, J.W.(Edited), op.cit., p.35.
39. Gulati, Ashok, Structure of Effective Incentives in Indian Agriculture, Some Policy Implications in *Political and Economic Weekly*, Volume XXIV No. 39, Bombay 1995, p.124.

suggested that the promoters are second generation farmers, who have investible surpluses available to them from the Green Revolution bounties of twenty years or so. For instance, companies like Nijjar Foods of Amritsar and Rana Sugars in Amritsar-Gurdaspur are examples of this agro-induced industrialization.

As agricultural production increased as a result of the Green Revolution it provided an impetus for the growth and expansion of engineering industries, already existent. While the development of agro-input industries spurted as a result of backward linkages; substantial increase in output and marketed surplus of agricultural commodities led to a rapid growth of agro-processing industries like flour mills and sugar.[40] In fact, it will be interesting to note that the Green Revolution even spawned the return of multi-nationals to India, for instance, Pepsi Cola decided to enter the Food Processing sector in the late 1980s in Punjab, looking at its prosperous agricultural base and potential.

On the eve of independence, Punjab had been relatively an industrially backward state. However, state activity for the rehabilitation of migrants, traders, entrepreneurs and workers - involving large investments in infrastructural sectors like power, industrial estates, transport and communications had created the necessary environment for industrial development which continued through the 1950s and 60s. The Industrial sector albeit small scale, got a fillip after the Goa-conflict, Chinese aggression and the Indo-Pak war of 1965 for fulfilling the defence needs in woollen textiles, hosiery sector, machine tools and the automobile sector. In the mid-1960s exports to the erst while USSR, gave a great

40. Shergill, H.S. and Singh, Gurmail, Scope of Development of Agro-Industries in Rural Punjab, Punjab Institute for Development and Communication, Chandigarh, 1996, p.6.

thrust to the small-scale industry because this was cheaper for the latter , as compared to the Western world. More so, the bilateral rupee trade between India and Russia increased because of India's dependence on the latter for defence suppliers. In the late 1960s, with the advent of the Green Revolution, the increasing demand from the rapidly growing agriculture-sector combined with a rise in export demand boosted the process of industrialization in 1971, raising its income from manufacturing to 8 per cent of the total state income.[41] Punjab made fairly rapid progress in industrial development and began to be known as the land of small-scale enterprises. In fact, the industrial development of Punjab became synonymous with small-scale sector growth in India.

As mentioned in earlier paragraphs, industrialization in Punjab received a big boost: a multiplier effect of the growth in agricultural output, consequent to the adoption of new technology during the mid 60s. The industries that witnessed the boom were agro-processing, agro-input and consumer industries like textiles, woollen products, food products, metal products, engineering and agricultural machinery. Most of these industries were set up in the small-scale sector, which has had a vibrant growth since the 60s.[42]

An analysis of the pattern of development of agro-processing industries in the state, reveals that the following industries dominate the agro-processing scene—contributing about 90 per cent of the total agro-processing output — edible oils, dairy products, hydrogenated ghee, cotton ginning, baling, woollen spinning, weaving, sugar, leather

---

41. Punjab Government, *Statistical Abstract*, Economic and Statistical Organization, 1971, Chandigarh.
42. NCAER, Techno Economic Survey, 1972, New Delhi, p.82.

and leather footwear, wooden furniture and cupboard manufacturing.[43]

The Punjab experience highlights the fact, that rapid agricultural growth became a powerful instrument for bringing about a significant transformation of the economy. There was a marked increase in the growth rate of agriculture, which in turn accelerated growth in other sectors of the economy through input, output and consumption linkages. In fact, the growth process strengthened the linkages and dependence of the rest of the country on the economy of Punjab. By now the state had become the food-supplier to the nation.

> Between 1967-68 and 1979-80, the production of wheat and paddy, the two principal crops of the state, increased by 136 per cent and 634 per cent respectively resulting in an eightfold increase in the state's contribution to the Central pool of foodgrains during this period.[44]

This enabled the state to derive a great deal of comparative advantage, through specialization both in certain crops and in some manufacturing areas — though in the small or medium scale sector. However, the historically determined regional distribution of manufacturing capacities, particularly, in agro-processing and agro-input industries, often does not conform with the present patterns of agricultural output of the state. There have been many snags and lags in the development of the manufacturing sector. Firstly, a lack of sufficient investment in agro-processing seems to be a major constraint, for example, in

43. Shergill, H.S. and Singh, Gurmail, op. cit., p.5.
44. Sidhu, D.S. quoted in S.S.Doosanj, Socio Economic Tensions as a Result of the Green Revolution, *The Punjab Past and Present*, Volume XVI-II, October, Serial No. 32, October 1983, Punjabi University, Patiala, p.305.

1988-89 with 24.4 per cent share in the production of raw cotton, Punjab had only 1.9 per cent of the total installed spindles and 0.6 per cent of the looms in India. With 23.4 per cent wheat output and a 62 per cent share in the wheat pool of the centre, the state had merely 5.4 per cent of the roller flour mill capacity in the country. Thus a lack of investment in agro-processing seems to be one important reason for the slower than expected growth rate of manufacturing, because this is the only sector of industry where probably the availability of raw materials would not be a constraint on the development of industrial activity.[45]

Secondly, in spite of much greater imports of raw materials and consumption goods, Punjab has become a highly export surplus economy after the advent of the Green Revolution during the mid-60s. This was primarily because of a phenomenal growth in agricultural output and the emergence of large marketing surpluses and export of wheat, rice and cotton, along with some industrial products. A large part of the balance of trade surplus is not being ploughed back into the state for investment in the non-agricultural sector.[46] Existing evidence suggests that surpluses arising out of prosperous agriculture in many parts of India, including Punjab are not being mobilized and are not flowing into manufacturing. This surplus either accounts for high consumption or increase in real estate prices or as idle bank deposits because otherwise agriculture does not contribute to the tax-revenue of the state. The high credit-deposit ratio explains this phenomenon to some extent.

---

45. Bhalla, G.S., Agricultural Growth and Industrial Development, A Case Study of Punjab, Paper presented at Taipei, China, Institute for Studies in Industrial Development, 4-7 September 1990, Published October 1990, p.51.
46. Ibid.

On the other hand, agriculture is receiving large subsidies on account of fertilizers, power, irrigation and credit.[47] In all developing countries, the large resources have to flow into agriculture from other sectors of the economy by the channel of investment in rural infrastructure, in order to accelerate its growth rate. Once agriculture starts growing rapidly and agricultural income rises sharply, it becomes important for surpluses to be mobilized from agriculture for investment in the non-agricultural sector.[48] This is happening because the rich farmers have now acquired economic and political clout and the mobilization of surpluses through raising input prices or taxation is becoming increasingly difficult. Moreover, it takes a long time for peasant societies to switch over to the regular rhythm and discipline of an industrial culture. The society of Punjab right through history has been primarily agricultural, they were mainly peasants or feudal landlords. Of course there were soldiers, who also preferred to till their land, which they got as grants if they were not at war. Interestingly, even in a Census of 1868, it was observed,

> The proportion of agricultural Sikhs to non-agricultural is very much greater than in other religions. The Sikhs do not follow industrial or commercial pursuits to the same extent as is done by Hindus and Muslims.[49]

A graphic study of Punjab would reflect pinnacles of success in agriculture despite the trauma of partition.

---

47. See Bains, G.S., Development of Agro-based and Food Industries in the Punjab State, Paper presented at the Seminar on Perspective Planning, Punjab Agriculture University, April, 1997.
48. Singh, Balwinder and Singh, J.N., A Study into the Existing Status and Potentials of Agro-based Industries in the Punjab, Paper Read at a Seminar, Department of Economics, Guru Nanak Dev University, April, 1980, p.42.
49. Census of the Punjab, 1878, Indian Public Press, Lahore 1870.

However, before the state could integrate the agricultural surpluses into the total economic rebuilding process it was vivisected into three parts as a consequence of reorganization. The Reorganization in 1966 on a linguistic basis was primarily the result of pressures from the Akali Dal. In the years to come communalism and the language issues got inextricably mixed, even after reorganization, the demands for Punjabi-speaking areas continued unabated.[50] The principles and mechanics of the 1966 reorganization still continues to perplex the political parties. It is not only the Akali Governments, but the Congress Government of Beant Singh, that vociferously declared that the injustice was done to the state in 1966 and later in the matter of territorial reorganization and river-water sharing. The rise of a stratum of rich Jat peasants and the concentration of Jat Sikhs in certain areas provided an opportunity for a dominant section within the Akali Dal to strengthen their support base, by identifying their politics with that of the interests of farmers (Jats mainly), in an indirect way. This also infused the caste factor in the politics of the state. The introduction of technical innovations in agriculture in Punjab in the mid-60s provided an impetus to agricultural development along capitalist lines.[51]

The rich Jat peasants now built forward linkages, in terms of branching out into agricultural trade and exploring lucrative avenues, which existed in industrial production and general trade. To enter the latter spheres of economic activity would mean coming into competition with Hindu traders,

---

50. See Chapter II, page 29.
51. Guru, H.S., Science and Technology Today and the Punjab Problem, in Technology for Development Perspective on Northern India, Volume I, Editors, Ragnekar S.B. and Malhotra, Rashpal, CRRID, Chandigarh 1990, p.169.

Sikhs traders and other established industrialists.[52] Mainly industry and trade remained the exclusive preserve of the latter two categories, while agriculture remained in the hands of the Jats. This primary division of the professions along these lines also affected the political and social fabric in the years to come.[53]

The impact of the Green Revolution was clear in politics, when in 1967 reorganized Punjab got its first elected government of the Akali Party and Jan Sangh, the urban opposition party to the Congress, joined them briefly. The Akali Government was first led by Justice Gurnam Singh, which was then followed by Parkash Singh Badal's government and again by that of Justice Gurnam Singh, which further was followed by a brief government of Akali defectors led by Lachchman Singh Gill and supported by the Congress. However, one thrust of policies of all these governments witnessed a direct slant towards providing an infrastructure for the rural economy of the Punjab. Whether it was the Ropar Thermal Plant or approval of the Thein Dam (during Akali regimes) or a crash rural link roads programme, all of these aimed at strengthening and integrating the rural and agriculture sectors in mainstreams of the economy.

Though the demand-pull of the agricultural sector and other external factors did lead to some increase in the share of large and medium industries in the period that followed, yet the small-scale industries continued to occupy the centre-

52. 'Bhapa' was a term which evolved in the mid 1950s to refer to the Khatri and Arora Sikhs who had come from West Pakistan.
53. D'Souza, Victor, Economy, Caste, Religion and Population Distribution in *Economic and Political Weekly,* Volume XVII, No. 19, Bombay, 1998, p.19.

stage in the industrial development of the state.[54] According to the 1971 Census, the number of registered working small-scale industrial units in Punjab was 14,827, while for the whole of India it was 1,59,000 and Punjab's share in this respect stood at 9.33 per cent. A large product-diversification had not yet set in and the concentration of the industry also remained limited to the Grand Trunk Road axis of Amritsar, Jullundur and Ludhiana, till the early 1970s.[55] The economic compulsions of the Green Revolution, bottled up enterprise and external demands of defence and exports resulted in a preponderance of low productivity small-scale units. These units had come up, despite, the related absence of opportunities of ancilliarization, due to the lack of large and medium-scale heavy industry. This lack of opportunities soon started acting as a constraint on the capacity of the industries in Punjab to compete with products of industrial units outside the state enjoying similar opportunities.

The small-scale units in Punjab were mainly engaged in the production of woollen textiles, hosiery, cotton textiles, cycle and cycle parts, agricultural implements, machine tools, sports goods, steel re-rolling and cotton ginning and pressing. In fact, the share of the small-scale sector increased from Rs. 4,082.5 million worth of output in 1973-74 to Rs. 29,950 million by 1988-89 which was nearly two thirds of the value of output produced by the medium and large scale units during that year.[56] The rapid growth of the small-scale industry has much to do with the enterprise of the West Punjab migrant urban population. A major segment of the small-scale industry which prospered, depended upon

54. Government of India, Ministry of Industry, DC(SSI), Report on Census of Small Scale Industrial Units, Volume I and II, New Delhi, 1971, pp. 10-25.
55. Sandhu, J.S. and Singh, Ajit, Industrial Development in Punjab, Edited Johar, R.S. and Khanna, J.S., op.cit., p.137.
56. Government of Punjab, Economic Survey of Punjab 1989-90, Economic Adviser, Chandigarh 1990.

the raw material imported from other parts of India and other countries. These industries included woollen textile and hoisery, steel re-rolling cycle and cycle parts. In 1966, when Punjab was reorganized, it was left with no mineral or forest resources, which went to the share of Haryana and Himachal. Punjab had only agricultural resources, Whereas Haryana had mineral deposits, as well as an agricultural base. So reorganization gave Haryana an edge over Punjab in resource distribution.[57]

In spite of these potential drawbacks, the state did make a spectacular revival, it reflected the highest per capita income of the Green Revolution with the sumultaneous impact. In Punjab, the income was Rs.1318 in 1978-79, as against an all India average of Rs.712; almost twice, as high as that of India as a whole. The poverty ratio steadily declined in Punjab from 16.4 per cent in 1977-78 to 13.8 per cent in 1983-84.[58] Despite all these positive figures, the lopsided development due to lack of industry, did not change in any perceptible manner.

In 1966-67, the Primary Sector comprising agriculture, animal husbandry, forestry and fishery accounted for 57.45 per cent of the net state domestic product, while the Secondary Sector, comprising registered and unregistered manufacturing, electricity, gas and water supply accounted for 15.25 per cent, and the Tertiary Sector comprising of transport, storage, communication, trade, hotels, restaurants, banking, insurance and public administration

---

57. Johar, R.S. and Khanna, J.S., Reflections on the Development of Punjab and Haryana (Edited), op.cit., p.261.
58. Government of India, Planning Commission 1986, A Technical Note on the Seventh Plan of India, 1985-90, New Delhi.

accounted for 27.95 per cent. The figures did not change much in 1978-79. Also, the Primary Sector contribution was 56.69 per cent, Secondary Sector was 15.19 per cent and the tertiary sector was 28.12 per cent. This clearly indicates that the structure of the Punjab economy remained primarily production-oriented.[59] From the above, it is clear that structural changes necessary for a continuous self-sustained sectorally balanced growth were not yet evident in the state. From a long-term perspective, the structure of the state economy was not well poised for a steady and higher rate of growth.[60] Over a period of time, the prospects of increase in agricultural production are not very optimistic, as there is no scope of further increase in area under cultivation, cropping intensity and yield per acre which are fairly high already. The only way out is a shift in cropping patterns and providing infrastructural facilities, uniformally, in all the districts, though even this will not result in a sufficient increase in agricultural production, unless some other technological breakthrough occurs. Hence the economy needs a reorientation towards industry to maintain the already achieved level of per capita income in the state.[61] Moreover in the agricultural sector, the state will soon face competition from other states in the country where the rate of growth in agricultural production is increasing rapedly.

The impact of industrial growth during the immediate post-Green Revolution period can be seen from the following table :-

---

59. Government of Punjab, *Statistical Abstract of Punjab*, 1989, Chandigarh, pp.434-435.
60. Bhalla, G.S., op.cit., p.30.
61. Bhalla, G.S. and Chadha, G.K., op.cit., pp. 87-89.

Table XXIII
Comparison of Different Variables in the Industrial Sector of Punjab

	Item	1970-71	1975-76	1980-81	1981-82	1982-83	1983-84	1984-85	1985-86	Percentage*
1.	Number of registered factories (No.)	4084	4358	5688	5946	5036	5380	5555	5862	2.58
2.	Productive capital(Rs.lakh)	96693	80997	188350	218206	263340	317633	372447	344475	12.02
3.	Workers (No.)	108480	140014	174947	209080	208797	218258	239410	247829	6.11
4.	Total number of employees (No.)	139084	138600	235141	261701	263367	275421	306273	312337	6.88
5.	Total input including depreciation (Rs. lakhs)	37081	84261	240748	265892	297357	313718	352485	4301292	27.61
6.	Total output (Rs. lakhs)	44185	101194	249106	308847	343148	368200	412948	511901	18.85

7.	Value added (Rs. lakhs)	7104	16933	38607	42955	45791	54482	60466	65909	17.12
8.	Output per worker	0.407	0.723	1.424	1.477	1.643	1.687	1.725	2.066	12.01
9.	Value added per worker	0.065	0.121	0.221	0.205	0.219	0.250	0.253	0.266	10.43
10.	Productive capital per worker	0.891	0.578	1.077	1.044	1.261	1.455	1.556	1.389	5.57
11.	Productive capital per reporting factory	23.676	18.586	33.114	36.698	52.292	59.04	67.047	52.864	8.85

Percentage rate of change $b = E\,xy/E\,xy^2$ Research Report of Bhalla, G.S.Chadha, G.K. Sharma, op.cit., p.223.

This table relates to the period 1970-71 to 1985-86. Though in gross-terms the percentage may seem very impressive, but the fact remains that the base level figures were too low, therefore the gross impact when related to low base figures of 1970-71 appear very impressive. However, a fact that cannot be denied that growth was the result of the Green Revolution because no substatical external position factors or investments came to change the industrial face of Punjab's economy.

The Green Revolution brought with it close input-output and consumption linkages with the industrial sector. As a consequence of which between 1967-68 and 1987-88, the income from the manufacturing sector in Punjab witnessed a growth rate of 7.6 per cent per annum compared with 4.5 per cent for agriculture and 5.2 per cent for manufacturing in India as a whole.[62] The Green Revolution in Punjab also affected the trend of political processes, with increased income levels. The Punjabi farmer started harbouring higher political ambitions especially in the context of democratic tools available to him and this led to the culmination of a new political culture.[63]

The Green Revolution has been a watershed in the history of Punjab. However, the logical historical corollary of the industrial revolution following an agricultural revolution, has so far not transpired. The Green Revolution led the state's per capita income soaring (the highest in the country since 1966) but the state has suffered from an anomalous situation because of an industrial lag. On the one hand, the agricultural growth is almost touching a saturation point and the growth rate is tapering off. On the other hand, there has been a failure of an industrial revolution to follow, so the growth rate of industry has not picked up as expected[64]

---

62. Government of Punjab, *Statistical Abstract,* 1975 and 1989.
63. Bhalla, G.S. and Chadha, G.K., etc. Research Report, op.cit., p.25.
64. Gill, K.S., Agricultural Development in Punjab, *PSE Economic Analyst*, Volume I, No. 2, December, 1980, p.8.

Table : XXIV

Characteristics of Six Major Industries in Relation to Output (1986-87) as 100

	Industry Code No.	Output (Rs)	Fixed Capital (Rs)	No.of Workers	Total Employment	Input (Rs)	Value added (Rs)
Food Products	20-21	100	10.56	34.09	41.19	90.97	9.03
Wool,Silk & Synthetic Fibre Textile	24	100	33.03	64.02	74.78	82.96	17.04
Chemical & Chemical Products	31	100	46.55	15.76	21.81	83.86	16.13
Basic Metal & Alloy Industries	33	100	9.25	23.99	28.83	94.16	5.84
Transport Equipment & Parts	37	100	13.35	49.68	60.42	85.26	14.61
Electricity Production	40	100	330.71	73.68	110.18	54.58	45.42

Source: *Department of Industries, Punjab 1987.*

Chapter IV

The Onset of Liberalization and its Impact on the State

The last two decades of the twentieth century, had seen a global resilience of the spirit of liberty pervasive to all human spheres of activity. This spirit unshackled politics, demolished political barriers, opened up the potential of information gathering through cyber space and brought about fresh ideologies of liberalization in the economic system of the world, to work towards converting this planet into a global village. In all these developments, it has been well recognized, that, political ideas and ideologies (minus the dogmas) may be pursued but not blindly. It is because of the omnipresence of the spirit of liberty, that the importance of transparent and accountable democratic institutions cannot be overlooked in a conscientious system of governance. It is universally recognized, today, that only such institutions can bring in self-corrections within the system to avoid it slipping into the morass of dogma. The breakdown of the totalitarian political and economic systems in Eastern Europe with an unbelievably rapid speed, proved that a liberal spirit cannot be contained by force. Ultimately, political freedom manifests itself into liberalized economic forces or market-led economic systems, because economics is at the nucleus of all human activity — social, political, cultural and in a broader context, even religious.

The genesis and culmination of economic liberalization at a macro-level in the Indian context, as well as in the states needs to be viewed at with some philosophic undertones. However, the perceptions about some government institutions, by economic experts, with different perception, leads to between economic needs, as worked out by the latter technicians and the politics of democracy, as perceived by the vote-bank, i.e. the common masses.[1] It is in this context, that, liberalization, has to follow the pace, which may be dictated by support to the political rulers of the day, if the masses themselves are not aware of the ramifications of such a process. Alternatively, the speed of such a process would also depend on the economic compulsions of political rulers and their capacity to convince the masses of the ideological route, which the former would follow. Thus, the trade-offs between the vote bank and political rulers, would determine or distort the shape of future policies. The fact remains, that the political masses have a predominant role in determining the pace of liberalization.

The Indian economy has undergone a structural transformation from a highly inward looking system to a more open market-oriented global economic order since 1991. Liberalization is a process of economic policy changes, India was forced to embark on this path by the most serious economic crisis in 1991. These economic reforms, in their current form had been initiated with the help of financial support from the IMF (International Monetary Fund) and the World Bank and lately ADB (Asian Development Bank).[2]

Drastic policy changes in the areas of trade, exchange rate, industry, taxation, foreign investments, the financial sector and capital market between 1991 and 1995, have led to a strong economic growth and a significant boom in exports. Foreign investment inflows, of about five billion dollars a year, reflecting a robust confidence in the future of the Indian economy, along with a steady rise in the volume

---

1. Bhaduri, Amit and Nayyar, Deepak, *The Intelligent Person's Guide to Liberalization*, Penguin Publishers, New Delhi, 1996, p.21.
2. Neogi, Chiranjit and Ghosh, Buddhadeo, Impact of Liberalization on Performance of Indian Industries : A Firm Level Study, *Economic and Political Weekly*, Volume XXIII, No. 9, 28 February - 6 March 1998, p.16.

of foreign trade are indicative of the country moving towards an era of globalization. The 1995-1996 annual report of the Finance Ministry, paints a rosy picture of the economy. The point repeatedly echoed is that far reaching changes brought about in the economy, during the crisis of 1991-92 are now bearing results. It is creditable that India had achieved an overall average growth rate of 5.9 per cent during the first four years of the Eighth Plan, higher than 5.6 per cent. The delicensing and the opening up of the industrial sector to competition induced a higher flow of foreign investment and technology into the country and contributed to higher industrial growth. The industrial growth was led by the manufacturing sector with a growth rate of 13.9 per cent during 1995-96.[3]

Macro policies, make a definite impact of liberalization on the Indian economy as a whole, controlled from Delhi, yet, the states have a role in shaping and determining the nitty-gritty of the implementation of such policies, which ultimately could smoothen the passage of investment flows, when a country integrates in a global economy. The policies of the State Governments, which could be relevant in the context would be those related to their labour laws, sales-tax laws, octroi duties, environmental regulations, law and infrastructural development, electricity transmission and generation, integration of their governance method through Information Technology and giving a larger role to the private sector in most of these areas.[4] In this context, the socio-political climate and policies of each state, have their own relevance in determining the pace and path of liberalization in the context of contemporary economic and political history. While for India, a conscious and definite

---

3. United News of India, Backgrounder XXI, 38, 19 September 1995, p.3.
4. Jagdish, Bhagwati, *India in Transition, Freeing with Economy*, Oxford Press, Delhi 1995, p.42.

policy of liberalization, came more as a fait accompli, in the context of the adverse balance of payments position of 1991, and almost akin to the fury of floods, it remains to be seen, whether the State Governments were prepared to swim with this current or not.[5] When a particular state, knows the art of swimming with the current, it will probably be a beneficiary of this flood of economic opportunities, while the others might mull-over their social, political and historical compulsions.

It is not only Punjab but India as a whole, which had suffered because of the delay in the ushering in of economic reforms, whereas other Asian Tigers, started reorienting their economies towards opening of the markets for the foreign investor through deregulation/delicensing in the early 80s. It was only in 1991, that P. V. Narasimha Rao's Government for the first time opted for the new policy and it was his pragmatic approach to revise the old Nehruvian policy of industrial protectionism. Manmohan Singh, the then Finance Minister succeeded in attracting foreign investments, though on a limited scale. Items requiring industrial licensing were reduced to 15 and public sector reservation reduced to 6 industries, but private participation was allowed on an ndividual case basis even in these sectors. Private investments were encouraged in the development of infrastructure like Power, Roadways, Telecommunication, Shipping and Ports. The automatic approval of foreign investment up to 31 per cent in 35 priority industries was given and thus foreign investments began.[6]

The impact of liberalization on the economy would have to be seen in the context of the complexity of contemporary

---

5. Bhaduri and Nayyar, op. cit., p.86.
6. UNI, op.cit., p.3.

historical developments of the last half century. Mercurial vicissitudes, so typical of Punjab's history — pre and post independence, kept the polity of the state, apprehensive of long-term stability.[7] It is a different matter, that due to social and historical compulsions, the pace of economic activity remained reasonably satisfactory, as compared to the rest of the country, though the prime mover of this pace was agriculture and this had also led to some extent in the industrial development of the state.[8]

In Punjab, fortunately, the period of national economic liberalization, almost coincided with a period of long awaited peace, after more than a decade of militancy and terrorism. This peace came within six months of the installation of a Congress Government led by Beant Singh.[9] Before this Punjab had been under Governor's rule for two spells, one from 1983-1985 and the other from 1987-1992. Right since the 1980s, from the appearance of Bhindranwale on the scene, the Congress was a house divided within itself, the Akalis and the Congress were politically at loggerheads. In Mrs. Gandhi's period, Giani Zail Singh, the former Chief Minister of Punjab and Darbara Singh, the Chief Minister were always clashing where as Bhajan Lal, the Chief Minister of the neighbouring state was a convenient pawn, in the negotiations. In the post Operation Blue Star phase, several attempts had been made for dialogues between the Prime Minister Rajiv Gandhi and the Moderate Akali Dal led by Harcharan Singh Longowal, to solve raging issues like the water sharing issue and the Anandpur Sahib Resolution. In 1985, Rajiv Gandhi and H.S. Longowal signed the historic

---

7. Grover, Verinder, op.cit., p.623.
8. Frankel, Francine R., Agricultural Modernization and Social Change, *Mainstream*, Volume VIII, No. 13, 1969, p.13.
9. Dang, Satyapal, Grover, Verinder, op.cit., Vol.II, p.558.

Longowal Pact. However, Punjab continued to be under the sway of militancy.[10]

In 1990, Mr. Chandrashekhar, the then Prime Minister of India, made an offer to hold direct talks with the militants and had a direct dialogue with three Akali factions of Mann, Badal and Longowal.[11] These factions on 26 December 1990 had passed a resolution to initiate a dialogue with the Centre for securing the right of self-determination for the Sikhs, and demanded Punjab elections to be held with UN supervision. These talks, also, got conditional support from the militant outfits of Wassan Singh Zafarwal, Dr. Sohan Singh and Mr. Gurbachan Singh Manochahal, They however, declared the then Akali leadership as irrelevant. This bold move of Chandrashekhar was welcomed by the people of Punjab, who had been reeling under the pressures of violence and wanted not only political peace but economic freedom as well to be able to walk in step with the rest of the country. However, it is interesting to note, that none of the militant or political outfits, an economic policy, barring a few schemes of Simranjit Singh Mann. (The State however, soon, thereafter started its move towards the restoration of democracy under Governor O.P. Malhotra).

In retrospect, during the period of Governor's rule, particularly during Siddharth Shankar Ray's tenure (1986-1991) industry was given a particular thrust but owing to prolonged militancy, and the states inability to raise additional resources for higher outlays in industry, the rate of growth did not reach the level, which it could have with

---

10. UNI Backgrounder Volume XVI, No. 3, *New Moves on Punjab*, 17 January 1991, page I.
11. Ibid.

available agricultural surplus and Punjabi enterprise.[12] Some flight of capital into the state, in the wake of the post 1984 riots, could not sustain here due to the unreceptive attitude of the locals towards the migrants. While on the one side, cultural differences were dampening such inflow, on the other side, the local industrialists felt they were their competitors and were diffident to extend normal business courtesies to new investors in the state. This was corroborated by Mr. H.S. Sarna, who set up a modern plant of packaged food in Ludhiana and was forced to close it down almost within two years of completion. There are many other similar stories of abortion of such inward capital flight, though, S.S. Ray brought the integrated Rail Coach Factory to Kapurthala. Yet in his tenure, it was difficult for him to convince the local industrialists within the state. While there was no perceptible flight of existing investments, except in the Cheharta area of Amritsar from where old established woollen mills closed their operations and preferred to shift to Bombay and Faridabad. In other parts of the state, the industrialists were hesitant to reinvest profits for expansion and opted for alternate bases elsewhere in the country. Oswal Agro, a major industrial house expanded in Maharashtra, Uttar Pradesh and West Bengal; even Hero Cycles set up a unit in Gujarat of bicycles and various automobile units in Delhi.[13] The Essma Woollen Mills of Amritsar set up units in Panipat and Sonepat. Probably, such houses were waiting for better times to return to Punjab, to reinvest their profit here or were looking for greener pastures, so they took advantage of the highly competitive

---

12. Conversation with Mr. Nair Secretary Industries, Punjab.

13. (a) Interviews with Mr. Sarna H.S., Managing Director, Sarna Fast Foods, New Delhi, (b) Sunil Munjal, Managing Director, Hero Cycles Ltd, Ludhiana, (c) Mr. Suresh Mehra, Managing Director, Essma Woollen Mills, Amritsar.

sops offered by other states, It was during Ray's tenure that the Industrial Policy of 1989 had been initiated.

Coming back to the early 1990s, in April-May, 1991, the first ever elections took place to the three Municipal Corporations of the state: Amritsar, Jullundur and Ludhiana — (ever since these were set up almost fourteen years ago) — with the participation of all the political parties.[14] The state witnessed the hustle and bustle of electoral activity, albeit, confined to the three big cities of Amritsar, Jullundur and Ludhiana. The election passed off peacefully and a democratically elected Municipal Corporation was installed. The people of the state, however, started looking forward eagerly to an elected Government at the state level also. This step under the Governorship of General O. P. Malhotra was reassuring enough to initiate the process of elections to the State Assembly. The national elections to the Parliament were announced for June 1991 and elections in Punjab for Parliament and Assembly were to be held a few days later.[15] The Governor enthusiastically, took upon himself the challenge of restoring democracy in the state. The Akalis, were equally enthusiastic about participating in the elections. However, after peaceful elections to the Municipal Corporation, the militants' apprehensive of a return to democratic rule in Punjab, issued warnings and threats to the candidates contesting the elections, accompanied by murders and a train blast. The Congress Party, however, unsure of its political future, started raising the demand for postponing the elections till the restoration of total peace in the state, General Malhotra's reassurances notwith-

14. Punjab Government, Director of Local Government Records, May 1991.
15. UNI Backgrounder 1991, op.cit.

standing. The Congress government of P.V. Narasimha Rao came to power at the Centre and within 24 hours decided to postpone the elections in Punjab, on the grounds of continuing militant activities. General Malhotra, was quite upset at this move of the Centre, which was taken without consulting him and he resigned from his post.

The next six months saw renewed political activities, with the Central Government's endeavours to hold elections in a peaceful atmosphere. After a few administrative changes, and some political initiatives, finally a notification was issued on 24 January 1992 to hold elections in Punjab to its 117 Assembly seats and 13 Lok Sabha seats. This time the Akali Party announced its' boycott of the elections, apprehending that the elections would not be fair with a Congress Government at the Centre; while at the same time, even the militants issued threats to those participating in the elections.[16] However, the Centre was adamant and decided to go ahead with the elections, which led to a massive mandate for the Congress Party, winning 87 seats out of 117 seats and leading to the formation of a popular Government under the Chief Ministership of Mr. Beant Singh on 25 February 1992. The Akalis had mainly boycotted these elections, except one faction under Capt. Amarinder Singh, which won three seats. The Beant Singh Government, was criticized by its detractors as a minority Government lacking a mandate of the people, on the argument, that the Akali Dal, a major political party of the state had boycotted the elections, yet it started functioning on all fronts, quite soon, with a declared first priority of law and order to peace restoration followed by economic

16. UNI Backgrounder, Punjab Polls, 1992, p.I.

development of the state.[17] Very soon, the tough policies of the State Government to restore peace in the state and wipe out terrorism, showed their result and within less than one year, there was an all round improvement in the general climate of the state. The people started experiencing the renewed bliss of peace.

The first priority of the Government, had been to establish peace, since normalcy would automatically boost activity it was time to consolidate the economy and join the national economic mainstream.[18] It would be interesting to recollect here, that Punjab had been the first state in the country to collaborate with Pepsi Cola, which later became the symbol of a liberalized economic climate in the country.[19] Thus the state had to pursue its programme of agricultural and industrial growth to integrate the two sectors to derive the optimum benefit for this.[20]

Initially, the new Government in Punjab had to focus on restoring law and order, yet soon, they began formulating progressive economic policies, so as to lure investment.[21] A conference, to this effect 'Punjab – 2002' was the first major initiative of the Beant Singh Government, wherein national and international investors were invited to acquaint

---

17. Singh, Beant, Chief Minister of Punjab, Miles to Go, in Verinder Grover, op. cit., p.599.
18. UNI Backgrounder, Volume XVII No. 9, Outcome of Punjab Polls, 27 February 1992, p.2.
19. Punjab, Haryana and Delhi Chamber of Commerce, Punjab Committee – Industrial Development of Punjab: New Realities, 22 July 1995, p.4.
20. Punjab Government, Punjab Agro Industries Corporation, Opportunities for Agro Business in Punjab, Chandigarh, 1992.
21. PHD Chamber of Commerce, op. cit., p.5.

themselves with a new and resurgent Punjab, and to dispel notions about the law and order situation in the state.[22] Delegates came from the USA, Canada and other European countries. The Government announced a major initiative in the field of industrial incentives and tax rationalization. It was also a period, when Punjab, being the primary agricultural state of the country had to make up its mind on the Dunkel Draft, with regard to Intellectual Property Rights on agriculture production and research.[23] This was a dilemma, because on the one hand, globalization interests at the macro level demanded that India sign the agreement after the Uruguay rounds of talks and the domestic compulsions in the interest of agricultural development, demanded otherwise. The prosperity of the agriculture of Punjab, could have been at stake with the acceptance of the entirety of such international pressure.[24]

Keeping the social, political and economic needs of the state and the new challenges thrown upon by the liberalization of the economy at the Centre, it became imperative for the new Government of Beant Singh to adopt a holistic approach to the situation as it existed.[25] The small-scale sector of the state, could soon be facing challenges from the competition of multinationals elsewhere in the

---

22. Punjab Government, Directorate of Industries, Literature Published by Udhyog Sahayak 19 December 1992.
23. Sharma, Devinder, *GATT and India, The Politics of Agriculture,* Delhi, 1994, p.X.
24. Ibid., Introduction.
25. Sahota, Gian, *Economic and Fiscal Gains from Liberalization in Punjab,* Institute for Development and Communication, Monograph series III, Chandigarh 1996.

country, the youth would be clamouring for jobs as per their education, and agriculture was not showing a large prospect of a higher rate of employment.[26]

The Government, therefore, had to make special studies to (a) identify those sectors, which had a higher and a faster rate of employment growth; (b) to make an assessment of the comparative costs of employment, in different sectors at different locations.[27] The conclusion, from most of these studies, would point out that in the short-run, the solution was to increase the growth of industrialization, provide special incentives for the development of industry and simultaneously, to ensure the small-scale sector against the competition of the multinationals, special efforts had to be made for Human Resource Development by increasing the technological capacity of the small-scale sector. In the infrastructural context the state support for liberalization required special attention, if it was to attract investments especially when it lacked natural resources.

A new industrial policy was devised which aimed at providing a modern infrastructure for the growth of the industry and tax concessions to the new large and medium sector units also. The State Government formulated a package of incentives, in modification of the Industrial Policy of 1989 which became effective from the tenth of October 1992. This policy did not merely provide incentives but

---

26. Krishan, Gopal, "Demographic Change in Punjab" in *Punjab in Prosperity and Violence 1947-1997*, Edited Grewal, J.S. and Banga Indu, K.K. Publishers, Chandigarh, 1998, p.177.
27. Government of Punjab, Department of Industries, Chandigarh, Punjab, 1993.

also stressed on making the freshly attained peaceful atmosphere conducive for industrial investments. The policy aimed at accelerating the rate of generation of employment opportunities, development of manpower, strengthening infrastructure and extension services for a better interface between industry and government. The Package of Incentives provided capital investment incentives upto Rs. 50 lakhs and sales tax exemption for a period upto 10 years to the units that would come up in the state on or after 1992.[28]

The Punjab Government initiated several measures to give an impetus to the development process. The 'Single Window Clearance Service' was revamped and a specific time-frame laid down for grant of the required approval/ clearance by the various Government Departments/ Agencies. In case, the clearance/approval was not accorded within the specific time, the case was placed before an empowered committee constituted under the Chairmanship of Chief Minister, Punjab. This Committee was empowered to take a final decision, if the concerned department/ agency did not decide the case within the stipulated time. The decision of this Committee, has been made binding on all the Departments/Government Agencies.

In line with the policy of the Government of India, the procedures were simplified and bureaucratic controls liberalized in Punjab. A new scheme with the nomenclature 'Inspector Free Raj' was introduced as a pilot project at Mohali. Under the scheme, the Inspectors from various departments were not visiting the industrial units for

28. Interview with Mr. Bindra I.S., Secretary, Industries, Punjab, August 1992.

enforcing the observance of different rules and regulations under the various Acts of the Government. Rather, the industry had been given an opportunity to self-discipline itself by voluntarily adhering to the various rules and regulations.[29]

The Government also introduced a new scheme in which 'Escort Service' was provided to the entrepreneurs. An officer of the Department was 'Escort' for providing every possible help and assistance to an intending entrepreneur in the setting up of a particular industrial project assigned to him. The performance of the officer is judged by the quality of service rendered by him to the entrepreneur.[30] The effect of the measures was that suddenly new investment started flowing into the state. Godrej in collaboration with Gist Brocades in the pharmaceuticals sector; Hitachi, Mazda, Oki and Fujitsu of Japan in the telecommunication sector; Ranbaxy in collaboration with Eli Lilly of USA, Westing House of USA, Olivetti of Italy, were a few of the new entrants in the industrial field of the state. The Indian Groups such as Birlas, Modis, JCT, Thapar Group, DCM, Godrej and Shri Ram made investments. All these were heralding the possibilities of multinational investments, not to say that domestic and local enterprise did not follow suit. The following Table XXV indicates the increase for industrial investments in various sectors of the state:

29. Information from officers of the Punjab Government, Department of Industries, Punjab.
30. Ibid.

Table XXV
Performance Figures on Investments, Production and Exports

Year	No. of Units	Employment (Nos.)	Production (Rupees	Fixed Capital Investment in	Exports Crores)
Small-Scale Sector					
1991-92	176378	711417	4437	499	545
1992-93	181563	732580	5345	1621	725
	(2.9%)	(3.0%)	(20.5%)	(8.1%)	(33%)
1993-94	184875	755883	7075	1764	1086
	(2.0%)	(3.2%)	(32.1%)	(8.7%)	(49.1%)
1994-95	188241	776763	9000	1973	1200
	(1.8%)	(2.8%)	(27.2%)	(11.8%)	(10.5%)
Large and Medium Sector					
1991-92	395	193789	7709	4552	356
1992-93	414	188034	9335	5194	490
	(4.8%)	(-3.0%)	(21.1%)	(14.1%)	(37.6%)
1993-94	440	200000	11000	5800	730
	(7.3%)	(6.3%)	(17.8%)	(11.6%)	(48.1%)
1994-95	475	06722	13500	6420	900
	(8.0%)	(3.4%)	(22.7%)	(10.7%)	(23%)
Total Industrial Sector					
1991-92	176773	905205	12146	6051	901
1992-93	181977	920614	14680	6815	1215
	(2.9%)	(1.7%)	(20.9%)	(12.6%)	(53%)
1993-94	185315	955883	18075	7564	1815
	(1.8%)	(3.8%)	(23%)	(11.0%)	(49%)
1994-95	188716	983485	22500	8393	2100
	(1.8%)	(2.9%)	(24.5%)	(10.9%)	(15.7%)

(Figures within brackets show percentage increase over the previous year).

Source: Government of Punjab, Department of Industries, Chandigarh, 1995.

The industrial development in the state during the period of liberalization was well documented by *The Economic Times* in its issue of 25 March 1995.

> The Beant Singh Government's Five Point Programme of economy in expenditure, mobilization of additional resources, administrative restructuring, improvement in performance of Public Undertakings and systematic reduction in subsidies, which began in May 1992, started paying dividends by 1995. In spite of the fact, that Punjab had a step up in police expenditure to maintain law and order, over and above the budgetary allocation, as well as an increasing burden on its exchequer for the security provisions of bigwigs.[31]

In this period, as the dark clouds of terrorism vanished, business boomed again, real estate prices soared and the pace of investments in the industrial sector accelerated to Rs. 25,000 crores. The exports surged to the Rs. 1,500 crore mark and the annual plan outlay, which stood at Rs. 700 crore three years ago rose to Rs. 1,675 crore in 1995-96. The state was in the third position in the matter of industrial growth from the 13th position, it held three years earlier.[32]

The Punjab State Industries Development Corporation since inception was performing well and was reckoned as one of the foremost State Industrial Development Corporations in India. In term lending portfolio, PSIDC registered a growth of 49 per cent when term loans (including bridge loans against

---

31. Kumar, Rahul, Punjab's Industrial Outlook Brightens in *The Economic Times*, 25 March 1995.
32. Punjab State Industries Corporation, Monograph, Published Chandigarh, 1995.

state subsidy) of Rs. 600 million were disbursed in 1994-95 against Rs. 403 million during the previous year. The PSIDC has also been maintaining a constant increase in its profits. The profit before tax during 1993-94 has been Rs. 327 million as compared to Rs. 115 million in 1992-93, having recorded an increase of 185 per cent. The earnings per share has been to the tune of Rs. 334 and the book value of Rs. 1588 of share of the face value of Rs. 1000.

During 1994-95, the effects of peace were percolating as PSIDC made an all time high investment in the equity capital promoted/assisted companies which had been of the order of Rs. 737 million as compared to investment of Rs. 414 million during the previous year, recording an increase of 78 per cent. Whereas, during the period of militancy fresh investments were suspended or were being made outside the state, as reflected above.

The Punjab State Industrial Development Corporation played a pivotal role in the development of industry in the state. Within three years of restored peace, the Government entered into 111 MOUs with various industrial houses and enterprises, which was to catalyze investments of Rs. 15,875 crore with an employment potential. In order to further improve the infrastructure, an essential input for the speedy development of industry, the Punjab Government made a plan to privatize the infrastructure development. The first project was set up by Shri Ram Industrial Enterprises Ltd., at Rajpura, about 40 kilometres from Chandigarh, another Industrial Park was set up at Lalru.[33]

---

33. PHDCCI, Meeting with M.Beant Singh, 22 July 1995, PHD House, New Delhi.

Table : XXVI

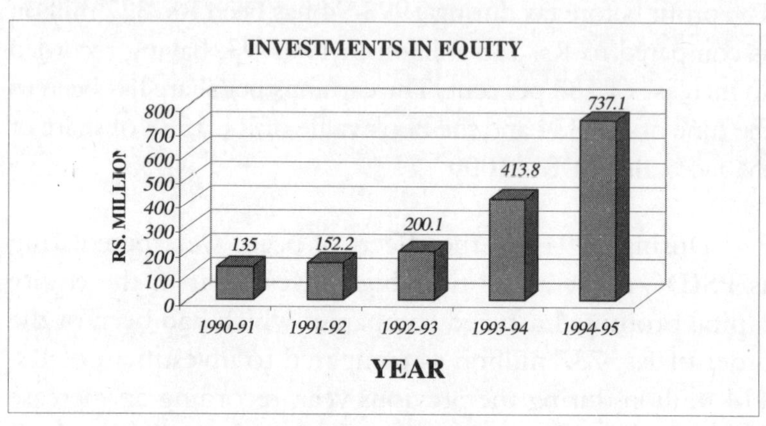

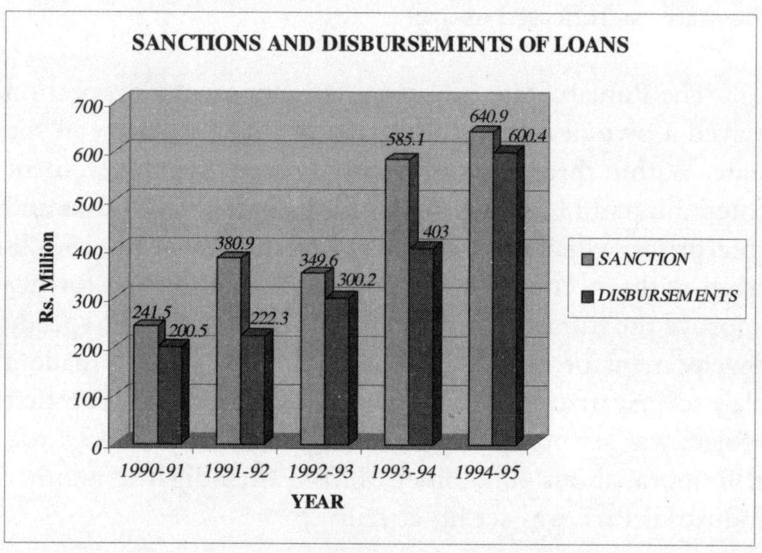

Source : PSIDC Monograph Figure 1995

The PSIDC was in dire straits as a post script of the populists policies to the previous Akali Government. The entire equity stands eroded, the investments in equity are for more than loan disbursements. In 2002, PSIDC had to meet liabilities to the extent of Rs. 297.62 crores. However, the Congress Government presently in saddle decided to give a boost to industrialization by making a token provision of Rs. 10 crores for equity investment during 2002-3.

While the process of economic reform generally in India was crisis driven, due to the condition of the economy in 1991, for Punjab, the new liberalization, also, required to be absorbed into the definite politico economic strategy for the future. Interestingly, the economy had witnessed a crisis due to internal as well as external factors. Internally, the Green Revolution had increased the income of the agricultural sector and aspirations of the rural youth, without a commensurate increase in the scope for employment potential, and externally, the international relations between India and Pakistan fuelled the frustrations of the youth, which further gave a fillip to terrorism spreading in the state.[34] Since terrorism was dealt with successfully the external challenge thrown by liberalization had to be encountered.

Therefore, it was imperative, that to permanently wardoff the spectre of militancy and terrorism, an affirmed economic policy in a liberalized industrial climate with concessional firm steps was required, which could probably be possible only with a firm leadership at the top. The strategies can always be successful in the long term, only if they are backed by strong political commitment backed by the involvement of the masses, in a democratic system. Beant Singh, as Chief Minister was successful to a large extent in

34. Ibid.

delivering the economic gains within a short span of the first three years of his chiefministership.[35] Once peace and liberalization prevailed in Punjab, endeavours at industrialization were made on an individual as well as governmental basis. In comparison to figures of industrial investments and ventures, the peace time figures showed a marked difference. However, in comparison to all India figures Punjab's performance was dismal. While others strode ahead and capitalized on major national and international investments, Punjab had lagged behind because of militancy.[36]

By 1995, there were 475 units in the large and medium sector with a fixed capital investment of Rs. 6,420 crores and employing 2.06 lakh persons. The small-scale industries sector, which is better entrenched in the state, had around 1.88 lakh units with a fixed capital investment of Rs. 1,929 crores and employs 7.74 lakh persons.

Punjab with a share of Rs. 18,477 crores, had only 2.4 per cent of the total proposed investment in the country. As on December 1994, it was still far behind states like Maharashtra and Gujarat, as indicated from Table I below. In per capita terms also, Punjab was behind other states and even the national average.

The low credit-deposit ratio in the state, as can be seen from Table II given below, is not a problem in itself, rather it is a manifestation of a larger problem, namely the low level of industrialization of the state. Though the credit-deposit ratio in the state has steadily improved, it still ranks 14th amongst the various states of the country, and is also significantly below the all India average.

35. UNI Service Backgrounder, Punjab Assembly Elections 1997, A Curtain Raiser, 30 January 1997.

36. Ibid.

Table XXVI

State-wise Proposed Investment as on December 1994

State	MFG.	MNG.	INF.	Total For all Industries	Per Capita Proposed Investment In Rs.
	Proposed Investment (Rs. Crores)				
1. Punjab	10023	NIL	8454	18477	9110
2. Maharashtra	33660	17395	46794	97848	12395
3. Gujarat	38392	16916	38076	93385	22606
4. Madhya Pradesh	20731	9393	54860	84984	12841
5. Orissa	14090	12534	55313	81937	25880
6. Haryana	2837	3886	10488	17211	10453
7. Rajasthan	6857	313	11552	18722	4254
8. Uttar Pradesh	18847	1213	37223	57283	4117
9. Himachal Pradesh	1948	NIL	22153	24102	46611
10. Andhra Pradesh	13385	18424	26184	57993	8719
11. Karnataka	17129	5965	24123	47217	10497
12. Kerala	3313	1836	9857	15006	5156
13. Tamil Nadu	14602	7101	22106	43809	7842
14. West Bengal	9765	2029	17964	29757	4371
All India	228948	106879	440617	776444	9174

Source: Centre for Monitoring Indian Economy, Shape of Things to Come, December 1994, p.32.

Table XXVII

Credit-Deposit Ratio of Public Sector Banks

	Credit Deposit Ratio (%)		
State	**June 1969**	**June 1980**	**March 1994**
Andhra Pradesh	100.8	70.4	73.3
Arunachal Pradesh	-	11.1	12.7
Assam	39.4	39.4	41.8
Bihar	30.8	41.4	34.7
Goa	40.8	36.2	25.4
Gujarat	48.6	51.7	46.3
Haryana	46.9	65.8	50.1
Himachal Pradesh	25.0	28.6	28.8
Jammu & Kashmir	5.6	36.4	25.8
Karnataka	76.1	78.7	72.7
Kerala	65.8	68.3	41.4
Madhya Pradesh	58.9	51.4	55.9
Maharashtra	100.9	77.3	69.9
Manipur	0.0	23.8	71.3
Meghalaya	33.3	14.3	15.3
Mizoram	-	0.0	18.1
Nagaland	0.0	23.5	43.4
Orissa	51.7	56.7	59.9
Punjab	**27.0**	**38.5**	**42.0**
Rajasthan	51.4	67.1	50.0
Sikkim	-	-	22.0
Tamil Nadu	133.5	90.0	87.0
Tripura	75.0	41.4	43.0
Uttar Pradesh	45.7	43.0	36.8
West Bengal	115.4	60.4	45.6
All India	78.0	66.9	57.5
Relatively rich states	86.5	68.1	62.5
Relatively poor states	45.0	47.3	42.8

Source: CMIE, April 1994.

Table XXVIII
Investment of Central Projects in Punjab and in India

Year (as on 31st March)	PUNJAB Gross Block (Cr. Rs.)	All INDIA Gross Block (Cr. Rs.)	% age Share in Punjab
1978-79	344.52	1567.89	2.20
1979-80	362.52	18166.14	2.00
1980-81	418.64	21171.78	1.90
1984-85	563.62	47323.27	1.20
1985-86	602.78	56806.42	1.00
1988-89	802.35	96880.67	0.83
1989-90	836.51	113430.90	0.74
1990-91	875.57	130655.10	0.67
1991-92	941-49	153893.02	0.61
1992-93	1230.89	174837.04	0.70
1993-94	1200.56	198912.48	0.60
1994-95	1393.24	229568.37	0.61
1995.96	1723.07	267259.64	0.64
1996.97	2077.85	284361.52	0.73
1997.98	2435.05	319829.16	0.78
1998-99	2950.33	354131.67	0.83
1999-2000	3004-01	381364.90	0.79

Source : Public Enterprises Survey, Government of India.

It is in disputable that the state has done well in terms of many socio-economic parameters due to its agricultural development. But, of late, the returns from the Green Revolution seem to be tapering off and approaching a plateau. Coupled with this is the fact, that, other relatively more industrialized states of the country are steadily catching up with Punjab and within a few years may overtake it in respect of several key socio-economic parameters. It is particularly true for per capita income.

In this era of sweeping market-oriented economic reforms, with the twin objectives of liberalizing and globalizing the Indian economy, a competition has emerged amongst the various states for attracting investment, both domestic and foreign, in a wide range of industrial activities. A state-wise comparison in this regard is given in Tables XXIX below. This gives the figures for proposed investment on the basis of Industrial Entrepreneurs Memoranda (IEMs) filed from August 1991 to December 1994.

What clearly emerges from the study of this data is the fact that the flow of investment to the Northern Region, particularly Punjab lagged behind the flow into other regions and states of the country, owing to prolonged militancy for almost a decade. The states which are attracting the larger share of investments are Maharashtra, Gujarat, Tamil Nadu, Madhya Pradesh and Orissa. Punjab's position does not compare too well even with other states in the Northern Region, including Himachal Pradesh. The proposed investment in the power sector, one of the major areas of concern and which is attracting a sizeable chunk of the investment, has been estimated at Rs. 3,41,066 crores, as on December 1994, of which Orissa and Madhya Pradesh account for Rs. 51.234 crores and Rs. 45,488 crores respectively. Against this, Punjab accounts for only 2.1 per cent of the total with a proposed investment of Rs. 6.996 crores.

Table XXIX

State-wise Breakup of Industrial Entrepreneurs Memoranda (IEMs) Filed from August 1991 to Decemeber 1994

State	IEMs Filed	Investment Proposed (Rs. Crores)	Employment Potential
Andhra Pradesh	100.8	70.4	73.3
Andhra Pradesh	962	26367	189454
Assam	39	1038	4125
Bihar	158	4057	24413
Gujarat	2446	59709	449189
Haryana	1105	13118	189639
Himachal Pradesh	169	4836	53208
Jammu & Kashmir	25	124	6924
Karnataka	610	13707	90668
Kerala	145	3547	27751
Madhya Pradesh	1048	34186	269362
Maharashtra	3049	67978	581922
Meghalaya	3	38	482
Nagaland	2	53	252
Orissa	105	3085	42804
Punjab	965	12657	276743
Rajasthan	997	16084	201344
Tamil Nadu	1324	18400	223508
Tripura	3	1038	1345
Uttar Pradesh	1779	38460	327258
West Bengal	576	8873	121555
Sikkim	8	22	680
Andaman & Nicobar	4	261	2180
Arunachal Pradesh	1	35	23
Chandigarh	12	121	3604
Dadra & Nagar Haveli	369	6458	51269
Delhi	370	5758	41581
Goa	103	2170	12410
Lakshadweep	1	4	278
Pondicherry	136	796	13756
Daman & Diu	190	1949	16722
Total	**17064**	**344929**	**3224449**

Source: State Industrial Association Newsletter, January 1995.

Beant Singh's assassination was followed by a lackadaisical approach of his successor H.S. Brar and an equally uneventful brief tenure of Rajinder Kaur Bhattal. The one and a half years of these two chief ministers suddenly put the politico-economic fabric in a disarray, since the leadership was weak and the new elections were forthcoming.[37]

In February 1997, new elections took place in the state, which gave a massive mandate to the Akali Government because the Congress Party was a house divided, after Beant Singh's assassination.[38] The Akali Government, particularly, is representative of the interest of the farming community in the state. In this regard, the speech of Prakash Singh Badal made to the PHD Chamber of Commerce on 18 March 1997 (within the first month of the Government) would be a pointer. His observations were.

> Punjab's economy is mainly agro-based. A large quantity of agricultural produce is marketed/exported as such without any value addition. My Government, therefore, will give special emphasis on the agro-industry, so as to establish a linkage between industry and agriculture, so that the benefit of industrial prosperity is shared by the agriculturist.
>
> Considering the significance of agro-industries to the state, such units are provided the highest quantum of incentives under Industrial Policy, irrespective of their location in the state. I shall welcome further suggestions from you for strengthening the state support to boost the agro-industry.[39]

---

37. UNI Service Backgrounder, Punjab Assembly Elections 1997, A Curtain Raiser, 30 January 1997.
38. Ibid.
39. PHDCCI, Seminar on Industrialization of Punjab, 18 March 1997, PHD House, New Delhi.

The Government under Mr. Badal had as one of its major policies announced free electricity and water for agriculture. However, in the year 2002, the Congress Government led by Captain Amarinder Singh is back in power and for industry it augurs well for the state. The chief minister is keen to perk up the industrial economy, he has initiated the process by holding meetings with industrialists and NRIS to promote investment in the core economic sectors. He has set up a high powered finance committee which would endeavour boosting agricultural and industrial production, by encouraging their partnership. Most importantly, he has done away with freebies like electricity, sheer, populism to garner votes but detrimental to industry and the state in the long run.[40]

40. Ibid.

Chapter V

Role of the Government: Five Year Plans and State Policies

As one embarks upon a study of industrial development, as a segment of a holistic historical process, it would be quite incomplete, without a perusal of the dominant role played by the Government: Central as well as State. In industrial development, the major determinants are: the extent of the facilitation role played by the Government, the approach of financial institutions in funding industry and the entrepreneurial spirit of the people.[1] In the post independence era, a closer interaction between industry and government has emerged as a part of a conscious policy of the Government. In modern times, the role was confined not only to the maintenance of law and order, but also as an active participant in economic development by not only assuming the role of an entrepreneur but also as a facilitator and catalyst through its institutions and policies.

The Government started playing a major role in steering industrial development by improving the industrial climate, attracting industrial investments, making things easy for entrepreneurs, thereby accelerating industrial growth leading to the prosperity of the state and its people. The Government has offered unique packages of incentives, infrastuctural and of capital subsidies and tax concessions.[2]

It developed industrial complexes, infrastructural facilities and an industrial network. In the Third World, the

1. *The Economic Times*, 1980, 16 September.
2. Khanna, S.S., *Government in Business*, Asia Publishing House, Bombay, 1963, p.3.

role of development of industrial infrastructure always devolves upon the Government, because it requires huge investments with low commercial returns and has a long gestation period in delvering benefits to the economy. Private investment is very hard to come by in heavy industry. Similarly, private investors do not only take into account social benefits in their investment decisions but look at the returns on their investments. Thus therefore, the Government has a major role to play in the promotion of infrastructural activities and heavy industries. Further in the annals of recent economic history, it is seen the world over that industrial development requires a stable, social and political environment, so that private entrepreneurs consider their investments safe and secure. Government investments always have a multiplier effect on the industrial development leading to overall economic growth.

Private investors because of their lack of knowledge and expertise may hesitate to invest in the beginning. The Government, therefore, has also to play the role of a friend, philosopher and guide to the private investors and create economic networking backwards and forwards, among suppliers of materials, producers and markets of finished products. Even credit facilities have to be developed to engineer smooth coupling of such networks. It is in this context, that the role of five year planning in industrial development needs to be historically examined.

In the foregoing chapters, various social, political, historical and geographical factors have been examined, which have influenced the pattern and scope of industrial growth of Punjab since 1947. It will, therefore, be worthwhile to examine as to how Government policies and plans, specifically targetted at industry, affected industrial growth. Since growth patterns, are affected by the legacy of their past, therefore, while discussing the effect of

Government policies, it is imperative to first recapitulate the legacy (or the lack of it) of industrial plans and policies, at the time of independence. These form a significant historical linkage, imperative to study the present as a culmination of its past.[3]

In the early days of British Punjab, the subject of "industries" formed but a small part of the Department of Agriculture, with which it was lumped at first, mainly because the existent industries were of a small-scale character and mostly associated with agriculture. The first structured state concern about planning and implementing, a scheme of industrialization in British Punjab (then known as the Province of Punjab) was seen in 1920, when a separate Department of Industry was set up in pursuance of the report of the Royal Commission on Indian Industry of 1918 saying that the demands of the First World War had made the development of industry an exigency for self-defence and economic necessity.[4] The Department was charged with the control of technical or industrial educational institutions, the survey of industrial possibilities, to advise factory owners, or future industrialists with regard to the cost and equipment of factories with engines and machinery. K.T. Shah was commissioned by the Government to prepare a plan, which in his view would have taken ten years for its proper implementation. He submitted his plan to the Government in 1941, this was the first structured plan, which was aimed at industrialization. It also considered such other facets of the economy in a macro perspective, as would have centrifugal effects on industrialization.[5]

---

3. Dubey, V. P. and Duggal, Bindu, Industrial Policy of Punjab, Centre for Research in Rural and Industrial Development, Chandigarh, 1995, p.4.
4. Shah, K.T., *Industrialization of the Punjab*, Government Printing, Punjab, Lahore, 1941, pp. 183-184.
5. Ibid.

Though this plan could not unfold itself and did not see the light of day, because of the Second World War and subsequent political turbulations ultimately culminating in the independence of the country - accompanied with the pangs of partition of the prosperous Province of Punjab. Yet a look at this plan would be immensely beneficial from the point of view of looking at the possible policy options, which were thought of and also, whether these policy options, later manifested themselves in the policy development of the state. This plan visualized industrialization as a policy incentive for economic development, with a view to :-

a) Increase the aggregate domestic product, as represented by the commodities or services produced, by either setting up of new industrial establishments or the development of the existing ones;

b) redistribute the burden of population from the agricultural to the secondary and tertiary sectors by making them complimentary and supplementary to each other;

c) to mop-up the potential of disguised unemployment by providing work for the labour force, shifted from the rural sector to manufacturing and servicing sectors, which in effect, would have meant a more even distribution of employment oppotunities in all sectors and an even distribution of additional wealth generated.

d) to effectively utilize the capital surplus available in the which manifested itself mainly in the rapid increase in the value of the agricultural lands. The return from the agricultural lands, therefore, was diminishing very fast. Therefore, to get optimum return upon the total capital available, the plan proposed investment of surplus capital in the industrial sector. Such a situation was also considered an opportunity for better utilization of agricultural produce as industrial raw-material: a situation which could develop a symbiotic relationship between agriculture and industry and consequently also increase returns from the agricultural land.[6]

The industrial plan implied the utilization of all industrial resources, whether in the form of land, water, power, forest wealth or human resources. Its broad enunciations would look similar to and a precursor of enunciations of subsequent industrial policies.

It said,

> whether, however, any given industry is large or small, worked with power driven machinery, or by means of human or animal energy; and whether it is spread over throughout the Province in small- scale establishments or concentrated in few places; every industry will, in a plan, have to be organized and interconnected carefully, as an integral part of the plan programme. No industry car be left to start, to grow, to work ad hoc , as its promotors, proprietors may choose ....each unit, each industry, each enterprise, must form an integral part, closely fitting into a carefully coordinate. whole. The interconnection of each option must be thought out and designed, so as to be for the advancement and benefit of all, and not result in any conflict or friction or needless over-lapping. The location of a unit, the size of options, the number of establishments, the nature of equipment, the labour and capital employed in each, the market served,

6. Ibid., pp.3-4.

the services needed of transport, banking, etc. must all form part of a common programme.[7]

It would be interesting to mention here, that the post Green Revolution industrial policies, also echoed similar themes, when they spoke of finding avenues for investment of agricultural surpluses in industries, correcting imbalances in credit-deposit ratios and generation of more employment opportunities.[8]

In a way, along with the stage being set for the independence of the country, in the pipeline were comprehensive development programmes for the economy, as well. In the proposed planning, the complementarity of the Primary and Secondary Sectors was duly recognized.

Shah visualized that,

> industrialization, moreover, must, in the ultimate analysis, depend upon, and be connected intimately with, the primary producer both for the materials of industry, and for the market for his finished goods.

The Plan did not only end here but it also aimed at the linkages between industry and services sector when it said :

> if the Plan is concentrated only upon the establishment or development of the industries, and neglects to take into account the incidental and indispensable service of transport, finance or marketing, it would be seriously handicapped at the outset.[9]

This Plan, was substantialized and framed to help the

---

7. Ibid., p.137.
8. See Chapter III, p.21.
9. Shah, K.T., op.cit., pp.15-16.

establishment of new industry since industrial encouragement and development of the existing industry in large as well as small sectors. In fact, the Plan even spoke of a proper employment development through an Apprenticeship Act, so that, while on the one hand, the labour would develop their skills. On the other hand, the industry would not face the shortage of skilled labour.

To tackle the crisis of financing for the industry, this plan even suggested specific financial institutions/banks for the financing of the industry for fixed, as well as working capital requirements, it went to suggest, the setting up of a special State Industrial Bank. The Plan even suggested some kind of subsidy for energy needs of industry and scientific research and development funds, specifically aimed at industrial research and development. In 1931, an industrial research laboratory was established to undertake investigation and experiments for assessing the possibilities of starting new industries, or developing the existing industry from the local raw-materials. The laboratory, was keen to carry-out research in the processes and materials of the existing industry encouraged by the success of this laboratory, it was made permanent in January 1937.[10] The state commissioned the services of experts in various industries like oil, textiles, hosiery, tanning, etc.to help in the technological industry. By now the Industries Department, was well recognized as a catalyst for industrial growth and it had started playing an important part in the development and promotion of industries.[11] It began promotional activities in the nature of one window service for industrial development by helping the industry in

10. Ibid., p.140.
11. Lal, Ram, *Report on the Department of Industries Punjab for the Year Ending 31 March 1938*, Superintendent, Government Printing, Punjab, Lahore, 1938, p.2.

acquisition of sites for factories; while at the same time it started promoting industry-related issues with other departments of the Government; prominent among those being:

a) Reduction in railway freight for transport of raw-material and finished goods.

b) Reduction in terminal taxes/octroi charged by local bodies on the raw materials or finished products.

c) Seeking canal water for industrial use at concessional rates.

d) General reduction in taxes imposed on industrial objects or activities.

In spite of all these measures, the British Punjab remained industrially backward.

First attempts at a structured date compilation of industries in the state can be seen in the Census of 1921, which contained a brief reference to Industry. In this context of the overall census, the data compiled mainly pertained to such of the concerns, which employed at least 10 persons on any normal working day. Though it was a rough compilation of data, but it showed only 80 per cent industrial establishments including mills, at work in the then Punjab, employing a total of 61.70 per cent male and 4,755 female workers, skilled and unskilled. Out of them only 430 were operated by mechanical power: steam, electricity, gas, oil or water, which aggregated to 40,000 horse powers, only 247 of these establishments came within the purview of the Factories Act.[12]

12. Census of India 1921, Volume XV relating to Punjab and Delhi, Report Part I, p.365.

The Census of 1931 merely gave fewer details than the Census of 1921. It only mentioned that now Punjab had 526 establishments coming within the purview of the Factories Act and had in addition: "A large number of smaller factories, chiefly soap work, hosiery factories, floor and rice mills, chemical works, printing presses, furniture making works, tanneries, etc."[13]

The next reliable information is the Annual Report on the Working of the Factories Act in the Punjab, for 1938, which shares 887 registered factories out of which 730 were actually working.[14] On the production of industry, the Department of Industries did a survey in 1932 which indicated gross value of products as 15,74,07,500,[15] which the value of agricultural products even in 1922-23 was estimated at Rs. 128 crores per annum.[16] The budget of the Industries Department was 3,50,912 in 1921 which went up to 21,90,150 in 1939, out of which 2134 went to technical education.[17] Thus it is more than apparent, that at the time of independence Punjab was principally an agricultural province.

It also needs to be seen that in the pre-partition Punjab, where there was a scope of development of industries, they were restricted by the policy of the then master to great monopolies to Biotech industry. The actual facts bore, "eloquent testimony to the utter disregard shown towards the material interests of............by the powers that have been".[18]

---

13. Census of India 1931, Volume XVII, Punjab, Report Part I, p. 363.
14. *Annual Report in the Working of the Factories Act, Punjab,* 1938, Department of Labour, Government of Labour (available at Punjab Archives, Patiala).
15. Ram, Lala, *Report on the Department of Industries, Punjab for the Year Ending 31 March 1938,* Superintendent Government Printing, Punjab, Lahore, 1939, p.40.
16. Darling, M.L, op.cit., p.16.
17. Shah, K.T., p.185.
18. Ibid., p.103

Though not adequate, these measures had spawned the process of industrialization. However, the most interesting aspect of the entire plan exercise of 1941, was a proposal for the constitution of a Statutory Development Corporation for carrying out the plan for the industrialization of Punjab.[19] The constitution, powers and functions of this body were proposed to be laid down by an Act of the Legislation. This body was supposed to execute and administer the entire industrialisation of the state. The exigencies of the Second World War and subsequently partition derailed the whole exercise. Barely when the British administration realized that emphasis on agriculture in Punjab now required to be supplemented with emphasis on secondary and tertiary sectors, as is apparent from the above Plan, came the misfortune of partition which threw every economic activity out of gear.

After partition, the major work, which prompted the State Government was the rehabilitation of refugees. As seen from the brief historical accounts of the effects of Partition in the East Punjab, in the foregoing chapters, the entire economy was disrupted, by this mass movement of population. The social and communal structure of this cross-migration completely distorted the economic equilibrium, because the employers moved in one direction and the workers in the opposite. Resultantly,

> Economic and social interdependencies were jerked out of balance, the Government and the people were faced with the colossal task of putting social and economic life again on an even level.[20]

Partition also affected the future progress of the border districts due to the fear-psychosis of the existing population of these districts and migratory population coming from

19. Ibid., p.140.
20. Luthra, K.L., op.cit., pp.71-72.

West Punjab. These areas, which were once throbbing with prosperity in the centre of undivided Punjab, were not attracting the migratory population, since they preferred to settle in the safer regions of Delhi and beyond or in rebuilding their fortunes, so grossly devastated by the aftermath of partition. Their economic life virtually came to a standstill due to the flight of labour and capital to safety zones, almost 54 per cent of skilled labour of the industries, which was Muslim, migrated to Pakistan from this region.[21]

The industry was also faced with a loss of market of raw materials, as well as of finished products, the deprivation of industrial infrastructure was another stumbling block. The desire of the industry to shift from the border towns of Amritsar, Gurdaspur and Ferozepur held another dangerous prospect for the future of the economy of the state and a possibility of structural imbalances. The state is replete with the examples of the structural ruination of many throbbing and historically important towns. These towns and cities have still not been able to stop their downward slide, despite over fifty years of independence.[22] For instance, the border town of Khemkaran, which had a municipality since the late 1860s (an index of its growth) has now been reduced to the level of a notified area committee. Similarly the fate of Ferozepur — even though, it is a divisional headquarter — is no better in the absence of economic activity, so is the town of Dera Baba Nanak, which despite being a historic place of the Sikhs, has not shown any hope for its economy. If the border towns of Abohar and Fazilka have been able to retain some economic standing, it is more

---

21. Government of Punjab, *Statistical Abstract of Punjab 1947-1950*, Government Printing Press, Simla, 1950.
22. Gazetteer of India, Punjab District Gazetteers, Amritsar 1976, Ferozepur 1983, Gurdaspur 1979, Published by the State Revenue Department Punjab.

because of the prosperity brought by their cotton crops than anything else.[23] To counter the adversities staring these towns, the Government of East Punjab immediately, passed the East Punjab factories (Control of Dismantling Act in March 1948), to restrict the shifting of factories registered in these areas, under the Factory Act. This was a comprehensively tough piece of legislation, to prevent the removal of even spare parts of machinery.[24]

At the same time, the Government, set up "The Board of Economic Enquiry" in 1949.[25] This committee recommended, that new industrial townships should be built near about and around Delhi, while suggesting some development measures for the industry, which would help cross-border trade between the East and the West Punjab, which has remained erratic due to the subsequent Indo-Pak tension. To fill up the gap of capital and skilled labour for the small and middle level migrant businessmen, the Government of India had set up a Rehabilitation Finance Administration in 1948, for providing medium and long term financial requirements. The Punjab Government opened up 34 Industrial Training Institutions (22 for men and 12 for women) in all the district headquarters and 32 training centres (23 for men and 9 for women), training upto 10,000 persons, to fill up the gap of vocational training.[26] All these efforts, were also being supplemented by the Punjab State Aid to Industry Act of 1932.

---

23. Ibid.
24. The Punjab Government Code: The East Punjab Act March 1948 Control of Dismantling Act, Government Printing Press, Simla, 1948.
25. Malhotra, V. P., *Economic Conditions of Displaced Persons Settled in East Punjab*, Part I, Ludhiana, 1940, p.51.
26. Technical Training in Punjab, The Industries Supplement 1.1., *The Tribune*, Ambala, 15 April 1954.

However, the task of industrializing the state was not easy, especially when partition had brought the industrial production to nearly half. The strain on the already brittle structure became almost unbearable. according to the Census of India. In 1951 only 7 per cent of the total workforce in Punjab was engaged in industries, construction and public utilities, as compared with 65 per cent in agriculture and allied occupations, 10 per cent in commerce and transport and 18 per cent in services.[27]

A substantial proportion of those employed in manufacturing, were using little or no power and working as independent workers with the help of family labour. The number of registered factories (employing more than 10 workers), did not exceed even one thousand and provided employment to not more than 50,000 people. As compared to many other parts of India, the new state inherited industrial backwardness. In 1950, Punjab accounted for only 1.8 per cent of the total value of output generated in the registered sector, as compared to 33.8 per cent for Bombay and 27.0 per cent and 12.2 per cent for Bengal and Madras respectively.[28]

Even in 1956, the proportion of work force employed in the factories' sector in Punjab, was far less than the national average and the only state below it, was Orissa. Table XXX below indicates that while the Indian average was 7.36 factory workers per 1000 of population, in Punjab it was 4.80. Another indicator of industrialisation is electricity consumption, here also Punjab was one of the lowest (only higher than Orissa) with 154.00 million kwh. against total for the country as 35.11.36 m.kwh.

(Table XXX on next page)

27. Census of India 1951.
28. Government of India, Ministry of Rehabilitation, 1951-52, n.79, pp.14-15.

Table XXX

Factory Employment Per 1,000 of Population (1956)

State	Total Factory Employment (Per 1,000 of population)	POWER Million KWH
India	7.36 (100)	3,511.36
Bombay	18.77	1,325.04
West Bengal	22.90 (22.7)	797.04
Madras	9.31 (9.1)	319.60
Orissa	1.39 (0.56)	19.52
Punjab	4.80 (4.3)	154.00

Source: National Council of Applied Economic Research Techno-Economic Survey of Punjab, op.cit., p.77.

At the national level, soon after Independence, the Government introduced the Industrial Policy Resolution (1948), and this outlined the approach to future industrial growth and development of the country. It emphasized the importance to the economy of securing a continuous increase in production and ensuring the equitable distribution of the wealth thus created. Further to ensure that the core sector does not suffer, the Government also introduced the concept of Public Sector investments by the Government. Once the pressures of refugee settlement started easing out, and was adopted the planning model of development and a clear, definite industrial policy became imperative. To serve these ends, therefore, the Central government adopted a new

Industrial Policy Resolution in 1956, which had as its objective, the acceleration of the rate of economic growth and the speeding up of industrialization, as a means of achieving a socialistic pattern of society. By 1956, capital was scarce and the base of entrepreneurship was not strong enough, hence, the 1956 Industrial Policy Resolution gave primacy to the role of the state to assume a predominant and direct responsibility for industrial development.[29]

The strategy of planning for industrialization, during the first four decades from the First Five Year Plan in 1951 was implemented under the framework of a mixed economy with a substantial role for the public sector and a state regulated private sector. At the national level, models of economic development were also being framed.[30] By the time, India went ahead with the Second Five Year Plan in 1957, the Mahalanobis model of economic growth was adopted, which laid stress on investment in heavy and the core sector industrially. Resultantly, there were investments in the Steel sector — Bhilai Steel, Bharat Heavy Electrical, Chitranjan Locomotives, Hindustan Machine Tool Corporation, etc., the industries which were infrastructure building. One such industry came up in the united Punjab at Panchkula (now in Haryana).[31]

The planned development of industries in Punjab, began with the Government announcing the establishment of industrial areas with the objectives (i) to rehabilitate the displaced persons from West Pakistan and to (ii) develop

---

29. Government of India, Ministry of Industry, Statement on Industrial Policy 1956, New Delhi, 1956.
30. Government of Punjab, First Five Year Plan, A Summary, Planning Department, Chandigarh 1953.
31. Uppal, J.S., Indian Economy and Five Year Plans in Uppal, J.S.(Ed.) *India's Economic Problems – An Analytical Approach*, Tata McGraw Hill Ltd., New Delhi, 1984, p.11.

small-scale industries. These areas were set up at Jullundur, Ludhiana, Phagwara and Patiala, they offered improved sites, as inducement for the establishment of industrial enterprises.[32]

In Punjab (not in its present form but as East Punjab and Pepsu) the First Five Year Plan essentially laid more emphasis on the development of agriculture, than on industries as was rooted in the state's history. The total plan was of Rs. 147.5 crores, made of an outlay of Rs. 138 crores for Punjab and Rs. 9.5 crores for Pepsu. The state spent only 63.62 lakhs (2.16 per cent of the total plan outlay) on industries during 1951-56. Out of this a major chunk of Rs. 48.13 lakhs (7.6 per cent) went to the development of cottage industries.[33] Pepsu, on the eve of the merger had a population of 35 lakhs and comprised the following states—Patiala, Nabha, Kapurthala, Jind, Faridkot, Malerkotla, Nalagarh and Kalsia. Punjab was actively considering the development of cottage and small-scale industries, in addition, to the development of industrial colonies and a number of training centres.[34]

In spite of these industrial strides, it was a natural consequence of the conditions prevalent in the area in 1951, that agricultural production was given the highest priority, in order to tackle effectively the shortage in food and raw materials. In the Plan for Punjab, irrigation and power claimed nearly 60 per cent of the total provision mainly because (i) 80 per cent of irrigation schemes in pre-partition went to Pakistan and large land resources of the state lay

---

32. Singh, Satwinder and Mann, Baltej, The Role of Government in Industrialization in Punjab, Vol.XXI-II, October 1987, *The Punjab Past and Present*, Punjabi University, Patiala, Serial No. 42, p.458.
33. Government of Punjab, First Five Year Plan, op.cit.
34. Singh and Mann, op. cit., p.41.

unproductive for want of water (ii) river water was the only source of power. Thus the First Five Year Plan began with an agricultural till.[35] The Second Five Year Plan showed comparatively more thrust on the development of industries, with the plan outlay raised to Rs. 1029.34 lakhs (6.20 per cent of the total plan outlay). However, in sectoral distribution, agriculture still claimed 18.8 per cent and industry claimed 6.14 per cent of the total provision. Even though, the plan outlay increase was 31 per cent over the First Five Year Plan, it compared unfavourably with the rest of India with 124 per cent increase.[36]

An attempt to group these 66 heads into 8 broad groups revealed that out of a total of Rs. 1029.34 lakhs of plan outlay, Rs. 370.63 (31.15 per cent) were spent by the Government on their own schemes for the development of industries followed by its programme on cottage industries training, which had an outlay of Rs. 240.80 lakhs (23.39 per cent). Other major heads were other schemes which constituted 20.31 per cent of the total plan outlay and a government subsidy which constituted 16.77 per cent out of the total plan outlay. Large land medium industries were allotted Rs. 1.6 crores, small scale industries Rs. 4.4 crores and cottage sector Rs. 2.1 crores.[37] The progress during the first four years was slow especially in the large- scale and medium sector. Cooperative Sugar Mills could not be started. A few other mills in which the Plan had provided for state participation were started in the private sector and hence the funds could not be used.

During the first two plans' period about Rs. 2 crores were disbursed as loans to about 8,000 industrial establishments. Five industrial establishments providing

35. NCAER, op.cit., p.105.
36. Punjab Government, Punjab State Integrated Second Five Year Plan, Planning Department, Chandigarh (1956-61), pp.23-25.
37. Ibid.

factory accommodation to 340 establishments, were to be set up during the Second Plan. Two common facility centres had been set up at Ludhiana and Bassi Pathana to provide facilities to small-scale industries. Nine Quality marking centres had been opened at different places for helping industries to improve the quality of products and major schemes for training were also formulated. To provide additional employment special schemes were drawn up for developing handloom, handicrafts, sericulture and Khadi industries, which included imparting training and the extension of credit and marketing facilities. The industrial programme envisaged a resettlement of the refugees as a primary aim. So there was no specific thrust on only large scale industry but with the given potential of Punjab, the emphasis was on small-scale industry. For instance, in this period, hosiery, textiles, sports' goods, paper, cycle parts and khadi manufacture registered good progress.

An important aspect of the Second Five Year Plan was the setting up of urban industrial estates at Ludhiana, Batala and Malerkotla at a cost of Rs. 57.50 lakhs. In this plan, there was a central provision of Rs. 20 crores for the Nangal fertilizers.[38] Up to the Third Plan, the responsibility of plan formulation in Punjab was with the State Planning Department. It was only by the Fourth Plan, that the Planning Department was reorganized and strengthened with the infusion of some technical expertise. Till then the proposals of various departments for inclusion in the Plan were scrutinized by a steering committee of senior officials of various departments.[39]

---

38. Mann, B.S., *Working of Industrial Estates in Punjab,* Unpublished Ph.D. Thesis, Meerut University, 1983, p.109.
39. Dhesi, A.S., Planning in Punjab : Planning Implementation and Formulation in Studies in Punjab Economy, Edited by Johar, R.S and Khanna, J.S., Punjab School of Economics, Guru Nanak Dev University, Amritsar, 1983, p.389.

The Third Five Year Plan period proved to be eventful in the industrial history and policy of Punjab. To begin with the Punjab Small Scale Industries Corporation was established in 1962, to assist and promote the small-scale industries in the state and to supply them essential raw materials. With a view to extend the benefits of industrialization to small towns and rural areas, the Government decided to set up 20 rural industrial estates during the Third Five Year Plan.[40]

The turning point, however, was the Reorganization of the State in November 1966, which brought about certain important changes in the overall industrial outlook. This historical turn was preceeded by the 1962 and 1965 hostilities with China and Pakistan respectively. Resultant instability was a setback to industrial activity. The state planners decided to take concrete steps for the development of industry in the states.[41] The period from 1966 to 1969 was that of plan holiday, instead of five year plans, three annual plans were followed, these on an average had a total plan outlay. The major developments during this period, were the setting up of focal points in 1967-68 at Mohali, Dhandari Kalan and Rajpura. Their number increased to 16 in 1986 and these 16 focal points had 2807 developed industrial plots in them.[42] The philosophy behind the establishment of industrial focal points was to ensure the integrated development of large, medium and small-scale industries in the state and the focal points were meant to provide the requisite infrastructure.[43]

---

40. Mann, B.S., op.cit., p.460.
41. Grover, Verinder (Ed.), op.cit., Sharma, P.K., Reorganization of Punjab, p.143.
42. Government of Punjab, Economic and Statistical Organization, *Evaluation Study of Focal Points of Industrial Growth*, Mohali, 1978, p.8.
43. Ibid., 1978, p.3.

At any rate, in joint Punjab, upto the Third Five Year Plan, the objective to industrialize the economy remained unfulfilled and whatever industrial progress had taken place it was in the small-scale industry. The dominance of the small sector in the industrial sector of Punjab in the early 1960s, is clear from the fact, that, the small enterprises contributed 81.8 per cent in the total net output of the industrial sector of Punjab in 1960-61. Whereas, the share of the large sector in India was 49.9 per cent in the net industrial output it was only 18.2 per cent in Punjab, small enterprises were further categorized into two-household and non-household. The household industry accounted for 34 per cent of the total net output of 81.8 per cent, whereas at the national level, it was only 16.9 per cent.[44]

The Fourth Five Year Plan document says, "All efforts made during the first three plans, though in themselves appreciable, could only touch the fringe of the problem. There was only some progress in small-scale industry."[45] Most of the state's expenditure, on industry under the three five year plans was Rs. 0.83 crores in the First Plan and Rs. 8.5 crores in the Second Plan, had been loan advances to small-scale industry. In making a sectoral allocation for the Third Plan, the state government had provided a relatively much larger amount of Rs. 37.5 crores, a part of which (Rs. 10 crores) was reserved for direct investment in industrial ventures.

After the Fourth Five Year Plan, the share of industry in the plan expenditure declined indicating that a still increasing proportion of plan expenditure is allocated to agriculture and industry has not got the increasing share,

44. Government of Punjab, *Punjab State Integrated Five Year Plan 1962-1967,* Chandigarh.
45. Ibid. Fourth Five Year Plan 1969-1974, p.56.

which is commensurate with the increasing contribution of the Net State Domestic product.[46]

While outlining the economic developments in the state, the historical occurrences must not be overlooked, as Punjab was passing through the Green Revolution. The Chief Minister Pratap Singh Kairon's policies and measures for the eight years of his tenure from 1956 to 1964 had contributed much towards development. Nehru was justified in saying, that Punjab had made greater progress under his guiding care.[47] His achievements were acquisition of land for seed farms outside the plan, consolidation of landholdings, provision of electric power to 5,000 villages, metalled roads loans for tubewells, introduction of poultry, farming and the establishment of the Punjabi University and the Punjab Agricultural University at Ludhiana. The tenancy decreased between 1955-1964 and the agricultural production increased by 42 per cent.[48]

After the creation of the Punjabi Suba, there were some changes in the overall industrial atmosphere of the state. The Punjab State Industrial Development Corporation which had been set up in 1966, was established as an undertaking of the Punjab Government, so as to promote planned Industrial Development in the organized sector. The wars with Pakistan had provided a major setback to the industrial development of the state. Some industrial establishments, which had their operations in border towns were Amritsar, Batala and Ferozepur which were faced with unused goods, accumulating due to transport bottlenecks during the war and pre-war period, due to fall in demand

46. Government of Punjab, *Statistical Abstract of Punjab*, Fifth Five Year Plan, 1974.
47. Grewal, op.cit., p.202.
48. Ibid.

and the consequent accumulation of a large stock of industrial products, whereas reorganization had its own impact.[49] When reorganization took place in 1966, Punjab had 93 units of which Ludhiana (26), Amritsar (16), Jullundur (8) and Rajpura (5) were the other important industrial centres. In all 28 places, had one or more large and medium scale industrial units.[50]

The erstwhile Punjab, was already deficient in mineral resources, some deposits of limestone and iron ore were available. As a result of reorganization, the mineral deposits in Kangra and other hilly areas went to Himachal Pradesh. The remaining deposits mainly of slate in Gurgaon, limestone in Ambala and iron ore in Mohindergarh district went entirely to Haryana, the reorganized Punjab thus, does not possess any mineral deposits. The position, in respect of forest resources was also similar, most of the forest areas, also, went to Himachal Pradesh. Punjab got only agricultural resources, Haryana on the other hand, got some mineral deposits, in addition to its agricultural base.[51] Haryana got the industrial complexes at Faridabad, Sonepat and Ambala. Further, all the major large-scale industries have gone to Haryana, viz. three paper mills one at Yamunanagar and two at Faridabad, six cotton mills, a well-established glassware industry at Ambala and Faridabad, two cement factories at Dadri and Pinjore and a big bicycle industry at Sonepat. Out of 13 urban and 24 rural industrial estates, 5 urban and 24 rural industrial estates fell to Haryana's share. Thus re-organization placed Haryana in a better position in the matter of resource distribution. (see Table XXXI)

49. Singh, Jaswinder, *Industrial Development in Punjab*, M.Phil. Thesis, Punjab School of Economics, Guru Nanak Dev University 1981, p.80.
50. Bhushan, Bharat, *Industrial Development in Punjab and Haryana, A Comparative Study*, Punjab School of Economics, Guru Nanak Dev University, 1983, p.148.
51. Ibid.

Table XXXI

Socio-Economic Conditions in Punjab, Haryana and Hilly Areas (After Reorganization)

	Punjab	Haryana	Hilly Areas
1. Rural Population as percentage of total population	75.3	82.8	89.9
2. Urban Population as percentage of total population	24.7	17.2	10.1
3. Working Population as percentage of total			
(a) Primary Sector	17.5	26.8	24.5
(b) Secondary and Tertiary Sector	14.0	10.9	11.5
4. Gross Area irrigated as percentage of total cropped area	63.0	30.0	17.0
5. Percentage of Electrified town/village to total town/ village in state	29.0	18.0	19.0
6. Number of registered factories per lakh of population	36.5	14.9	6.6
7. Literacy as percentage of total	26.7	19.8	27.1

Source: B.S.Bhatia, Pattern of Industrialization in Punjab since Independence, Unpublished Ph.D. thesis, submitted to Punjab University, Chandigarh, 1970, p.324.

At the time of the formulation of the Fifth Five Year Plan, the planning machinery was further strengthened with the establishment of the State Planning Board, which worked independently of the Planning Department. The Fifth Five Year Plan lamented at the unbalanced industrial development of the state. It was stated that in Punjab, there were about 29,000 small-scale industrial units providing employment to 1.50 lakh workers, as compared to only 94 large and medium scale units employing approximately 0.47 lakh workers. Therefore, high priority was given to large and medium scale industry in the Plan. Incentives were given to entrepreneurs for setting up industries in backward and border areas. A sum of Rs. 37.56 crores was set aside constituting 5.22 per cent of the total plan expenditure was spent on industrial development.[52]

By the time, the Sixth Five Year Plan was passed the State Planning Board and State Planning Department were merged and the formulation procedures improved.

The Sixth Five Year Plan (1980-1985) outlined its objectives:

1. Accelerated growth and realization of economic benefits of already created infrastructure for industries.
2. Diversified rapid industrialization of the state.
3. To promote rural industries for which separate incentives are envisaged to ameliorate the economic conditions of the weaker sections of society.
4. Special emphasis on small-scale industrial units to create maximum employment.
5. Incentives to industrialists for setting up industries in Punjab.
6. Export of industrial products of the state and exploring new markets for exports.[53]

---

52. Government of Punjab, *Fifth Five Year Plan 1974-79, Draft Outline,* Planning Department, Chandigarh, 1974, p.41.
53. Ibid.

In spite of these industrial inclinations, the earlier five year plans of Punjab, reflect that the power sector received a major share of the total plan outlay.[54] Of course, the consumption pattern of electric power is biased towards the agricultural sector, while in other states, a greater share of power is consumed in the industrial sector.[55]

For instance, some of the points delineated in this plan were :

1. The energization of tubewells/pumping sets and replacement of diesel engines by electric motors.
2. The electrification of post harvest operations, cottage and small-scale industries.
3. The improvement of supply conditions by augmentation and improvement works.

In 1978, Punjab decided to frame its own industrial policy which aimed at generating more employment opportunities, regional balance industry-wise, balanced resource development and encouraging resource-based units were given a high priority.[56]

This Industrial Policy Statement was followed by the rules for the grant of incentives as notified in 1978. The incentives, which were provided under these rules were interest-free loans, which were repayable in the 11th, 12th and 13th years of their disbursement. The maximum amount of these loans was Rs.5 lakhs and 7 lakhs depending upon the location of the industry. The other incentives were a

54. Bhalla, G.S., Political Economy since Independence in Indu Banga, (Edited) *Five Punjabi Centuries*, Manohar Publishers, Delhi, 1997, p. 386.
55. Singh, Jaswinder, op.cit., pp.47-48.
56. Government of Punjab, *Punjab: The Only Answer, Economic and Statistical Adviser Report,* Chandigarh, 1978.

subsidy upto 25 per cent of the power tariff for a period of 5 years, exemption from electricity duty for a period of 5 to 10 years, depending upon the location of the industry, exemption/refund of octroi/terminal taxes, subsidy at 15 per cent of the fixed capital investment in the border districts, sub-mountain areas and backward districts declared by the state. Apart from these interest bearing investment loans to bridge the gap of the promotors contribution in capital formation were also allowed. Liberal land subsidy and subsidies for the preparation of feasibility reports were some features of this Policy, special incentive and facilities were also given for non-resident Indians at this juncture.[57] After 1978, the next policy was announced in which the State Government realized that Punjab's performance in industry is not as spectacular, as its success in agriculture and the reasons for this lag are historical, geographical and cultural, and the concentration is more on small-scale industrial units.

> Even for an agriculturally based economy, the development of industries is essential. The continuously high rate of growth in the economy of the state is the goal of the Government and this can be achieved by diversifying the state economy. As such, more emphasis is being laid on the development of the industry.[58]

The Industrial Policy introduced in 1987 aimed at giving a push to the process of industrialization, through the development of infrastructural facilities for the growth of village, small and tiny industrial units, with deliberate emphasis, on the setting up of large and medium scale industries. However, the industrial scene in the country had undergone

---

57. Government of Punjab, Directorate of Industries, To Non-Resident Indians Punjab offers a package of Incentives and Facilities for setting up new Industries in Punjab, Punjab, 1978, p.18.
58. Government of Punjab, Directorate of Industries, *Industrial Policy and Incentive Code 1987,* Chandigarh, 1987, p.23.

a sea change, during the last 10 years, the introduction of a graded package of incentives, diluted in favour of no industry districts and certain special areas under the Central Policy about backward areas, had put states like Punjab in a disadvantageous position.

The state was divided into three categories of areas for various benefits, to ensure a balanced development, the areas within the municipal limits of Jullundur and Ludhiana were debarred from any incentives. The incentives were capital subsidy, sales tax concessions, land subsidy and exemption from electricity duty. To ensure social justice, a new category of incentives was introduced for units belonging to Scheduled Castes to push up the exports so were 100 per cent Export Oriented Units (EOUs) also given subsidies.[59]

It is worth mentioning, that gradually the Punjab State Industrial Development Corporation (PSIDC) became a more active catalyst for the promotion of large and medium scale industries in Punjab. The PSIDC (i) identifies and investigates projects and obtains letters of intent from the government (ii) Undertakes feasibility studies for various identified projects (iii) Provides financial support (iv) Acts as an agent of the Industrial Development Bank of India and State Government for providing assistance and incentives to industry under various schemes.[60]

Then came another review of the Industrial Policy of the State in 1989, which stated that :

---

59. Government of Punjab, Directorate of Industries, Report of the Committee constituted to study the Problems of Industrial Development in Punjab, 1983, Chandigarh, 1985, p.8.
60. Punjab Government, Punjab State Industrial Development Corporation Brochure, A State Government Undertaking Chandigarh 1986, p.4.

"The Industrial Policy has been under review with the State Government, with the objective of providing a conducive industrial environment, strengthening of infrastructure, identifying thrust areas, developing skills and encouraging entrepreneurship, for accelerating the rate of industrial development and generating employment opportunities, particularly for the educated unemployed rural youth, to provide for a minimum 10 per cent of the total annual plan outlay in the industrial sector, to take up the rate of industrial growth to go upto 20 per cent by the end of the Eighth Five Year Plan and to take up the share of the industrial sector to 20 per cent in the State domestic product during the same period. The objectives of this policy were :

a) building up of a conducive industrial climate for fresh investment;
b) providing technical facilities, financial assistance for technological upgradation, modernization and setting up of nucleus units for promoting ancillarization;
c) strengthening institutional arrangements for the development of need-based skills and encouraging youth to enter into business;
d) developing an equity cult by promoting units in assisted Joint Sector with a view to channelizing investible surpluses in industry;
e) strengthening of extension services for interface between industry and the Government on a continuing basis;
f) ensuring proper coordination between State Government Corporations and Apex Cooperative Institutions for optimal utilization of State resources and channelizing investments in less developed areas."[61]

The main components of this policy were :

61. Government of Punjab, Industrial Policy and Incentive Code, Udhyog Sahayak Publications, Directorate of Industries, Chandigarh, 1989.

a) Providing an attractive Package of Incentives.
b) Planning for manpower development.
c) Strengthening of infrastructure.
d) Modernization and Technological Upgradation.
e) Providing Financial Support.
f) Strengthening of Extension Services, Administrative Improvements and Simplification of Procedures.
g) Attracting Non-Resident Investment.

The main incentives were similar to the earlier ones but a new category of incentives was provided to pioneer units. This policy of the State Government was further modified by a new code of incentives in 1992 with minor variations in the eligibility for incentives. However, in 1996, a new Industrial Policy, was proposed which diluted the targets of growth set for industry as follows :

a) Increase the annual industrial growth rate from the present 8 per cent to 12 per cent.
b) Increase the present share of industry in Gross Domestic Product (GDP) from 17 per cent to 25 per cent.[62]

This policy introduced a new objective of diverting 15% of the present rural population to manufacturing and related occupations. However, if we look at the share of the producing and manufacturing sector in the GDP it will be seen from the tables below, that the targets still remained to be achieved. Similarly, the Central Public Sector Investment even today is below a figure of 2 per cent, there is hardly any investment in the large-scale Central Public Sector units. The three units which the state got, Nangal Fertilizers, Heavy

62. Government of Punjab, *Industrial Policy and Incentive Code 1996, Udhyog Sahayak,* Directorate of Industries, Chandigarh, 1996.

Water Plan at Nangal and Bhathinda Fertilizers Unit have not contributed much to the overall growth either by generating any extra employment or by creating any multiplier effect. Of course, the state developed Industrial Focal Points in the vicinity of Hoshiarpur, Sangrur, Kotkapura, Moga, Tarn Taran, Nabha, Nawanshahr, Bhatinda and Jullundur and encouraged some medium and large-scale units, while some large-scale units like textiles, milk processing, etc. are directly the result of the economic factor of the availability of raw-materials. Yet looking at the growth rate of the contribution of industry to GDP and the contribution of agriculture to this should be abundantly clear that industrial policies still leave a lot to be desired. (In the earlier chapter, I have discussed the industrial policy of 1992. I thought it would be appropriate as a part of liberalization)

Meanwhile to pick up the historico-political threads after 1966 and 1967, the Gurnam Singh ministry came to power in 1968, Punjab was put under President's Rule in 1969, then it went to the polls and Gurnam Singh returned to power. In spite of all these changes, there was a constant discontent simmering within the Akali Dal over the linguistic reorganization and there was a fresh demand that Chandigarh should come to Punjab. In 1970, the Union Government made an award giving Chandigarh to Punjab but in lieu of this Haryana was given Rs. 20 crores and 110 villages in Fazilka to Haryana. The Punjab Government claimed over 1,000 Punjabi speaking villages, on a linguistic basis from Haryana and Himachal Pradesh.[63] The Gurnam Singh ministry resigned on 26 March 1970, an Akali-Jan Sangh coalition ministry headed by Prakash Singh Badal came to power. In 1971, Lachman Singh Gill with a splinter group of Akalis and Congress support came to power, the major contibution was linking every village

63. Grover, Verinder, op.cit., p.6.

with a link road. This was a major infrastructural support to link agricultural growth with future industrial development.

In 1972, Giani Zail Singh headed a Congress ministry, followed in 1975 by the Emergency. In 1977, in a mid-term poll the Akali Janata alliance got an absolute majority in Punjab. In 1980, Darbara Singh was sworn in as the Chief Minister of Punjab by the Congress Ministry. In 1981, came the advent of Sant Jarnail Singh Bhindranwale and the wave of militancy swept Punjab for over a decade, doing irretrievable damage to the state in every sphere. In 1985, there was an Akali Government led by Barnala, the major accomplishment was that the agriculture minister, Capt. Amarinder Singh opened the doors for the multinational, Pepsi Cola to enter Punjab. Thereafter, the state went under Governor's rule till 1992 till a Congress ministry under Beant Singh was sworn in as mentioned earlier and an Industrial Policy was formed in 1996.

A study of the plans and policies reflects that the share of Central Government investment in Punjab in large scale industry had been meagre.[64] In 2002, the Congress Government under Capt. Amarinder Singh, brought the focus on to the industrial lag. They set up an advisory committee under former chief secretary A.S. Chatha, which recommended a proactive industrial policy and stressed on refurbishing government credibility and confidence building among entrepreneurs to attract investment. Suggestions were made for an efficient and cost effective infrastructure, human resource development, positive, policy environment, good governance, resuscitation of existing units particularly small units that are burdened with outdated technology, and equipment and suffer from inadequate market linkages. (*The Tribune,* July 2002)

64. Industrial Policy and Incentives Code, Government of Punjab, 2002.

They apportioned a part of the blame for sluggish industrial development on financial institutions, particularly the state- related Punjab Financial Corporation and the Punjab State Industrial Development Corporation. They have suggested salvaging the PFC and PSIDC by improving their cash flow upgradation of existing units and helping new ones. The steps include the introduction of a mechanism similar to the BIFR (Board for Industrial and Financial Construction) exclusively for the state to, cover such units, that are not covered under this. They propose that if some states have done this, why not Punjab, likewise, SIDBI and and the IDBI should share some of the financial burden of the state when loan and equity cases are decided.

Table XXXII illustrates the role of major financial institutions in the country, in financing industry in various states in the past. Surprisingly, the rest of the country apart, even Haryana remained ahead of Punjab in getting funding from these by 1975, while Punjab had, only 8 per cent share of ICICI funding. Haryana got 2.3 per cent of, ICIC funds, the latter bagged 3.5 per cent as compared to 3.2 per cent of the former. This reflects a poor institutional investment support to Punjab's industry. The figures of the year 2000, reflect the same trend, the cumulative investment in Haryana was 13,897 crores, whereas in Punjab it was 13,622 crores. Irrespective, of these figures, the performance indices of financial institutions, the reasons could be a policy lag, a locational disadvantage and a neglect of upcoming sectors like IT and bio technology.

Table XXXII

State-wise Distribution of Financial Assistance/ Investment by ICICI and LIC (Rs. in Crores)

States	ICICI Assistance Sanctioned by Dec.1975	Percentage	LIC Investment by 31.3.78	Percentage
Maharashtra	229.43	34.0	379.40	14.6
Gujarat	80.25	11.9	264.50	10.1
Tamil Nadu	77.73	11.5	248.90	9.6
Bihar	46.07	6.8	162.72	6.2
Karnataka	43.47	6.4	140.63	5.4
West Bengal	41.52	6.2	216.83	8.3
Uttar Pradesh	32.72	4.9	256.92	9.9
Andhra Pradesh	22.11	3.3	159.27	6.1
Rajasthan	15.45	2.3	143.96	5.5
Haryana	15.24	2.3	91.91	3.5
Kerala	14.27	2.1	124.56	4.8
Madhya Pradesh	13.06	1.9	111.53	4.3
Orissa	12.03	1.8	110.79	4.2
Punjab	5.18	0.8	83,04	3.2
Other States/ U T	25.65	3.8	110.79	4.2
Total All India	674.18	100.00	2605.95	100.00

Source: *1. ICICI Report 1978*
2. Reports on Activities of Life Insurance Corporation of India 1977-78.

The latest figures are of loans sanctioned during 1999.

Gujarat	Rs. 13,049 crores
Maharashtra	Rs. 23,872 crores
Karnatka	Rs. 5,418 crores

Tamil Nadu	Rs. 8,771 crores
Punjab	Rs. 2,498 crores

Data relates to LIC< UTI and retail finance of ICICI

Source : Statistical Outline of India 2001-2002, Tata Services, Ltd., Mumbai, 2001.

Table XXXIII

Investment of Selected State Governments in Public Sector Undertakings (Financial and Promotional) at the Beginning of 1976-77 (Rs. in Crores)

States	Financial	Promotional	Total	Percentage
Andhra Pradesh	15	24	39	15.54
Bihar	12	7	19	7.57
Gujarat	11	14	25	9.96
Karnataka	13	2	15	5.98
Kerala	6	9	15	5.98
Maharashtra	17	26	43	17.13
Punjab	8	7	15	5.98
Tamil Nadu	7	38	45	17.93
Uttar Pradesh	7	28	35	13.94
Total for 9 States	96	155	255	100.00

Source: *Report of the 7th Finance Commission, 1978, p.172.*

The meagre role played by the state government has also been responsible for the slow industrial growth in Punjab, they virtually did not do anything till the early 1970s. It was mainly after the mid-70s that many corporations were set up in the Public Sector to promote industrial development. It is reflected that investment made by the Punjab government is very low as compared to Tamil

Nadu, Maharashtra, Andhra Pradesh and Gujarat. The share is not commensurate with the high level of per capita income and high incidence of taxation in the state.[65]

At the current level of knowledge and technology, electric power is the most important requirement to run industry. However, the state is suffering from a shortage of electricity. During 1981-82, the availability of power supply was 12.23 per cent short of requirement in Punjab.[66] The power shortage in both the states is not only hindering the industrial development, but agricultural development, as well.

The following Table XXXIV shows the position of installed capacity in both the states. The table reveals that the installed capacity in both the states had increased during 1971-72 to November 1981.

Table XXXIV

Comparative Power Position

State	1971-72	1975-76	Nov. 1981 (MW)
Punjab	697	988	1537
Haryana	486	546	1141

Source: 1. *Government of Punjab, 1971-72 Electricity Statistics of Punjab.*
2. *Government of India, Central Electricity Authority, Power Supply Position in the Country, Nov. 1981.*

In Punjab however, the installed capacity of electricity increased by 120.52 per cent between 1971-72 and

65. Centre for Monitoring Indian Economy, Basic Statistics Relating to Indian Economy, Volume II, Table 9.62, p.33.
66. Government of India, Central Electricity Authority, Power Supply Position in the Country, November 1982.

November 1981, whereas this capacity increased by 134.77 per cent in Haryana during the same period.

The power position, availability, demand and gap has been shown in Tables XXXV and XXXVI for Punjab and Haryana respectively for the coming years upto 1984-85. The tables reveal, that both the states were not able to overcome the problem of electricity shortage till the year 1984-85. However, the problem is more acute as far as Punjab is concerned.

Table XXXV

Power Position in Punjab (M.W.)

Year	Availability	Demand	Gap
1980-81	986	1485	499
1981-82	1036	1636	600
1982-83	1111	1814	703
1983-84	1284	2021	737
1984-85	1535	2259	724

Source: Sixth Five Year Plan 1980-85, Government of Punjab Planning Department, Punjab, p.71.

Table XXXVI

Power Position in Haryana (MW)

Year	Availability	Demand	Gap
1980-81	745	929	184
1981-82	763	1035	272
1982-83	780	1162	382
1983-84	920	1278	358
1984-85	1034	1403	369

Source: Sixth Five Year Plan, Planning Department, 1980-85 Government of Haryana, p.82.

Contd.

As has been seen during discussions in the foregoing chapters, the economic development of Punjab, during the First Four Plans revolved around refugee resettlement. So accordingly, agricultural development and the construction of the Hydro Electric - Irrigation Project of Bhakra Nangal got priority in planning. The Bhakra Nangal Project was given priority because this canal network was to carry water to Rajasthan and especially its Ganga Nagar District where a large number of Punjabi farmers had settled in the post-independence period. The industrial development which took place during that period was more in and around the areas near Delhi (Faridabad) and Chandigarh (Panchkula). Though there was some growth in small-scale industries in Jullundur, Phagwara and Ludhiana areas, yet there was no perceptible large-scale investment during the first three Plans, in industry, in the areas which constitute the present Punjab. Therefore, while surveying the history of industrial development in the present Punjab, a meaningful comparison can be made only from the Fourth Five Year Plan onwards. Table XXXVII below indicates the outlay and expenditure on industry in the various plans in the state since 1969 (Fourth Plan). The table also gives the percentage of the outlay and expenditure to the gross outlay and expenditure in the respective plans. From this table it will be seen that during the period of the Fourth, Fifth and Sixth Plans, the actual expenditure always fell short of the approved outlay on industry. For the first time in the Seventh Five Year Plan, the actual expenditure exceeded the approved outlay. The trend also continued during the period of the Eighth Five Year Plan. In the latter's first three years, the actual expenditure exceeded the outlay by almost 70 per cent at this junctive state received an elected Congress government after a gap of almost five years, under the Chief Ministership of Beant Singh.

Punjab has the highest capita consumption of power in industry with the exception Daman, Diu, Dadra and Nagar Haveli. Against corresponding national figures of 359.57 kwh and 129.04 kwh, Punjab's figures are 860.81 kwh and 332.27 kwh respectively. Coming back to the power sector performance of the Punjab economy from a historical perspective, the total per capita consumption in 1970-71 was 158-52 kw while in 1998-99 it became 844.91 kw. Correspondingly in agriculture per capita consumption went

Table XXXVII

Outlay and Expenditure of Five Year Plans in Punjab, Industry and Minerals

Plans	Approved Outlay	% to Total Outlay	Actual Expenditure	% to Total Expenditure
Fourth Plan 1969-74	1615.00	5.50	1125.95	2.64
Fifth Plan 1974-78	6615.00	6.42	3756.12	5.22
Sixth Plan 1980-85	8183.00	4.18	7413.98	3.93
Seventh Plan 1985-90	12474.00	3.79	14901.46	4.20
Eighth Plan 1992-97	16292.00	2.48	184.66	3.00 (approx.)
Ninth Plan	3004.00	0.21	598.85	.29

Source: Statistical Abstract of Punjab, 1997.

up from 34-73 kw to 325.05 kw in this period, while industry saw an increase of 104.90 kwh to 332.27 kwh. This is a major index of the lag between industrial growth and agricultural growth in this period. Coming to percentage figures, the industrial consumption went up from 30.96 per cent to 36.78 per cent while agricultural consumption rose from 38 per cent to 39.33 per cent generation increase of 2364.08 million kwh to 20880.13 million kwh comparing the gross figures with relative figures. Historically it is apparent that the industrial sector consumption has grown at a rate less than total generation as well as agricultural consumption. This proves that the economy depends upon agriculture than industry.

Further Table XXXVIII is given below which shows the yearwise growth in small-scale, large and medium scale industries separately.

This table indicates the number of units, fixed capital employed, employment generated and production. It may be a sheer coincidence or it may be a matter of policies of the respective governments, but from the table it appears that during the years, when a Congress led government was ruling, the statistics regarding industrial development have shown a higher rate of growth. If we look at the index of industrial growth of the state for the years since 1976 to 1994, it is apparent that during the period 1981 to 1986, the index rose from 176.66 to 214.76 and similarly in the subsequent five years it jumped to 328.35. Thereafter in 1991-92, 1992-93 and 1993-94 the trend remained quite steady. During the Plan period, further, it is clear that industry really started looking up when the agricultural surpluses were made available to it. However, one more

Table XXXVIII

A comparesion of Small and Medium Scale Industries

Year	Growth Index	No. of Units	Fixed Capital	Employees	Production (Crores of Rs.)	No. of Units	Fixed Capital	Employees	Production (Crores of Rs.)
1976-77	108.63								
1980-81	176.66	43338	332.12	264869	1118.44	228	727.42	109767	1141.07
1985-86	214.76	97517	738.94	464809	2150.99	292	1489.72	132174	2534.53
1990-91	328.35	160368	1348.78	668845	4049.82	373	4003.08	187311	7163.69
1991-92	333.09	176378	1498.60	711417	4434.45	395	4552.30	193789	7709.33
1992-93	360.17	181563	1620.99	732580	5345.13	414	5193.64	188034	9335.25
1993-94	394.37	184875	1763.61	755883	7074.95	440	5697.41	195343	10438.87

factor which is noticeable is that somehow the employment in the industrial sector did not keep pace with the increase in the number of industrial units/increase in investments, while on the other hand in gross terms the unemployment figure was increasing due to (a) mechanization of agricultural and (b) the influx of seasonal Bihari labour. A mis-match between increase in employment, industrial growth and overall development rate of the state, was the an important reason for the on set of the militancy/terrorism. In fact, it became a Catch-22 situation because for almost a decade rising unemployment fuelled by political factors led to militancy, which curbed industrial investment further accentuating the frustrations.

However, the figures of industrial development did not suggest massive capital outflow or any major migration of capital into the state in the post 1984 situation, though there was a setting up of parallel ventures in other states and stagnation in the prevalent set up in Punjab. The policy failure in industrial growth is indicated by the factor that sectoral allocation for agriculture in government budgets have far acceded those for industry.

Conclusion

As one unravels Punjab's history, it is evident, that the state traditionally served as a bulwark for India, against almost all the military invasions from the North - Western frontiers of India. The tribulations caused by religious, cultural and ethnic movements have had their repercussions on this region. Owing to its precarious geographical location, this region was impacted by a synthesis of varied cultures. In a long term historical perspective, Punjab has survived the instabilities caused by marauders coming from the West, be they Greeks, Persians, Turks, Mughals or Pathans. Post independence, destiny, in this regard, did not change for the state substantially, even, within the Indian Union, it had to go through an unstable period for the determination of its boundaries, as well as due to its contiguity to the international boundary line.

Punjab should have had no justifiable reason to lag behind Maharashtra, Gujarat, Karnataka or Tamil Nadu, in different industrial sectors, nationally or behind Taiwan, Korea, Malaysia or even Japan internationally. In some of these regions and countries, industrialization was far behind or started, at the same time when Punjab started (industries with sugar, food processing, hosiery, engineering goods, cycle-parts, textiles, etc.,) they have paced ahead, while Punjab has lagged behind. It is not a mere economic analysis but with a fusion of other currents too, flowing in their historical perspective. As the state endeavours to move out of its mould of a purely agrarian economy to one of a multi sectoral economy, industrial growth is important for agricultural growth because it creates a demand for agricultural output. It reduces the burden of population on agriculture and provides improved agricultural machinery, fertilizers and insecticides. Industrial growth leads to the growth of the tertiary sector, as means of transport and communication are to be expanded commensurately. For industrial development, a crucial factor is a stable, social and political environment and an allied sense of security for entrepreneurial investment. However, while unfolding the pages of Punjab's history, stability for a substantial span in its historical records is missing.

A study of this period of almost fifty-four years, reflects a partition of the state, a further vivisection in reorganization, Indo-Pakistan wars and militancy. Post partition recuperation, which could have immensely fructified the infrastructural input, saw the state rock with political instability and border disturbances. Reorganization hacked away some industrial gains and the dividends of the Green Revolution never culminated in a spectacular industrial revolution, as elsewhere because eventually militancy arose. A World Bank and Confederation of Indian Industry Report of 2002 had classified Gujarat and Maharashtra as possessing the best investment climate states, whereas Punjab has a mediocre rating in this respect. It ranks seventh in the country, as far as industrial growth is concerned.

A historical synopsis of events, reflects that whenever the state, would bask in peaceful progression conducive for industrial development, some tremor would perturb it. The British came to Punjab in 1849 with no commercial inclinations, since they had concentrated industrial activity around the port towns of Bombay, Calcutta and Madras. After they laid out a canal and railway network, the state was brimming with agricultural activity though commercialized, but at their whims. Then came the two wars, which shook the world, as never before, in response to the increased demands the town of Lahore, Amritsar, Dhariwal, Sialkot, Wazirabad, Batala and a few others, were industrialized.

The impact of the historical torrent of partition were major scars which took years to heal, the entire economy was shattered and industrial production came to a halt. Owing to efforts at reconstruction and rehabilitation begun by the Government some manufacturing started by 1950. However, in the early Five Year Plans, a high priority was given to investment in basic infrastructure and agriculture to cope with the food deficit.

An increased agricultural output in the 1950s created a demand for agro-processing, agro-input and machine goods and was supplemented by an increased demand from the rest of India for such products as machine goods, hosiery knitwear, textiles and sporting goods. Some industrial development began, particularly in the small-scale sector, by the 1960s and agricultural implements, bicycles and foundry products were being produced. A few towns which emerged as industrial centres — Ludhiana, Amritsar and Jullundur, did so because they were on the Grand Trunk Road to Delhi. Whatever industrial activity had begun, was disrupted temporarily by the Indo-Pakistan war of 1965, particularly, in border towns like Amritsar.

The next major historical occurrence on Punjab's soil was the usage of the Borlaug seed, which propelled the miraculous Green Revolution taking Punjab to unprecedented agricultural prosperity. This triggered some manufacturing activity particularly, in agricultural implements and consumer products as the buying capacity of the people accelerated with increased agricultural inflows. While Punjab was in the throes of the Green Revolution, it was bifurcated in 1966 stripping it of some important industrial clusters.

The gains of the Green Revolution were reflected in rapid agricultural growth, accompanied by an even faster growth in the secondary and tertiary sectors of Punjab's economy. Consequently, between 1967-68, the income from manufacturing grew from 9.04 per cent per year compared to 4.5 per cent in agriculture and 5.2 per cent for manufacturing in India as a whole. The net per capita income originating in manufacturing rose from a ranking of sixth among the major states in 1960/61 to third in 1989/90. Before industry could take an upswing trend, history intervened with monstrous militancy with its communal overtones creeping into the state's previously unperturbed cultural composite.

Of course, the socio-cultural complexion of Punjab has had many distortions, which were again rooted in its history. Going back to the colonial rule, the British had used caste and religion based martial skills to promote their own ends. For instance, they boosted the chauvinism of the Sikhs by calling them a "martial race" to fight their wars. A major division was also created in Punjab's social fabric by the Act of 1901, the Alienation of Land Act, which gave the landowning lobby a distinctive air of superiority for the future and in later years, they formed a powerful political lobby. A few years later the language issue took communal overtones, as the two major communities clashed in the post partition era. However, the Punjabi Suba Movement and the wave of militancy which came later ruptured the social fabric to alarming proportions. During militancy, industry suffered and there was a flight of capital outside the state and entrepreneurial investments slowed down. Though, industry picked up again when peace returned with Beant Singh in 1991.

During the British period, Punjab was considered one of the most prosperous regions in undivided India, owing to the structural changes introduced in the previous century. To develop its agricultural base and to effectively utilize the surplus capital resources generated, the British Government had created a Directorate of Industries in 1920. In 1935, the Government had passed a State Aid to the Industries Act to provide multifarious assistance and aid to the industry. However, that canvas of history got washed away by events, that besieged the destiny of the state. At any rate, industrial development was not a priority of the British in Punjab. In the following half-century, before any clear pattern could emerge, the tumults of partition caused ripples in the flow of history.

The British endeavour at agricultural colonization, produced a significant economic growth in Punjab. In a space of fifty years, human settlement spread over the erstwhile barren and scantily populated doabs of West Punjab, transforming the region into one of the most important areas of commercial farming in Asia, even though eventually this turned out to be a lopsided development. The genesis of Punjab being essentially an agrarian society was seeded in its history dating back to the Alienation of Land Act of 1901, whereby they socially demarcated the farming strata and endowed them with agricultural benefits. This situation, in the first half of this century, led to the emergence of strong politically vested interests of the agricultural class in the Unionist Party and with its agricultural bias, clouded the aspirations of other segments of society, for their economic development. In Punjab, the British were not interested in setting up any business or commercial venture, so industrial development suffered from the disadvantages of a late start. Besides other areas, which had infrastructural and other facilities concentrated in the port town states as initial centres of production, through a process of cumulative causation a la Myrdal the state was confined to industrial backwardness. While in undivided India areas like Mumbai, Madras, Ahmedabad and Calcutta were developing industrially, in the process a corporate culture was emerging, Punjab could only develop as an appendix and supplier of industrial raw materials like, cotton. The industry that could take shape here was either related to local consumer needs or to processing and packaging of the industrial raw-material coming from the agriculture sector.

Owing to the geographical location of Punjab, its history was constantly in a state of flux. In 1947, migration was not yet complete when the Pakistan aggression of Kashmir in 1948, compounded the scars and apprehensions of the Punjabis. They wondered whether they would ever achieve economic stability. Twice again, the Indo-Pak War of 1965 and the 1971 war, confirmed the doubts and insecurities, that proximity to an internationally volatile border could cause. The result of this, has been that the three important border districts have never been able to develop. In fact, Gurdaspur, which at one time was important horticulturally, has never been able to even set out on the path of industrialization, the district of Ferozpur has also seen a decadence in whatever it had. The district of Amritsar, has been no less a victim, because no substantial industry has been able to come up in the entire border belt of the district. It was once a thriving commercial city, virtually a twin to Lahore. In fact, after the Indo-Pak wars, the textile industry of Chheharta, a suburb of Amritsar was shifted to distant places like Faridabad, Ahmedabad and Mumbai. Chheharta would have developed as much as Faridabad if the wars of 1965 and 1971 had not taken place.

Tension always mounted at Punjab's frontier, particularly, with the wars. Some industrial establishments were faced with unused goods accumulating due to transport bottlenecks during the war and pre-war period, also due to fall in demand and large stocks of industrial products. Since the state was exposed to constant war threats, there was an absence of a well developed stock exchange market, business houses and port facilities which are helpful in promoting large- scale industrial investments. Owing to this brittle stability, banking institutions were also wary of financing industrial ventures.

The reorganization of the state had repercussions on the industrial scene which were not conducive to industrial growth because whatever efforts had been made in the late 1950s and early 1960s to develop new clusters of industry around the national capital of Delhi, were taken away. Of 13 urban and 24 rural industrial estates, 5 urban and 24 rural industrial estates fell to Haryana's share. For instance, Faridabad was one such area, which was the result of the vision of the late Sardar Partap Singh Kairon, Chief Minister of Punjab. Similarly, the loss of industry in Sonepat and Panipat, adversely affected the economy. The entire forest potential went to Himachal Pradesh, depriving the Punjab of its wealth of forests.

Shuttling back and forth in Punjab's volatile history, in the immediate post-partition phase, the Punjabi language issue controversy triggered the Punjabi Suba Movement, disrupting the body politic of the state. The resultant instability, which the movement caused to the economy only compounded the lag in industrialization. For some time, industrial investment and trade suffered, the instability and the injection of communal politics into linguistic issues being major obstacles. The only industry that could develop, during this period was the legacy brought by post-partition migrants of sports goods' and some low-end engineering industry. However, the political environment was not yet conducive for the flow of large-scale investment.

In the mid-1960s, the Green Revolution, generated capital surpluses in the state, along with a politico-economic instability. In 1966, a reorganized and truncated Punjab became the only area, where a majority Sikh population resided and the established political fulcrum lost its balance. The local political parties, i.e. the Akali Party joined hands with the Jan Sangh and fought on a common platform to the Congress Party. The Akali Dal and the Jan Sangh also comprised the newly rich social segments in the state, viz. the Jat farmer and the Hindu trader in the urban area. However, in this they became the targets of their political adversaries, who tried to destabilize any strong political configuration. The following period saw many political turbulations at the level of Government formation but in the post-emergency period, many factors arose which muddled the political scene of the state. The Emergency had enveloped the social tensions arising from the Green Revolution, and some communal tension was brewing in the otherwise, calm social fabric of the state. certain inimical international forces, also, fished in troubled waters. So unfortunately Punjab, could not witness a quick capital formation, which should normally follow a successful Green Revolution.

The Green Revolution led to a rapid agricultural growth, which created surpluses, flowing from the agricultural sphere into the hands of capitalist farmers and rich peasants. The rural rich, felt the need for fresh avenues of investment but generally they were conditioned to siphon their surpluses into agricultural amenities or at the most into small and medium industry. The lopsided character of economic development in general and industrial development, in particular, inhibited opportunities for investment in large-scale industry.

Punjab is often compared to Japan and Taiwan, where resource transfers from agriculture led to massive industrial growth. These two countries invested heavily in rural infrastructure, which resulted in a buoyant agriculture. Similarly, in both these countries, public investment in irrigation and other infrastructure was supplemented by large private investments. Agriculture grew rapidly and prospered a great deal, so were specific policies to extract large agricultural surpluses for investment in manufacturing. Even though in Punjab, according to J.W. Mellor's thesis, the peasants became rich and had political clout, yet they could not act in a similar manner because of different political conditions. The balance of political forces is quite different in a democracy, where farming interests that benefit from public and private involvement in agriculture might command a predominant voting strength. Moreover, in Punjab, as Dr. G.S. Bhalla has said an "industrial culture did not develop."

In the post-Green Revolution phase, new investments within the state, as well as investment flows from other parts of the country were reduced. On the other hand, during this entire period, national policy and the planning process were not conducive to industrial development. Sizeable agricultural resources have been mobilized from this sector by the commercial banking sector. It is another matter, that these resources had not been used to finance industrial development in Punjab, instead these have flowed out to finance industrial and other investments in other states. The figures of the total public sector investment in Punjab, when compared with other States of the Union are dismal as shown in the Table below:

Table XLI

Distribution of Assets of Central Government in States

(Rs. in crores)

Name of State/Union Territory	Value of Gross Block as on 31.3.1976	31.3.1981
1. Andhra Pradesh	310.9 (3.41)	987.56 (4.66)
2. Assam	271.9 (2.98)	666.88 (3.15)
3. Bihar	1882.8 (20.66)	3541.40 (16.73)
4. Gujarat	432.5 (4.75)	1068.45 (5.05)
5. Haryana	51.6 (0.57)	261.15 (1.23)
6. Himachal Pradesh	4.2 (0.05)	147.80 (0.70)
7. Jammu & Kashmir	7.2 (0.8)	10.03 (0.05)
8. Karnataka	212.0 (2.33)	844.64 (3.99)
9. Kerala	246.8 (2.71)	481.96 (2.28)
10. Madhya Pradesh	1366.3 (14.99)	2634.67 (12.44)
11. Maharashtra	371.5 (4.07)	1826.80 (8.63)
12. Orissa	619.6 (6.79)	1038.99 (4.91)
13. Punjab	165.2 (1.81)	418.64 (1.98)
14. Rajasthan	187.7 (2.59)	361.56 (1.71)
15. Tamil Nadu	498.6 (5.47)	922.57 (4.36)
16. Uttar Pradesh	305.6 (3.35)	1017.90 (4.81)
17. West Bengal	566.0 (6.21)	1731.11 (8.18)
18. Delhi	274.9 (3.02)	604.16 (2.85)
19. Goa	3.9 (0.03)	6.94 (0.03)
20. Other States/Union Territories	-	176.43 (0.83)
21. Unallocated	1334.1 (14.63)	2422.14 (11.44)
Total	**9112.2 (100.00)**	**21171.78 (100.00)**

Source: *Centre for Monitoring Indian Economy, Basic Statistics Relating to Indian Economy, Vol.States, August 1982.*

Similarly, there was a capital flight from the state though

not at the individual level but at the institutional level. A comparison of credit deposit ratio of the state with other states would highlight this trend : as a sample :

To balance this high Credit Deposit Ratio, there was no reversed flow of capital in the industrial sector in the state for a long period. If the figures of investment by financial institutions are analysed, Punjab has almost a negligible share of these. In spite of the fact, that large surpluses were generated in agriculture, these were not transformed into industrial capital. Out of the amount deposited in the banking institutions in the state, a major part of the capital was not invested in it, rather it helped economic development outside the state.(See Table II) The Credit Deposit Ratio for the state, was only about 40 per cent in the 1980s. The Punjab average was much lower than the all India average and the 60 per cent fixed by the Reserve Bank of India from 1972 to 1978, the advance deposit ratio in Punjab increased from 33.2 to 37.0, whereas this increase was from 51.1 to 61.4 in Haryana, 48.7 to 60.8 in Rajasthan and from 67.2 to 69.9 at the all India level. As the figures from the Directorate of Institutional Finance and Banking Punjab (2000) reflected. In the matter of foreign investment, also, the state remained at a loss. During the period 1966 to 1990, the industrial licence granted to the state, does not suggest a very high rate of growth of industrialization.

Punjab, of course, has paced the course of industrialization at a faster rate than India as a whole. Yet its relative share in all India net value added by manufacturing is low as compared to other states like Maharashtra, Gujarat, Tamil Nadu and East Bengal. Moreover, the percentage of shares of the state in regard to registered factories, fixed capital total workers, gross output and net value added by manufacture have declined to some extent. Thus, despite planned development and investment by the Government there has been very little structural change in

Table II

Advance-Deposit Ratio in Selected States and Union Territories in India

States	1969	1970	1971	1972	1973	1974	1975	1976	1977	1978	1979
Haryana	47.23	60.21	48.05	51.1	59.8	65	62.6	61	61.5	61.4	65.1
Punjab	33.2	35.04	29.99	33.2	41.3	43.8	38.1	37.7	42.3	37	37.6
Rajasthan	49.86	55.35	48.67	48.7	55.4	58	59.5	62.2	62	60.8	66.5
Chandigarh	63.84	114.92	123.44	138.7	69.6	158.8	211.1	254.3	283.7	346.7	313.2
Delhi	40.61	55.57	77.59	53.3	75.8	48.8	92.70	138.2	123.9	117.5	110.7
West Bengal	100.6	93.33	81.96	76	82	81.5	72.9	70.4	69.1	63.9	60.3
Gujarat	50.61	59.37	55.32	56.4	57.5	62.6	61	59.7	54.1	50.4	52
Maharashtra	92.08	90.89	84.8	83.5	84	87.9	86	82.5	76.1	72.5	76.4
Karnataka	72.69	78.38	74.59	88.4	89.7	94.2	100	98	83.4	81.8	75.5
Kerala	68.7	72.28	69.01	70.7	70.8	71.1	71.7	67.5	61.3	61.9	65.3
Tamil Nadu	133.52	132.78	108.57	110.1	105.8	104.6	109.1	110.5	96.7	94.2	92
All India	72.1	75.86	69.74	67.2	70.3	71	73.5	77	72.7	69.9	69.5

Source: *Reserve Bank of India, Report on Trend and Progress of Banking in India - Various Issues.*

the state economy and barely any occupational diversification occurred.

It was a repetition of a historical error, when like the British, who wanted Punjab to be primarily agriculturally developed, the Central Government in free India, too, propped Punjab as the 'bread basket' or the 'granary of India'. The irony of the situation, was that political and other compulsions conditioned the planning process in such a way, that there was a focus on agriculture in the state, as a national priority, which led to the neglect of other areas of infrastructure conducive for industrial development.

Agriculture grew rapidly due to massive planned public investment undertaken by the Government for a rural infrastructural base in Punjab. For example, during the First Five Year Plan per capita plan expenditure was Rs. 174 in Punjab as compared with Rs. 26 in Bihar and Rs. 38 for India as a whole. During the Seventh Plan, the corresponding figures were Rs. 1729 for the Punjab, Rs. 622 for Bihar and Rs. 980 for India as a whole. Further, nearly 70 per cent of the plan outlay in Punjab was devoted to basic rural infrastructure like irrigation, power, research and extension. During all plans, the highest expenditures in Punjab were for power and irrigation. The figures of the indices of industrial production, also, highlight this factor. This could probably be attributed to the faltering political leadership which probably remained bogged down with mainly non-economic issues, while the policy makers and planners at the Centre, conveniently ignored Punjab in a macro perspective, on the basis of its otherwise, high per capita income on account of the Green Revolution.

The case of Punjab for financial assistance given to the states by the Centre for industrial development has also been neglected. A report prepared by NCAER regarding the industrial programme for the Fourth Plan in Punjab pointed out that the share of the state (even before reorganization) in Central Government projects was negligible and recommended that the State Government should continue pursuing the Centre for siting more Central Government industrial projects in the State. Till 1975, the share of Punjab in Central investment, among all the states in non-departmental undertakings, was only about 1per cent. It was only at the end of March 1979, with the commissioning of the fertilizer plant at Bhatinda, that such Central investment in Punjab increased to 2.2 per cent of the total total level of investment. In the years 1999-2000, it continued to be a mere 0.79.

Another aspect of the Indian economy is the development of the public sector to promote industrialization. However, the state has been bypassed in the location of public sector enterprises currently, there is a move for disinvesting the public sector units since the previous ones are at a loss. It is the private sector, which dominates the industrial structure of the Punjab economy, with only a marginal role of the public sector. In fact, whatever industrial strides are prevalent are primarily based on private enterprise inherent in the basic psyche of the people, even though a corporate or institutional industrial culture does not prevail. The apprehension of the public sector investment are causes again, rooted in the tumultuous currents of the state's history. Even the leadership of the state and the successful governments need to be blamed, that they did not form any conscious policy for the development of industry, till as late as 1976. It is not intended to brush aside the growth of industrial estates set up during 1950s and 1960s but these primarily aimed at the small-scale sector, not the large-scale sector. The Akali Government, largely composed of agriculturists, always sought the votes of the farmer by populist measures.

In the early 1980s before militancy soared, various

ventures had been initiated. 'Eltop', the industrial estate for electronics had been set up at Mohali near Chandigarh. Another large industrial focal point was set up at Shri Goindwal Sahib in the Tarn Taran sub-division. This was India's first nucleus industrial complex. It had 450 industrial and 160 residential plots spread over 500 acres. With the assistance of the Punjab State Industries Corporation and PFC, a few small and medium units were promoted. BHEL, and SPINFED also set up units, among the private large units was Bawa Shoes. However, soon thereafter, the area stopped attracting private investment because it became the hotbed of terrorism. In spite of the fact, that the industrial complex did not succeed, a paradigm of individual Punjabi entrepreneurship is the success of Bawa Shoes. Eltop has degenerated into a failure, and is today a veritable ghost town. Almost all the government subsidiaries floated here like Punjab Power Packs Ltd., Bio Medicals, others like consumer Electronics Punjab Ltd., which launched a laudable Government of India Project to manufacture and install TVsets in gram panchayats was later abandoned. Even the central government entity, Semi Conductor Complex for making chips for supply, to schools, is not doing well. The Punjab Communications Ltd. (PUNCOM) is making a telephone exchange on C-DOT technology but it seems to be heading for a collapse. The onset of militancy in the 1980s capsized the entire state, destabilized the body politic from the 1980s till 1995, when people were subsumed by apprehension and phobia. The battles were fought on several planes in a blend of religious, economic and political issues. Whatever may have been the precise cause but the repercussions were tremendous. The state suffered a mammoth setback, instead of soaring ahead with the prosperity of the Green Revolution. At the end of the study, one simple fact emerges that without peace and stability for a prolonged span any concrete industrial measures are impossible. If we look at the figures in the above tables, we will see that Punjab did well industrially in a relatively substantial manner in phases, when a relatively stable political climate prevailed. If Punjab had experienced a span of prolonged peace after the spectacular dividends of the Green Revolution, it would have achieved tremendous success. On the base provided by agricultural surpluses, fresh investments could have come from outside and catapulted the state as a major industrialized state of the country. However, the malaise of terrorism, which was rooted in its history was a major setback to the progress. Though in the 1990s, no doubt peace returned under Beant Singh's Government and liberalization swept all over the country, the impact undoubtedly was there. However, the disturbances which had pervaded the infrastructural base for over a decade did not have the desired impact as elsewhere. Particularly, states like Maharashtra pursued a prolonged and peaceful industrial process.

Various studies have been conducted, suggesting a better growth for the state by redefining its priorities for investment in industry, education and infrastructure. A study by economic consultants led by Dr. Raghavan Parthasarthy had suggested that since agricultural affluence was prevalent, it should now go in for full-fledged industrialization in order to not only absorb excess farm labour but also to promote the agro business sector in a big way to exploit the enormous farm productivity. As power generation, at present is insufficient to meet any programme of rapid industrialization, the state will have to implement its power generation programmes speedily. In the case of Punjab, the consumption pattern of electric power is biased towards the agricultural sector as the provision for free electricity for farmers by the Akali Government led by Badal. The percentage of consumption of electric power in the industrial sector had remained static. On the other hand, consumption of electric power in the agricultural sector increased. In 1999-2000, the agricultural consumption was 39.33 per cent whereas the industrial one was 36.789.

The group had emphasized that there should be a new

shift of focus of heavy investment from agriculture to industry since agriculture has reached a saturation point. The agro business should take into account the volume of production and the demands of the consumer market. Growth in this field will naturally bring more economic prosperity to the farmers. As three-fourths of Punjab's productive workforce is employed in farming, this workforce will look for a bright future in the agro-industrial sector.

For development in any sphere, the infrastructural growth is imperative, though, some progress exists in critical areas like the communication network, which is almost of international standards and the emergence of new technologies like cellular phones, wireless paging and internet. However, roads need to be modernized to provide for the rapid movement of goods and services. A further updating in, terms of globalization and information technology is necessary, so that the progress achieved in the agricultural sector can be sustained.

The formation and development of industrial clusters, industry specific and including upstream and downstream industries should be encouraged by the State Government. These clusters should be provided with all the infrastructural facilities like adequate power, a well developed transportation network and telecommunication facilities. Some natural industrial clusters are already emerging and they should be encouraged to develop industrial corridors like Dhandari, Kalan, Ludhiana, Khanna, Mandi Gobindgarh and Dera Bassi, Banur, Rajpura and Patiala. Instead of setting up new economic zones, the Punjab should first strengthen the existent industrial hubs, frame positive industrial policies to create an atmosphere conducive for NRI investment as well as other local enterpreneurs. A host of other reforms are registered institutional, regulatory and infrastructural to foster a good investment climate. The Government must make provision for the aftermath of reckless globalization like the influx of Chinese goods, crippling some of Punjab's industry like hosiery, worsted spining and rerolling industries. For instance, Ludhiana with its concentration of hosiery and engineering industries had closed down a number of spinning units because of the flooding of cheap Chinese and Korean polyester yarn. Earlier, the knitwear industry had faced the onslaught of the stoppage of exports to Russia.

In spite of scores of multipronged, multifaceted studies delineated, the primary causes for industrial lag rooted in history are : a volatile border state with an agricultural focus steered by historical currents. Punjab was in the forefront of the Green Revolution, when its success was liquidated as it fell into the grip of militancy for over a decade. The resultant fear psychosis did stunt the state's progress in certain spheres of economy, particularly, industry, especially the largescale sector. With the resumption of peace and stability there is the fructification of the Bhatinda refinery commissioned years earlier, which after the Bhakra Nangal Dam is the first mega project. The state's problem is one of growth in the right direction by a rapid transformation to industrialization, viz. large-scale industry. However, through the major crises seeded in Punjab's history, the people have always reflected a pronounced resilience and enterprise, which is consequential to the volatile history, as post partition and post-militancy phases reflect. To make the optimum use of this potential, surplus capital should be reinvested in the state, a backdrop of stable conditions should prevail to increase industrial activity. This is only a prognosis and hope, the rest depends on the history of the future.

Bibliography

Primary Sources

I. Private Papers and Collections

(a) All India Congress Committee Proceedings 1885, 1917-1967, Nehru Memorial Museum and Library, New Delhi.

(b) Ganda Singh, Some Confidential Papers of the Akali Movement, Shiromani Gurdwara Prabandhak Committee, Amritsar, 1965.

(c) Hukam Singh, Memorandum by him, Member Parliament, Shiromani Akali Dal, Amritsar, 1964.

(d (i) Jawaharlal Nehru's Private Papers 1905-1964 on microfilm at Nehru Memorial Museum and Library, Teen Murti House, New Delhi.

(ii) Telegram to Congress Sikhs of Lahore, Pratap Singh Kairon and Bhim Sen Sachar (2315).

(e) Master Tara Singh, Presidential Address at Ninth All India Akali Conference, Shiromani Gurdwara Prabhandak Committee Records, Amritsar.

(f) Lord Mountbatten's Private Papers 1947-1948 on Microfilm in Nehru Memorial Museum and Library, Teen Murti House, New Delhi.

(g) Sant Fateh Singh, Our Stand on Punjabi Suba, Shiromani Akali Dal Papers, Amritsar, 1963.

II. Personal Interviews with Businessmen of Punjab

1. Mr. Neelam Oswal, Managing Director of Vidyasagar Oswal Group of Industries at Ludhiana on 18 September 1997.

23. Punjab Administration Report, 1934-35, Superintendent, Government Printing Press, Punjab, Lahore, 1937.

24. Report on the Exhibition of Silk Cocoon, Department of Commerce and Industry Punjab, File No. 84.

25. Report on the Working of the Departments of Industries, Punjab 1949-1953, Simla, 1953.

26. Report on the Indian Tariff Board Regarding Grant of Protection to the Cotton Textile Industry, 1932.

27. Report on the Indian Tariff Board on the Woollen Textile Industry III, 1936.

IV. Census Reports

1. Rose, H.A., Census of India, 1901, Volume XVII, The Punjab and its Feudatories and the North-West Frontier Province, Part I, The Government Central Printing Press, Simla, 1902.

2. Kaul, Pandit Hari Kishan, Census of India, 1911, Volume XIV, Punjab, Part I, The Civil and Military Gazette Press, Lahore, 1912.

3. Middleton, L. and Jacob, S.M., Census of India, 1921, Volume XV, Punjab and Delhi, Part I, The Civil and Military Gazette Press, Lahore, 1923.

4. Khan, Ahmad Hasan Khan, Census of India, 1931, Punjab, Part I, Volume XVII, The Civil and Military Gazette Press, Lahore, 1933.

5. Anand, R.L., Census of India, 1961, Vol. XIII, Punjab, Part II-A, General Population Tables, Government of Punjab, Chandigarh.

6. Anand, R.L., Census of India, 1961, Vol. XIII, Punjab, Part III, Household Economic Tables, Government of Punjab, Chandigarh.

Bibliography

Primary Sources

I. Private Papers and Collections

(a) All India Congress Committee Proceedings 1885, 1917-1967, Nehru Memorial Museum and Library, New Delhi.

(b) Ganda Singh, Some Confidential Papers of the Akali Movement, Shiromani Gurdwara Prabandhak Committee, Amritsar, 1965.

(c) Hukam Singh, Memorandum by him, Member Parliament, Shiromani Akali Dal, Amritsar, 1964.

(d (i) Jawaharlal Nehru's Private Papers 1905-1964 on microfilm at Nehru Memorial Museum and Library, Teen Murti House, New Delhi.

(ii) Telegram to Congress Sikhs of Lahore, Pratap Singh Kairon and Bhim Sen Sachar (2315).

(e) Master Tara Singh, Presidential Address at Ninth All India Akali Conference, Shiromani Gurdwara Prabhandak Committee Records, Amritsar.

(f) Lord Mountbatten's Private Papers 1947-1948 on Microfilm in Nehru Memorial Museum and Library, Teen Murti House, New Delhi.

(g) Sant Fateh Singh, Our Stand on Punjabi Suba, Shiromani Akali Dal Papers, Amritsar, 1963.

II. Personal Interviews with Businessmen of Punjab

1. Mr. Neelam Oswal, Managing Director of Vidyasagar Oswal Group of Industries at Ludhiana on 18 September 1997.

23. Punjab Administration Report, 1934-35, Superintendent, Government Printing Press, Punjab, Lahore, 1937.

24. Report on the Exhibition of Silk Cocoon, Department of Commerce and Industry Punjab, File No. 84.

25. Report on the Working of the Departments of Industries, Punjab 1949-1953, Simla, 1953.

26. Report on the Indian Tariff Board Regarding Grant of Protection to the Cotton Textile Industry, 1932.

27. Report on the Indian Tariff Board on the Woollen Textile Industry III, 1936.

IV. Census Reports

1. Rose, H.A., Census of India, 1901, Volume XVII, The Punjab and its Feudatories and the North-West Frontier Province, Part I, The Government Central Printing Press, Simla, 1902.

2. Kaul, Pandit Hari Kishan, Census of India, 1911, Volume XIV, Punjab, Part I, The Civil and Military Gazette Press, Lahore, 1912.

3. Middleton, L. and Jacob, S.M., Census of India, 1921, Volume XV, Punjab and Delhi, Part I, The Civil and Military Gazette Press, Lahore, 1923.

4. Khan, Ahmad Hasan Khan, Census of India, 1931, Punjab, Part I, Volume XVII, The Civil and Military Gazette Press, Lahore, 1933.

5. Anand, R.L., Census of India, 1961, Vol. XIII, Punjab, Part II-A, General Population Tables, Government of Punjab, Chandigarh.

6. Anand, R.L., Census of India, 1961, Vol. XIII, Punjab, Part III, Household Economic Tables, Government of Punjab, Chandigarh.

7. Census Reports of 1971, 1981, 1991.

8. Vashishta, Lakshmi Chandra, Census of India, 1951, Vol.VII, Punjab, Pepsu, Himachal Pradesh, Bilaspur and Delhi, Part IA Report Army Press, Simla, 1953.

9. Vashishta, Lakshmi Chandra, Census of India, 1951, Vol.VIII, Punjab, Pepsu, Himachal Pradesh, Bilaspur and Delhi, Part IIB, Economic Tables, Himalya Press, Simla, 1953.

10. Census of India, 1951, District Census Handbook, Volume XIII (Simla Controller, Printing & Stationery, Punjab, 1953).

11. Census of India, 1951, Vol.III, Part 5A (Simla, The Army Press, 1953.)

V. **Regulatory Acts and Reports** (Available at Punjab Archives, Chandigarh).

1. The East Punjab Holdings (Pros and Cons of Fragmentation Act of 1948) Punjab Government Legislative Department, Printed by Controller Printing & Stationery Punjab, 1961.

2. U53/1 Punjab Alienation of Land Act No. XIII of 1900 504 U44 (A collection of Acts passed by the Lt. Governor of Punjab in Council 1918-1919).

3. The Punjab Government Code: The East Punjab Act, March 1948 (Control of Dismantling Act).

4. Report on the Administration of Punjab for the Year 1851, Calcutta Gazette 1853.

5. Report on the Punjab Exhibition of Arts and Manufacturers 1881-1882, Lahore Secretariat Press, 1882.

6. Report on the Evaluation Study of Focal Points of Industrial Growth; Economic and Statistical Organization Publication No. 248.

16. Annual Reports of Major Industrial Houses in Punjab, Oswals, Munjals, Essma, Trident Group, 1970-1991.

17. Annual Administration Report, 1994-1995, Department of Industries, Punjab.

18. Directory of Punjab Large and Medium Industries, 1996, Punjab.

VII. Pamphlets of Industries Department

1. Reports on the Working of the Department of Industries, Punjab 1949-53, Simla, 1954 - Financing Small-Scale Industries in Punjab, Directorate of Industries, Udhyog Sahayak Publications, Chandigarh, 1984.

2. To Non-Resident Indians Punjab Offers a Package of Incentives and Facilities for Setting Up New Industries in Punjab, Directorate of Industries, Punjab, Chandigarh, 1979.

3. Industrial Policy and Incentive Code 1989, 1996, Opportunities for Agri Business in Punjab, Udhyog Sahayak Publications, Chandigarh, 1989.

4. Punjab State Industries Corporation Brochure, Chandigarh, 1986.

5. Reports of Punjab, Haryana and Delhi Confederation of Indian Industry 1996 and 1997.

VIII. Board of Economic Enquiry Available at Punjab Archives, Chandigarh.

1. Anand, R.L., Tanning Industry in Punjab, Lahore, 1939.

2. Bhalla, T.R., Oilseeds Crushing Industry in the Punjab, Economic and Statistical Organization, 1954.

3. Bhalla, T.R., Production and Marketing of Wool in the Punjab, 1958.

4. Luthra, K.L., Impact of Partition on Industries in Border Districts of East Punjab, 1949, General Editor, Trilochan Singh, Publication No. I.

5. Malhotra, V., Economic Conditions of Displaced Persons Settled in East Punjab, Part I (Town) Ludhiana, 1949.

6. Prakash, Om

- A Factual Survey Relating to the Employment of Camp Dwellers in the Punjab Relief Camps, Ludhiana, 1950.

- An Economic Survey of Industrial Labour in the Punjab, Ludhiana, 1952.

- Survey of Refugee Camps in East Punjab, Ludhiana, 1949.

- Social and Economic Survey of Refugee Camps in East Punjab, Ludhiana, 1949.

7. Monthly Survey of Economic Conditions in the Punjab, Controller Printing and Stationery, Chandigarh, 1961.

IX. Punjab Government Publications

1. Punjab Legislative Assembly Debates 1937-1947 at Punjab Civil Secretariat, Chandigarh.

2. Speeches of the Hon'ble Gopi Chand Bhargava, Finance Minister, East Punjab, 8 March 1948, Simla.

3. Statistical Abstracts of Punjab, 1947-50, Simla, 1950.

4. Statistical Abstracts of Punjab, 1966-1996, Economic and Statistical Organization, Government of Punjab, Chandigarh.

5. Progress Report on First Five Year Plan and other Development Schemes in Punjab, April 1952 to March 1956.

6. Government of Punjab, Planning Department, Chandigarh

Sabha Secretariat, February, New Delhi, 1956).

12. Report on the Linguistic Provinces Commission, 1948 (Government of India Press, New Delhi, 1948).

13. Government of India, Punjab Boundary Commission Report, 1966, Manager of Publications, Government of India Press, New Delhi, 1966.

14. Resolutions on Economic Policy and Programme 1924-54 (New Delhi, All India Congress Committee, 1954).

15. Government of India, Bureau of Public Enterprises, Ministry of Finance, Annual Report on the Working of Industrial and Commercial Undertakings of the Central Government, New Delhi, 1975-1976.

16. Directorate of Industrial Statistics, First Census of Manufacturers, India, 1946 (Statistics by Industries and Provinces, Vol. I and II, Government of India Press, New Delhi, 1946 & 1949.

17. Government of India, Parliamentary Committee Report on the Demand for Punjabi Suba, Appendix VB, Lok Sabha Secretariat Library, Government of India Press, New Delhi, 1966.

18. Government of India, Planning Commission, The First Five Year Plan, a Summary, 1952, Government of India Press, New Delhi.

19. Government of India, Indian Munitions Board Industrial Handbook, Superintendent, Government Printing, Calcutta, 1919.

20. Government of India, Planning Commission, Five Year Plan, Progress Report for 1953-54, Government of India Press, New Delhi, 1954.

21. Government of India, Planning Commission, Second Five Year Plan, A Draft Outline, Government of India Press, New Delhi, 1957.

22. Government of India, Ministry of Labour, Annual Reports of the Department of Labour and Employment 1979-81; Volume II, Government of India Press, 1982, Volume II, Reports 1987-88.

23. Government of India, Planning Commission, A Technical Note on the Seventh Plan of India 1985-90, New Delhi, 1986.

24. Government of India, Economic Survey (1987-88), Public Enterprises Survey.

25. Government of India, Jawaharlal Nehru's Speeches, Ministry of Information and Broadcasting, New Delhi, 1954.

26. Handbook of Industrial Statistics, Office of the Economic Adviser, Ministry of Industry, Government of India, New Delhi, 1987.

27. Government of India, Statement on Industrial Policy, Ministry of Industry, New Delhi, 1956.

28. Government of India, Annual Report on the Working of Industrial and Commercial Undertakings of the Central Government, New Delhi, 1980.

29. Government of India, Report of Punjab Commission, Manager, Government of India Press, New Delhi, 1963.

30. Government of India, DC(SSI) Report on Census of Small Scale Industrial Units, Vol.I and II, New Delhi (1977).

31. Government of India, Ministry of Planning, Central Statistical Organization, Annual Survey of Industries, New Delhi, 1979.

32. Indian Election Commission Report on the First General Elections in India, 1951-1952, Volume II.

33. Dar Commission Report – Report of the Linguistic Provinces Commission Government of India Press, New Delhi, 1948.

and Military Gazette Press, Lahore, 1884.

2. Gazetteer of the Jullundur District 1883-84, Arya Press, Lahore, 1884.

3. Punjab District Gazetteer, Volume XXA and Volume XXII Amritsar District, The Civil and Military Gazette Press, Lahore, 1914.

4. Macfarguhar, A. Punjab District Gazetteers, Amritsar District, Controller of Printing and Stationery, Punjab, Chandigarh, 1947.

5. Gazette of India, 4 November 1961, Government of India Press, 1961.

6. Gazetteers of the Canal Colonies, Jhelum and Chenab 1883-1884, Government Printing Press, Lahore.

Secondary Sources

Articles, Papers, Books and Theses

Articles

Agha, Zaffar, "Punjab Crisis Calls for Early Solution", *The Patriot*, 20 June 1984.

Ahuja, Charnjit, "Punjab: The Unresolved Issues", *The Indian Express*, 8 December 1985.

Ahuja, Harvinder, "Reflections on Punjab", *The Indian Express*, 23 July 1984.

Aiyar, Swaminathan S, " The Hindu Factor", *Mainstream* XXIII 37, 11 May 1985, Delhi.

Akbar, M.J., "Politics of Fear, Precarious Punjab : A Review", XXVIII, 24 May 1985 - *Far Eastern Economic Review* XXVIII 17, Singapore, May 1985.

Alagh, Y.K., "Regional Industrial Development in India", *Economic and Political Weekly,* Vol.XVI, No. 5, 10 April 1974, Bombay.

Ankleswaria, Shahnaz - "Punjab Fall Out of Army Action: A Field Report," *Economic and Political Weekly,* XIX, 28 July 1984, Bombay.

Arora, Jagjit Singh – "Government Policy - A Grave Error", *The Sikh Review,* XXXII 370, Calcutta, October 1984.

Aulakh H.S. and P. S. Raiky, "Linkages between Agriculture and Industry in Punjab Economy", Punjab School of Economics, *Economic Analyst*, Guru Nanak Dev University, Vol.II, Amritsar, December 1980.

Azad, N.S., "Agrarian Production Relations in Punjab", *Mainstream*, Vol.XIX No. 35, May 1981, New Delhi.

Bains, G.S., "Development of Agrobased Feed and Food Industries in the Punjab State", Paper Presented at the Seminar on Perspective Planning, Punjab Agriculture University, April 1997, Ludhiana.

Bajaj, Y.P., - "Genesis of the Bhakra Dam Scheme 1914-1948", *The Punjab Past and Present*, Vol.XI, Part I and II, Punjabi University, Patiala, October 1993.

Bal, S S. - "Character of Ranjit Singh's Kingdom as seen by the British", *The Punjab Past and Present*, Vol. XXII-X, Serial No. 43, Punjabi University, April 1988, Patiala.

Banga, Indu, "Polity, Economy and Urbanization in the Upper Bari Doab (1700-1947)" *Studies in Urban History*, Edited by J.S. Grewal and Indu Banga, Guru Nanak Dev University, Amritsar, 1978.

Bannerjee, A.C., "An Aspect of Guru Gobind Singh's Career", *Indian Historical Quarterly,* Vol.I, New Delhi, 1995.

Barnala, S.S., "Policy Statement on Science, Technology and Industrial Development in Punjab" (Edited), S.B. Ragnekar and Rashpal Malhotra, *CRRID Publications*, Chandigarh, 1990.

Barrier, N.G. - "The Punjab Disturbances in 1907", *Modern Asian Studies* Sussex, 1967.

Bawa, R.S. and Sharma, M.K. - "An Analysis into the Inter District Variations in Industrial Development in Punjab, Punjab School of Economics", *Economic Analyst*, Vol. III and IV, No. 1 and 2, December - June, Amritsar, 1982.

- "Urbanization in Punjab, A Causal Analysis" (Edited), S.N. Mishra, *Urbanization and Urban Development in Punjab*, Guru Ram Das School of Planning, Amritsar, 1985.

Bhalla, G.S., "The Role of Small and International Towns in the Regional Development of India, Paper Presented at the Indian Institute of Advanced Studies", May 1992, Simla.

"Agricultural Growth and Industrial Development - A Case Study of Punjab", Paper Presented at China on 4 July 1990. Available at Institute for Studies in Industrial Development, Delhi, October 1990.

"Political Economy since Independence" (Edited), Indu Banga, *Five Punjabi Centuries*, Manohar Publications, Delhi, 1977.

Bhalla, G.S. and Chadha, G.K., Green Revolution and the Small Peasant: A Study of Income Distribution in Punjab, *Economic and Political Weekly*, Vol.XVII, No. 22, 15 May, Bombay, 1983.

Bhalla, G.S.; Chadha, G.K.; Kashyap and Sharma, "Agricultural Growth and the Structural Changes in the Punjab Economy, An Input and Output Analysis", *Research Report No.* 82, Centre for Regional Development, Jawaharlal Nehru University, New Delhi, 1980.

Bhatia, Kabal Singh, "The Punjab Land Alienation Acts, 1900, Circumstances Leading to its Passage and its Impact on Congress Politics in Punjab". *The Punjab Past and Present*, Vol.XXI-1, Serial No. 41, Punjabi University, Patiala, April 1987.

Bhatnagar, S and P.S. Verma, "Coalition Governments, 1967-1980", *Punjab Journal of Politics*, Vol. V, No. I, New Delhi, January-June 1981.

Bhushan, Bharat, "Punjab Politics and the Farmers", *Business India* 165, 22 July, Bombay 1984.

"Industrial Development in Punjab and Haryana, A Comparative Study", Punjab School of Economics, Guru Nanak Dev University, Amritsar, 1983.

Branhan, P., "The Green Revolution and Agricultural Labour", *Economic and Political Weekly,* July, Bombay, 1970.

Brass, Paul, R., "Coalition Politics in North India", *American Political Science Review*, 62, P. 1174, No. 4, 1968

Chadha, G.K., "Planning Implications of Transformation of Agriculture in a Developing Area", A Case Study of Punjab, India, Paper Read at Berlin, 1976.

Chadha and Johar R.S., "A Strategy for Industrial Development of Punjab", Paper Presented at Seminar on Punjab Economy in Retrospect and Prospect, Guru Nanak Dev University, Amritsar, 1980.

Chandan, Amarjit, "Power Crisis in Punjab", *Economic and Political Weekly,* Bombay, March 1980.

Chatterton, Alfred, - "Hand Weaving in India", *Indian Review*, Vol.III, Calcutta, 1902.

Chopra, Pran, "Last Chance in Punjab", *Sikh Review* XXX, Vol.No. 1359, November, Calcutta, 1983.

Chopra, V.D., "Significance of Punjab Poll", *The Patriot*, 28 January, New Delhi, 1992, Punjab : A Leadership Crisis, *The Patriot*, 6 June, New Delhi, 1992.

Chum, B.K., "Sikh Standpoint: Punjab Crisis", *The Sikh Review*, Vol. 31, No. 336, December, Calcutta, 1981.

Dang, Satypal - "Punjab: Religion against Politics", *Mainstream*, Vol.XXII, No. 17, 24 , New Delhi, 1985.

Datar, Kiran, "The Trader of Punjab and Asian Trade, 17th to Early 19th Centuries", *The Punjab Past and Present*, Volume XX A, Serial No. 39. Punjabi University, Patiala, April 1986.

Dhesi, A.S., Planning in Punjab: Plan Implementation and Formulation in Studies in Punjab's Economy, Edited Johar, R.S. and Khanna, J.S., Studies in Punjab's Economy, Punjab School of Economics, Guru Nanak Dev University, Amritsar, 1983.

Domain, Dolores, "Some Aspects of the British Land Policy in the Punjab, After its Annexation in 1849", *The Punjab Past and Present*, Volume VIII, Part I and II, Punjabi University, Patiala, October 1974.

Doosanj, S.S., "Socio-Economic Tensions as a Result of the Green Revolution" in *The Punjab Past and Present* Volume XVI-II, Serial No. 32, Punjabi University, Patiala, October, 1982.

D'Souza, V.S., "Economic Transformation, Mobility and Social Structure in the Rural Areas of the Punjab", Punjab School of Economics, *Economic Analyst*, Vol.III, IV, Nos. I and 2, Amritsar, 1982-83.

- "Economy, Caste, Religion and Population Distribution - An Analysis of Communal Tension in Punjab", *Economic and Political Weekly*, Vol.XVII, No. 19, Bombay, May 1986.

Frankel, F., "Agricultural Modernization and Social Change", *Mainstream*, Vol. 8, No. 13, New Delhi , 1969.

Gajrani, S.D., "Agrarian Unrest in British Punjab", *The Punjab Past and Present*, Serial No. 39, Punjabi University, Patiala, October, 1990.

"Agrarian Structures and Economic Condition of Peasantry in Punjab (1920-47)", Punjab History Conference, Proceedings, Punjabi University, 15, 17 March, Patiala, 1991.

Ganda Singh, "Introducing the Punjab", *The Punjab Past and Present*, Vol.V, Part I and II, April 1967 and October 1967, (Ed.) Ganda Singh, Panjabi University, Patiala, October 1967.

Ghosh, Tirthanthar and Sharma, Rita, "Destination Punjab", Sunday XII 12, 20-26, New Delhi, January 1985.

Gill, K.S., "Agricultural Development in Punjab", Punjab School of Economics, *Economic Analyst*, Vol.II, December, Amritsar, 1980.

Gill, M.S., "Pakistani Punjab vs Indian Punjab" in *The Illustrated Weekly of India*, 10 August 1975.

"The Green Revolution, Success in the Indian Punjab", Centenary Celebrations of Birmingham University, 1975.

Gill, S.S. and Bedi M.S., "Punjab's Industrial Backwardness", *Mainstream* Vol.XX, No. 47, 24 July, New Delhi, 1982.

Gill, Sucha Singh, "Punjab Crisis and the Political Process", *Economic and Political Weekly*, 27(5): 1 January, Bombay, 1992.

Gopal, Krishan, "Reaction of Hindus towards the Punjabi Suba Movement", *The Punjab Past and Present*, Volume XXVII, Part II, Serial No. 54, Punjabi University, Patiala, October 1993.

Gour, Sanjeev, "Punjab: One Year After", Sunday XII: 32 (9-15 June 1985), "Sunset in Punjab", *The Statesman*, 29 June 1981.

Graham, A.S., "Opposition Shift on Punjab: A Shortlived National Consensus," *The Times of India*, 13 July 1984.

"Politics of Violence: Varieties of Terrorism", *The Times of India*, 18 May 1984.

Grewal, J.S., "Business Communities in the Punjab", *Journal of Regional History*, Vol.III, Guru Nanak Dev University, Amritsar, 1982.

Grewal, S.S. and Kahlon, A.S., "Impact of Mechanization on

Farm Employment in the Punjab", *Indian Journal of Agricultural Economics*, Vol.XXVII, No. 4, 1972.

Grover, B.R, "Approach and Methodology to the Study of Medieval Punjab", 28-29 February, Punjab History Conference, Proceedings, Patiala, April 1976.

Gujral, I.K., "Punjab's Anguish", *Mainstream* Vol.XX, No. 50, 14 August 1982.

"Unravelling the Punjabi Knot", *Mainstream* XXIII, 22 Republic Day Special 1985.

"Never ending agony of the Punjab", *The Indian Express*, 16 December 1991.

"The Economic Dimensions", Amrik Singh (Edited) *Punjab in Indian Politics: Issues and Trends*, Ajanta Publications, New Delhi, 1985.

Gulati, Ashok, "Structure of Effective Incentives in Indian Agriculture Some Policy Implications", in *Economic and Political Weekly*, Volume XXIV No. 39, Bombay, 1995.

Gupta, Shekhar, "Punjab: The Rule of the Gun", *India Today* 16(1): 1 January 1991.

Gupta, Ved Prakash, "Punjab: Politic Raj, all the way", *Frontier*, 24 (14), 16 November 1991.

Guru, H.S., "Science and Technology and the Punjab Problem" in Technology for Development Perspective on Northern India, S.B. Ragnekar, Malhotra, Rashpal, *CRRID*, Chandigarh, 1990.

Habib, Irfan, "Essays in Indian History, "Towards a Marxist Perception", (Edited) Irfan Habib, Tullika, New Delhi, 1995.

Handa, Devendra, "The Pre-Harappan Settlements of Ancient Punjab", *The Punjab Past and Present*, Punjabi University, Vol. V, Part I and II year, Patiala, 1973.

Hazlehurot, Leighton W., "Entrepreneurship and the Merchant Castes in a Punjabi City", Monograph No. I, Programmes in

Comparative Studies on Southern Asia, Duke University, North Carolina, 1966.

Hira, B.S., "Agrarian Prosperity and Rural Poverty in the Upper Bari Doab" (1849-1947), *The Punjab Past and Present*, Vol. XXVII, Part II, Punjabi University, Patiala, April, 1970.

Hundal, Simran, "Woollen Textiles Industry in the Punjab Under the Raj", *The Punjab Past and Present*, Vol.XXVII, Panjabi University, Patiala, April 1993.

Hutchinson, J., "A Note on the Passage of the Hydaspes" - by Alexander, *The Punjab Past and Present*, Vol. II, Part II, Punjabi University, Patiala, October, 1968.

Inderjit, "Punjab: Towards a Solution", *The Tribune*, 14 February 1989, "Punjab: The Inside Story", *The Economic Times*, 19 June 1984.

Jain, Girilal, "Failure of the Sikh Intellectuals to Recognize the Bhindranwale Menace", *The Times of India*, 9 July 1984.

Johar, R.S., "Decentralization of Industrial Development with Special Reference to Punjab" in Johar and Khanna (Edited), Studies in Punjab Economy, Guru Nanak Dev University, Amritsar, 1983.

Johar, R.S., and Khanna P., "Aspects of Growth in the Small Scale Engineering Industry at Batala", A Note in Punjab School of Economics, December, *Economic Analyst*, Vol.III, No. 2, Guru Nanak Dev University, Amritsar, 1982.

Johar, R.S. and Khanna, J.S., "Reflections on the Development of Punjab and Haryana" (Ed.), Studies in Punjab Economy, Guru Nanak Dev University, Amritsar, 1983.

Kairon, Partap Singh, "Bright Future for Industries in Punjab, Underdeveloped Regions to be Developed", *The Tribune*, Ambala, 4 April, Ambala, 1958.

Kapoor, Satish, Punjab and the Freedom Struggle, *The Tribune*, August 1997.

Kaur, Mandeep, "The Partition of India: A Case Study", *The Punjab Past and Present*, Vol.XXII-II, Serial No. 42, Punjabi University, Patiala, October 1987.

Krishan, Gopal, "Jobless in Punjab" in *The Economic Times*, 21 May 1995.

Kumar, Pawan, "Judicial Administration in Punjab During 1897 - 1919", Punjab History Conference, Proceedings, 18 - 20 March, 26th Session, Punjabi University, Patiala, 1994.

Kumar, Rahul, "Punjab's Industrial Outlook Brightens", in *The Economic Times*, 25 March 1995.

Kumar, Ravinder, "Future of Punjab, Consolidating Gains of Peace", *The Times of India*, 8 May 1995.

Ladejinski, Wolf, "Green Revolution in Punjab: A Field Trip", *Economic and Political Weekly*, 28 June, Bombay, 1969.

Mukherjee, Mridula, "Some Aspects of Agrarian Structure of Punjab, 1925-47", *Economic & Political Weekly* XV, Vol. 26, Bombay 1984.

Mukherjee, "Difficulties in the Way of Cotton Textile Industry", *The Tribune*, 7 March, Ambala, 1953.

Nanda, I., *Punjab Uprooted – A Survey of Problems Riots and Rehabilitation Problems*, Hind Kitab, 1948, Bombay.

Nayyar, Gurcharan Singh, The Dynamics of Maharaja Ranjit Singh's Policies, *The Punjab Past and Present*, Vol. XXII-I, Serial No. 40, Punjabi University, Patiala, April 1988.

Nijhawan, P.K., "Genesis of the Punjab Problem: The Language Question", Man & Development, Vol.IV, No. I, March, 1982.

Oberoi, A.S. and H.K. Manmohan Singh, "Migration and Flows in Punjab's Green Revolution" Belt *Economic and Political Weekly*, Volume 15 No. 13, 29 March, Bombay 1980.

Panchmuklu, V. R. 1975 - "Linkages in Industrialization: A

Study of Selected Developing Countries in Asia", *Journal of Development Planning* 8: 121-165.

Pandit, M.L., "Some Lesser Known Factors Behind Recent Industrial Changes in Punjab and Haryana", *Economic and Political Weekly* XIII, 47, No. 75, Bombay 1975.

Patnaik, Prashant, "Industrial Development in India", *Social Scientist*, June 1979.

Paul, R.R. and Myer R.M. - "Structure Growth and Potential of Hosiery Industry in Punjab", *Economic Analyst*, Punjab School of Economics, Vol.III and IV, No. 1 and 2, Amritsar, December - June (1981-82)

Paul, Samuel, "Industrialization Goal's without Policies", *Economic and Political Weekly* Vol.XV No. 3, January 19, Bombay 1980.

Paul, Satya, "Integrated Punjab as an Industrialist Sees it", *The Tribune*, 9 November 1956.

Pradip, "Punjab Impasse", *The Deccan Chronicle* 8 August 1984.

Rai, Satya M., "The Structure of Regional Politics in Punjab" in *The Story of Punjab* Volume II Edited Verinder Grover, Deep and Deep Publications, New Delhi, 1995.

Randhawa, M.S., A Case Study of Green Revolution in Punjab, *The Punjab Past and Present*, Volume XVI-II, Serial No. 32, October 1982.

Sandhu, J.S. and Singh, Ajit, "Industrial Development in Punjab, Some Features", in *Studies in Punjab Economy,* Punjab School of Economics, Guru Nanak Dev University, Amritsar, 1983.

Seth, N.G., "A Review of Research in Industrial Relations in India" *Journal of Industrial Relations*, Sydney, Vol. 9, No. 3, November 1967.

Sharma, Harish, "Handloom Weavers of the Punjab under British Rule: A Study of Socio-Economic Change", - *The Punjab*

Past and Present, Punjabi University, Vol.XXIII, Serial No. 42, Patiala, April 1989.

Sharma, Raj Kumar - "The Unrest of 1907 in the Punjab", Punjab History Conference, Proceedings, Punjabi University, 19-20 March, Patiala, 1971.

Singh, Attar,"Punjab's Recurrent Themes," *The Tribune*, 25 June, Chandigarh, 1980.

Singh, Amandeep, "Impact of the British Rule on the Social Scene of Punjab and the Rise of Communalism", Punjab History Conference, Proceedings, Volume XXVI, Punjabi University, Patiala, April, 1992.

Singh, A.J. and Harjinder Singh, "Industrial Focal Points and Regional Imbalances in Punjab", Punjab School of Economics, *Economic Analyst* Vol.II, GNDU, Amritsar, December 1980.

Singh, Balbir, "Pattern of Industrial Development in Punjab", Punjab History Conference, Proceedings , Punjabi University, 18-20 March, Patiala, 1994.

Singh, Balwinder and Singh, J.N., "A Study into the Existing Status and Potential of Agrobased Industries in the Punjab", Paper read at a Seminar, Department of Economics, GNDU, Amritsar, 1986.

Singh, Bharpur, "Punjab comes Under President's Rule", *The Spokesman,* Vol. 22 No. 7, 17 October 1983.

"Punjab Tangle Stalemate," *The Spokesman*, Vol.33, No.6, 10 October 1983.

Singh, Chauhan, "Strained Economy of the Punjab", *Link* XXVII, 28 April.

Singh, Fauza, "Akalis and the Indian National Congress" (1920-1947), *The Punjab Past and Present*, Volume XV-II, Serial No. 30, Punjabi University, Patiala, October, 1981.

Singh, Gopal, "Economic Basis of the Punjab Crisis", *Economic and Political Weekly*, Vol.XIX, 7 January 1984.

Singh, Gopal, *The Punjab Past, Present and Future* (Edited) Ajanta Publications, New Delhi, 1994.

S.Gopal, *Selected Works of Jawaharlal Nehru*, Orient Longmans, Vol. X, New Delhi, 1972.

Singh, Gurcharan, "Indus Valley Civilization and Drama", Punjab History Conference, Proceedings, 28-30 October 1966, Punjabi University, Patiala.

Singh, Gurcharan, "The Punjab Alienation of Land Act", 1900, Its Background", Punjab History Conference, Proceedings Ist Session, 12-14 November 1965.

Singh, Gurcharan,"Culmination of the Sikh Movement", *Spokesman* XXXIV: 33, 20 May 1985.

Singh, Gursharan, "Industrial Development in Pepsu", Punjab History Conference, Proceedings, 17-19 March, Punjabi University, Patiala, 1989.

Singh, Gursharan, "Rehabilitation of Refugees in Pepsu", *The Punjab Past and Present*, Volume XXII Serial No. Punjabi University, Patiala, 1986.

Singh, Harbir, "Sant Fateh Singh's Role in the Creation of the Punjabi Suba, A Study in Charismatic Leadership", *Indian Political Science Review*, Vol.VII, No.2, 1974.

Singh, Hukum, "The States Reorganization in the North", Paper with Shiromani Akali Dal, Publication Sikh Reference Library, Amritsar.

Singh, Inderjit (1983), "Punjab Situation", *Mainstream*, Vol. XXI, No. 18, 1 January. "Punjab Situation Clouded Perception".

Singh, Jagjit K., "Punjab Tangle: A Probe", *Spokesman*, Vol.32, No. 51, 22 August 1983.

Singh, Jagmohan, "Agony of Punjab", *Link*, VIII, 3 October 1985.

Singh, Khushwant, "In the Aftermath of Operation Blue Star", *The Indian Express*, 25 October 1984.

Singh, Kirpal, "Partition of the Punjab 1947", *The Punjab Past and Present*, Volume XXII, No. 42, Punjabi University, Patiala, October 1986.

Singh, Satwinder and Mann, Baltej, "The Role of Government in Industrial Development in Punjab" Vol.XXI-II, Serial No. 42, *The Punjab Past and Present*, October, 1987.

Singh, Shaukin, "Punjab in Pain", *Link* XXVII-2, 19 August 1984.

Singh, Sucha, "Economic Development and Structural Change in Punjab, Some Policy Issues, Echo Publishers, Ludhiana, 1994 and Genesis of Akali Agitation As a Sikh Scholar Sees it", *The Times of India*, 15-16 March 1984.

Singh, Sukhwant, "Canalization and Colonization in the Punjab, 1849-1901", Volume IV, *Journal of Regional History*, Guru Nanak Dev University, Amritsar, 1996.

Singh, Tarlok, "Rural Resettlement in Punjab, The Background, A Transfer of Population", *The Statesman*, New Delhi, 6 July 1950.

Singh, Tarlok, "Rural Resettlement in Punjab, The Background, A Transfer of Population", *The Statesman*, New Delhi, 25 July 1950.

Sohal, K.S., Evolution of Well and Tubewell Irrigation in Punjab, 1950-51 to 1990-91, Punjab History Conference Proceedings, 18-20 March, Punjabi University, Patiala, 1994.

Sohal, S.S., "Western Research on Political Economy", *Journal of Regional History*, Vol.III, Guru Nanak Dev University, Amritsar, 1982.

- "Professional Middle Classes in the Punjab", *Journal of Regional History*, Vol.III, Guru Nanak Dev University, Amritsar, 1982.

Suri, V.C., "Political, Territorial and Administrative Changes in the Panjab, from Earliest Times upto 1947" in *The Punjab Past and Present* , Volume I, October I, Punjabi University, Patiala, 1967.

Tiwana, S.S., "The Issue of Linguistic Reorganization in Punjab 1947-66, A Study of Administration Strategies", *The Punjab Past and Present*, Volume XXVII, Part 5, Serial No. 53, Punjabi University, Patiala, April 1993.

Uppal, J.S., "Indian Economy and Five Year Plans", in J.S.Uppal (Edited), India's Economic Problems, An Analytical Approach, Tata Hill Ltd., New Delhi, 1984.

Warner, Lee, Dalhousie's Administration, *Calcutta Review*, Vol.XXVII, 1856.

Wasti, Razi, The Punjab Colonisation Act 1907, reprinted in *The Punjab Past and Present*, Vol.I, Part I and II, Punjabi University, Patiala, 1967.

Yadav, K.C., "British Policy Towards the Sikhs 1849-1859, Punjab History Conference, Proceedings, 28-30 October, Punjabi University, 1996, Patiala.

CRRID Publications, Chandigarh

1. V. P. Dubey and Bindu Duggal: Industrial Policy of Punjab: A Critical Evaluation, Chandigarh, 1995.
2. Editors S.B. Ragnekar, Rashpal Malhotra, Technology for Development Perspective on Northern India, September 1990.
3. Man and Development, Volume IV, No. I, March 1982.

Books

Adirapu, Venkateshwar Rao, *The Sikhs and India, Identity Crisis*, Satya Publications, Hyderabad, 1991.

Aggarwal, A., *The Economics of Underdevelopment*, Oxford University Press, 1962.

Ali, Imran, *The Punjab under Imperialism 1885-1947*, Oxford

University Press, New Delhi, 1988.

Anstay, Vera, *The Economic Development of India*, Longmans Green & Co., London, 1957.

Arora, R.C., *Turmoil in Punjab Politics*, Mittal Publications, New Delhi, 1980.

Badenoch, A.C., *Punjab Industries 1911-17*, Superintendent, Government Printing, Punjab, Lahore 1917.

Bagchi, Amiya Kumar, *Private Investment in India*, 1900-1939, Cambridge University Press, Cambridge 1972.

Bajwa, H.S., *Fifty Years of Punjab Politics* 1920-70, Modern Publishers, Chandigarh, 1979.

Bali, A.N., *Glimpses of Punjab History*, Manohar Publications, New Delhi 1969.

Banga, Indu, *Agrarian System of the Sikhs*, New Delhi: Manohar Publications 1978.

Bannerjee, Indu Bhushan, *Evolution of the Khalsa*, Calcutta, 1962.

Baran, Paul A., *The Political Economy of Growth*, New Age Printing Press, New Delhi, 1958.

Barrier, N.G., *The Sikhs and Their Literature*, Manohar Book Service, Delhi, 1970.

Barrier, N.G., *The Punjab Alienation of Land Act 1900*, Duke University, Carolina, 1966.

Bawa, H.S., *Plea of Punjabi Speaking Provinces*, Hindu Union Press, New Delhi, 1948.

Bawa, R.S. and P.S. Raikhy, *Structural Changes in Indian Economy*, Punjab School of Economics, Guru Nanak Dev University, Amritsar, 1993.

Bhaduri, Amit and Nayyar, *The Intelligent Person's Guide to Liberalization*, Penguin, New Delhi, 1996.

Bhagwati, Jagdish, *India in Transition, Freeing the Economy*, Oxford Press, New Delhi 1993.

Bhalla, G.S. and Chadha, G.K., *Green Revolution and the Small Peasant*, Concept Publishing Co. New Delhi, 1983.

Bhalla, G.S., Agricultural Growth and Industrial Development in Punjab (Edited) J.W. Mellor, Agriculture towards Industrialization, John Hopkins Press, New York, 1995.

- Structure of Punjab Economy: Inter Industrial Flows and Pattern of Final Demand (1969-70) (Mimeo) Centre for Regional Development, Jawaharlal Nehru University, New Delhi, 1975.

Brij Pal Singh, Educational Progress and Economic Development in Punjab, Punjabi University Press, Patiala, 1974.

Buchanan, D., *The Development of Capitalist Enterprise* in India, Frank Cass, London 1934.

Budwood, C.B., *A Continental Experiment*, London, 1945.

Burnes, Alexander, Travels into Bukhara Being the Account of a Journey from India to Cabool, Tartary and Persia, also Narrative of Voyage on the Indus from Sea to Lahore, Volume I (Karachi 1973, 4th edition).

Calvert, H. , The Wealth and Welfare of the Punjab, Civil and Military Gazette Limited (1936), Punjab Civil Secretariat, Lahore, 1936.

Chadha, G.K., *The State and Rural Economic Transformation, The Case of Punjab*, 1950-85, Sage Publications, New Delhi, 1986.

- The Off Farm Economic Structure of Agriculturally Growing Regions: A Study of Indian Punjab in Off Farm Employment in the Development of Rural Asia papers presented at a conference held in Chiang Mai, Thailand, 23-26 August 1983.

- Production *Gains of New Agricultural Technology*, Chandigarh, Punjab University Press, 1979

Chandra, Bipin, *Nationalism and Colonization in Modern India*, Orient Longmans, New Delhi, 1979.

Chopra, G.L., *Punjab as a Sovereign State* 1799-1839, Hoshiarpur, 1960.

Clark, Colin, *The Conditions of Economic Progress* (3rd Edition, 1951, reprinted 1983) Macmillan & Co., London.

Cooper, Frederic, *Crisis in Punjab*, Sameer Prakashan Chandigarh, 1979.

Cunningham, J.D., *A History of the Sikhs*, reprinted by S.Chand & Co., New Delhi, 1972.

Dalip Singh, *Dynamics of Punjab Politics*, Macmillan, New Delhi, 1981.

Danewallia, B.S., *Police and Politics in Twentieth Century Punjab*, Ajanta Publications, New Delhi, 1997.

Darling, M.L., *The Punjab Peasant in Prosperity and Debt*, Manohar Publishers, New Delhi, 1977.

Dator, A.L., *India's Economic Relations with the USSR and Eastern Europe*, 1953-1969, Cambridge 1972.

Divyendra Tripati, *Communities of India*, Manohar Publishing House, New Delhi, 1984.

Domain, Dolores, *India in 1857-1858: A Study in the Peoples' Uprising*, Berlin 1975.

Douie, Sir James, *The Punjab Settlement Manual*, Lahore 1907-1930.

- *The Punjab, North-West Frontier Province and Kashmir*, Seema Publications, Delhi (1974).

Dutt, R.P., *India's Green Revolution*, Princeton University Press, New Jersey, 1971.

Dutt, Romesh, *The Economic History of India in the Victorian Age*, 1837-1900 Volume II (reprinted) 1960 Tribnex Press, London.

Farmer, B.H., *Agricultural Colonization in India* since *Independence*, London, 1974.

Forster, W., *English Factories in India 1637-1647*, Claredon Press, Oxford 1912.

Fox, Richard, *Lions of the Punjab Culture in the Making*, Low Price Publications, New Delhi, 1950.

Fox, Sir Cyril, *Economic Mineral Resources of Patiala State and Their Industrial Possibilities*, Punjabi University, Patiala, 1946.

Frankel, Francine R., *India's Green Revolution: Economic Gains and Political Costs*, Princeton University Press, New Jersey, 1971.

Gadgil, D.R., *The Industrial Evolution of India in Recent Times (1860-1939)*, Oxford University Press, New Delhi, 1971.

Ghosh, Ravindranath, *Agriculture in Economic Development with Special Reference to Punjab*, Vikas Publications, New Delhi, 1977.

Gilmartin, David, *Empire and Islam: Punjab and the Making of Pakistan*, Berkeley, University of Carolina Press, 1988.

Gordon, S. and Ojha, B.S., *Agricultural Use in Punjab: A Special Analysis*, New Delhi: 1967.

Grewal, J.S., *The Sikhs of the Punjab*, The New Cambridge History of India, Cambridge University Press, 1990.

- "Essays on Sikh History", Essay on Cunningham, Amritsar, 1984.

Grewal, J.S., and Indu Banga, *Punjab in Prosperity and Violence*, 1947-1997, K.K. Publishers, Chandigarh, 1998.

Grover, Verinder, Punjab , *The Story of Punjab, Yesterday and Today,* Vol.I and II, Deep & Deep Publications, New Delhi, 1995.

Gustafson, W.E. and Jones, K.W., Sources of Punjab History: A Study Sponsored by the Research Committee on the Punjab, Manohar Publishers, New Delhi (1975).

Hamilton, W., A Geographical, Statistical and Historical Description of Hindustan and Other Adjacent Countries, Vol.II,

Oriental Publishers, New Delhi, 1971.

Hanson, A.H., *The Process of Planning: A Study of India's Five Year Plans*, London, 1966.

Hazari, R.K., *Essays on Industrial Policy*, Concept Publishing Company, New Delhi, 1986.

Hicks John, *A Theory of Economic History*, Oxford University Press, Oxford 1969.

Hoffman, W.G., *The Growth of Industrial Economics*, Manchester University Press, Manchester, 1958.

Jammu, P.S., *Changing Rural Structure in Rural Punjab*, Sterling Publishers, New Delhi, 1975.

Johar, R.S. and Khanna, J.S., Studies in Punjab Economy, Punjab School of Economics, Guru Nanak Dev University, Amritsar, 1983.

Josh, Bhagwan, *Communist Movement in Punjab* (1926-1947), Anupama Publications, Delhi 1975.

Kapoor, T.N., *Industrial Development in States of India*, Sterling Publishers, New Delhi 1967.

Kaur, Amarjit, Arun Shourie, Lt. Gen. J.S. Aurora, Khushwant Singh, *The Punjab Story*, Roli Books International, Delhi, 1984.

Khara, S.S., *Government in Business*, Asia Publishing House, Bombay, 1963.

Kohli, Sita Ram, *Sunset of the Sikh Empire*, New Delhi, 1967.

Kothari, Rajni, *Politics in India*, Orient Longman, New Delhi, 1970.

Kuldip Nayyar and Khushwant Singh, *Tragedy of Punjab*, Vision Books, New Delhi, 1984.

Kulkarni, M.R., *Industrial Development*, National Book Trust, New Delhi, 1971.

Kumar, Dharma, *The Cambridge Economic History of India*, Vol.II, 1757-1970, Cambridge University Press, 1975.

Kumar Pramod and Manmohan Sharma, Atul Sood and Ashwini Handa, *Punjab Crisis, Context and Trends,* CRRID Publications, Chandigarh, 1984.

Kumar, Ravinder, *Essays in the Social History of Modern India*, ICHR Delhi, 1983.

Lal, Bhiwani (Claims Officer for Punjab) and Mittal, Harbans Lal, Advocate, An Encyclopedia of Laws Relating to Evacuee Property and Displaced Persons in India and Pakistan, Federal Law Deport, Second Edition, Delhi, 1951.

Lal, Shiv, Dateline Punjab, Lifeline Sikhs, Election Archives, New Delhi, 1994.

Latifi, A., *The Industrial Punjab: A Survey of Facts, Conditions and Possibilities*, Longmans, Green and Company, London, 1911.

Malik, I.A., *The History of the Punjab*: 1799-1947, Neeraj Publishing House, New Delhi, 1983.

Marshall, Alfred, *Principles of Economics*, Oxford University Press, London, VIIIth Edition.

Mcleod, W.H., *Who is a Sikh? The Problem of Sikh Identity,* Clarendon Press, 1987, Oxford.

Moon, Penderel, *Divide and Rule*, Chatto & Windus, London, 1961.

Mountjoy, Alan B., *Industrialization and Underdeveloped Countries*, Hutchinson and Company Ltd., London, 1965.

Myrdal, Gunnar, *Economic Theory and Underdeveloped Regions*, Indian Edition, New Delhi, 1978.

- *Asian Drama - An Enquiry into the Poverty of Nations*, Allen Lane, Penguin Press, Great Britain, 1968.

Nafziger, E.Wayne, *Class Caste and Entrepreneurship: A Study of Indian Industrialists*, University Press, Hawai, Honolulu, 1973.

Nair, Kusum, *Blossoms in the Dust: The Human Element in Indian Development*, Gerald Duckworth, & Co., London, 1961.

Narain, Brij, The Agricultural Worker and the Punjab Land Revenue Committee, The Institute of Agrarian Reform, Lahore, 1939.

Narang, Gokul Chand, *The Transformation of Sikhism*, New Book Society, 5th edition, New Delhi, 1960.

Nayar, B.R., *Minority Politics in the Punjab*, Princeton University Press, Princeton, 1966.

Nijjar, Bakshi Singh, *Punjab under the Sultans* (100-1526 A.D.) Sterling Publishers, Pvt. Ltd. New Delhi, 1968.

Pandit, M.L., *Industrial Development in the Punjab* and *Haryana*, B.R. Publishing Corporation, New Delhi, 1985.

Pavate, D.C., *My Dayas Governor*, Vikas Publishing House, New Delhi, 1974.

Pavlov, V. I., *The Indian Capitalist Class: A Historical Study*, People's Publishing House, New Delhi, 1964.

Phillip, C.H. (Ed.), *The Evolution of India and Pakistan : Select Documents 1858-1947*, London, 1982.

Powell, B.A. Baden, *Handbook of Manufactures and Arts of Punjab*, Vol.II, Punjab Printing Press, Lahore, 1872.

Prakash Singh, *Changing Social Structure in Rural Punjab*, New Delhi: Sterling Publishers, New Delhi, 1974.

Rai, Satya M., *Partition of the Punjab*, Asia Publishing House, Bombay, 1965.

Randhawa, M.S., (a) *The Green Revolution, A Case Study of Punjab* (b) *Out of the Ashes*, Vikas Publishing House, Chandigarh, 1954.

Rostow, W. W., *The Process of Economic Growth*, W.W. Norton & Co., New York, 1952.

Saini, B.S., *The Social and Economic History of the Punjab, 1901-1939*, Vikas Publishing House, Delhi, 1975.

Sen, Sunil Kumar, *Studies in Economic Policy and Development in India*, Calcutta, 1966.

Shah, K.T., *Industrialization of Punjab*, Government Printing Press, Punjab, Lahore, 1941.

Sharma, Devinder, *GATT and India, The Politics of Agriculture*, New Delhi, 1994.

Sharma, R.A., *Entrepreneurial Change in Indian Industry*, Sterling Publishers, New Delhi, 1980.

Sharma, S.R., *Punjab in Ferment*, Delhi: S.Chand & Co. New Delhi, 1971.

Sharma, S.C., *Punjab: The Crucial Decade* (1911-20), New Delhi, 1987.

Shergill, H.S and Gurmail Singh, Scope of Development of Agro Industries in Rural Punjab, Institute for Development & Communication, Chandigarh, 1996.

Singh, Bakhtavar, *The Social and Economic History of Punjab* (1901-1939), Punjab University, Chandigarh 1964.

Singh, Dalip, *Dynamics of Punjab Politics*, Macmillan Ltd. New Delhi, 1981.

Singh, Fauja, *Some Aspects of Sikh Society under Ranjit Singh*, Master Publications, Patiala, 1982.

Singh, Jasbir, *The Green Revolution in India, How Green is it?* Vishal Publications, Kurukshetra, 1995.

Singh Teja, *Gurdwara Reform Movement and Sikh Awakening*, Jullundar, 1922.

- *Essays in Sikhism*, Siddharth Publications, New Delhi, 1989.

Singh, Ganda (Ed.), *Maharaja Ranjit Singh's Correspondence*, Punjabi University, Patiala, 1977.

- *A Brief Account of the Sikhs*, Amritsar 1965.

- Maharaja Ranjit Singh: First Death Centenary Memorial Volume , Khalsa College, Amritsar, 1939.

Singh, Giani Kartar, *The Case for a New Sikh Hindu Province in the Punjab*, New Delhi, 1946.

Singh, Gursharan, *History of Pepsu - Patiala and East Punjab States Union*, Konark Publishers, New Delhi, 1991.

Singh, *Harbans, Heritage of the Sikhs*, Manohar Publications, New Delhi, 1985.

Singh, Khushwant, *History of the Sikhs*, Vol.III, Princeton University Press, Princeton, New Jersey, 1966.

- *Ranjit Singh*, Allen & Unwin Ltd., London, 1962.

Singh Kirpal S., *Partition of Punjab*, Punjabi University, Patiala 1972.

Singh, Mohinder, *The Akali Struggle*, Macmillan Press, New Delhi, 1978.

Sinha, N.K., *Ranjit Singh*, A. Mukherjee & Co., Calcutta, 1968.

Steinbach, Johan, *The Punjab*, Punjabi University Press, Patiala, 1970 (Reprint).

Suttcliffe, R.B., *Industry and Underdevelopment* Addison, Wesley Publishing Company, London, 1971.

Talbot, Ian, *Punjab and the Raj*, Manohar Publications, New Delhi, 1988.

Talbot, Ian and Gurpal Singh, *Punjabi Identity and Social Change*, Manohar, Publications, New Delhi, 1996.

Tandon, Prakash - *Punjab Century : The Fascinating Story of a Virile People* (1857-1947) Orient Paperbacks, New Delhi, 1961.

Tully, Mark and Jacob, Satish, *Amritsar, Mrs. Gandhi's Last Battle*, Rupa Publications, New Delhi, 1985.

Vakil, C.N. (ed.), *Industrial Development of India - Policy and Problems*, Orient Longman, Ltd., New Delhi, 1973.

Vera, Anstay, *The Economic Development of India*, Longmans Green, London, 1957.

Weber, Alfred, *Theory of Location of Industries*, English Edition, 1949.

M.Phil. Dissertations and Ph.D. Theses

1. Bhatia, B.S., *Pattern of Industrial Development of Punjab University*, Chandigarh, 1970.

2. Deol, H.S. Analysis of Political Elite in Punjab with special reference to the Legislature, Ph.D. Thesis, Panjab University, 1979.

3. Hundal, Simran, "Small Scale Industries in the Punjab, Under the Raj 1901-1994, M.Phil. Thesis, Punjab University, 1979.

4. Kumar, Pramod, Violence and Indian Politics, Unpublished Ph.D. Thesis, Punjab University, Chandigarh, 1980.

5. Mann, B.S., *Working of the Industrial Estates in Punjab*, Unpublished Ph.D. Thesis, Meerut University, 1983.

6. Singh, Jaswinder, *Industrial Development, Problems and Prospects,* M.Phil. Dissertation, Guru Nanak Dev University, Amritsar, 1981.

7. Sidan, Meena, *Growth Performance of Industrial Sector in Punjab*, M.Phil. Dissertations, Guru Nanak Dev University, Amritsar, 1991.